Public Libraries in the 21st Century

Recent Titles in
Library and Information Science Text Series

Public Libraries in the 21st Century

Ann E. Prentice

Library and Information Science Text Series

LIBRARIES UNLIMITED

AN IMPRINT OF ABC-CLIO, LLC
Santa Barbara, California • Denver, Colorado • Oxford, England

Library of Congress Cataloging-in-Publication Data

Prentice, Ann E.
    Public libraries in the 21st century / Ann Prentice.
        p. cm.
    Includes bibliographical references and index.
    ISBN 978-1-59158-854-2 (acid-free paper) -- ISBN 978-1-59158-853-5
(pbk. : acid-free paper) -- ISBN 978-1-59158-855-9 (ebook) 1. Public
libraries--United States. I. Title. II. Title: Public libraries in the
twenty-first century.
    Z731.P924 2011
    027.473--dc22   2010040786

15 14 13 12 11   1 2 3 4 5

This book is also available on the World Wide Web as an eBook.
Visit www.abc-clio.com for details.

Libraries Unlimited
An Imprint of ABC-CLIO, LLC

ABC-CLIO, LLC
130 Cremona Drive, P.O. Box 1911
Santa Barbara, California 93116-1911

This book is printed on acid-free paper ∞
Manufactured in the United States of America

Contents

Preface

I have always been passionate about public libraries since I was a small child in rural Vermont, anticipating the arrival of the bookmobile. After moving to the city, the public library was my second home, and it continues to have an important place in my life. I have been a public library director, a trustee, and a consultant, and in each of these roles there has been something special about working with public libraries. It's where everyone, regardless of age, education, economic status, and ethnic or cultural background, is welcome and where new ideas and new adventures beckon. You don't need to join a club or pay a fee, and if you don't know how to use a computer or find a book or find the answer to a question, someone will help you.

In the beginning stages of writing this book, it was intended to be a fairly traditional discussion of the public library at the start of the 21st century. And then it became something else. As I was researching and writing, I found that what I was describing was an institution that, in the second half of the 20th century, had reinvented itself to become a leading player in the information revolution while staying true to its mission of bringing people and information together for the benefit of the individual and society. The book became less a description of how the public library is managed and more of an exploration of how the public library reinvented itself and what we need to do to continue its reinvention so that it can hold its place ahead of the curve.

I would like to thank Chris McDonald, library director extraordinaire of the Crandall Library in Glens Falls, New York, and the many other public librarians I have listened to and of whom I have asked questions. They are examples of the best in librarianship, whose hard work and creative efforts are responsible for the continuing process of reinvention. They are the librarians who, as one writer said, will blast us into the future.

I would also like thank the students in the Public Libraries Seminar I taught during spring 2010, who had a first read of several chapters. If they are representative of the next public librarians, we are in very good hands. Many thanks to Gary Videlock for his skill with charts and to Blanche Woolls for her kind words as I struggled toward deadlines. And to my husband, Don Surratt, a former president of ALTA, for his patience and understanding. And now we are going sailing.

Chapter 1

Introduction

In the late 18th and early 19th centuries, the new United States of America began an experiment in democratic government in which citizens had the vote and therefore the power to direct their government. The key to success was an informed electorate, and the public library was key to ensuring an informed electorate. From the beginning of our republic, the public library has been an integral part of activities to provide information to everyone, not just the elite. The belief that information should be freely available to all is a core value of a democratic society and of the public library movement.

The concept of a library that would be available to more than a few individuals first appeared in England in the late 17th and early 18th centuries. Dr Thomas Bray, an English clergyman, started a free lending library in England under the auspices of the Society for Promoting Christian Knowledge, and his efforts spread to the colonies, particularly in Maryland, Virginia, and South Carolina. Little remains of this early effort. By the second half of the 18th century in England, book clubs of various sorts had become popular among the growing middle class. At the same time, similar efforts had begun in America.

Benjamin Franklin was among the first to establish social libraries, also called subscription libraries, and his particular audience was young men wishing to improve themselves through self-education. Individuals would set up a book club; pay a subscription fee, which would be used to purchase books; and then share these books held in common. This would greatly increase the availability of reading materials over what one individual could afford. Wealthy businessmen often contributed to these libraries, as it was in their interest to support the education of the growing urban workforce. This emphasis on self-improvement provided seeds for continuing education programs, which became important elements of public libraries as they developed.

Another early form of public library was the circulating library. Books were purchased by an individual or organization such as a bookstore and then rented out to readers. A third format was the reading room, in which a range of newspapers was available to readers.

Although the initial concept of the public library began in England, it truly flourished in America and has become "one of the most characteristically American of our major cultural institutions . . . as it fit so well into the prevailing and rising patterns of thought, conditions of living, and social needs."[1] The need for an informed electorate was in contrast to the attitudes of the privileged in England, many of whom feared that public education might upset the social balance. The level of general education in the United States was higher than in many other countries, the political duties in a democracy required education, and the growing middle class also required that means be made available for individuals to continue to learn after they completed their required schooling, which usually ended with the eighth grade. It was recognized that political participation required an informed electorate, which was in contrast to the attitudes of the privileged in England, many of whom feared that public education might upset the social balance.

In the United States, "the public library it is often said, has been dedicated from its earliest days to the economic and cultural improvement of the common man."[2] The early colonists had a sense of obligation to help others help themselves through education and information, the recognition that education is a way to succeed and to lead. George Tichnor, one of the leaders of the public library movement, said that "the building and maintenance of a great nation rested on the wisdom of the masses who controlled it."[3] Each public library is very important to its community, as it signifies that the community values learning and that learning should be available to all regardless of their economic or social status.

Concurrent with the growth of library collections that would become public libraries, school district libraries were instituted as part of the Common School movement of the 1830s. This movement championed the availability of a tax-supported education for all children and was seen as a way to ensure that children were educated properly. Although school district libraries varied widely in size and quality, they were accepted as an integral part of the educational system. Because they were tax-supported libraries, they set a precedent for tax support of other types of libraries available to the public.

Tax support of public libraries was discussed throughout the first part of the 19th century, and in 1833 the public library in Peterborough, New Hampshire, was the first library to receive tax funds and thus became a model for others to follow. In 1848 the Massachusetts State Legislature enacted legislation to permit "Boston to tax the citizens for the support of a public library," thus making the Boston Public Library the first public library to receive municipal funds.[4] In 1852 the Boston City Council appointed a librarian and a board of trustees to govern the library. With these actions, a model for the organization of a tax-supported public library was formed.

The public library movement in New England and nearby states continued to grow. From 1851 to 1875, each of the New England state legislatures passed laws permitting the use of tax monies to support public libraries. New libraries were often begun with a gift from a resident or former resident who had become wealthy and wished to do something for his community as a strong statement of his personal success and desire to give something back. Despite the important role of philanthropy in the establishment and growth of public libraries, libraries grew in size and number "only when commerce and industry were operating with eminent success [and] surpluses were available for new public institutions."[5]

During the latter half of the 19th century, many of the great public libraries were established by individuals who had built their fortunes and wished to contribute to the good of their community and country. The Enoch Pratt Library in Baltimore, Maryland; the New York Public Library based on donations by Astor, Lennox, and Tilden; and many other libraries in cities large and small and in small towns grew. The great library philanthropist Andrew Carnegie donated more than $41,000,000 to build libraries in the United States, the United Kingdom, and many corners of the British Empire.

Carnegie believed that if one had access to books, one could become educated and thus become a more productive citizen. For a community to receive support from Andrew Carnegie, it was required to provide evidence that if it received funds from Carnegie, continuing support of the library would be assured by taxation. "Popular initiative, participation and control were the desired aims for they were basic to America's fluid, evolutionary social organization."[6]

Another factor that influenced the rapid development of the public library during this period was the increase in the availability of books and other reading materials. Unlike earlier decades, when books were rare, expensive, and highly prized, the publishing industry experienced rapid growth. Books were printed on cheaper paper, were relatively inexpensive, and were widely available. A library could assemble a respectable collection and maintain it much more easily than in earlier years. Publishers had positive relationships with the public libraries and often gave them titles to be included in their collections, while booksellers, fearful that a source of freely available books would cut into their sales, were concerned by the growth of the public library movement. Once it became apparent that libraries stimulated book buying, the booksellers began working with libraries to provide them with materials at discounted rates. The developing relationship between librarians and booksellers is recounted in early issues of *Publishers Weekly* (1876–1877) and the *American Library Journal* (1876–1877) and is a fascinating story.

PUBLIC LIBRARY DEVELOPMENT INTO THE FIRST HALF OF THE 20TH CENTURY

The public library movement responded to many social and educational interests during the years that spanned the latter part of the 19th and the early 20th centuries: those who supported an informed electorate, those who understood that an educated workforce prepared to deal with the new science and technology was becoming increasingly important to industrial growth, and those who saw education as a steadying social force that would "blunt the edges of differences . . . and [produce] a unified nation based on the free informed choice of individuals rather than on measures of indoctrination in behalf of any particular group."[7] Supporters saw many specific roles for the public library: to provide adult education programs and courses, to champion women's rights and continued education, to provide books and learning as an escape from the tedium of the factory, and to provide everyone an upward path toward achieving the American dream. The public library could be the working man's university. It could also be the transitional cultural environment for the immigrant who was trying to find a firm footing in this new and different culture.

As the public library movement grew, it needed individuals skilled in the art of building and maintaining collections and in the art of bringing user and reading together so that the goal of society to educate everyone would be achieved. This was a new professional area, and although its beginnings were dominated by men from early in its development, it was staffed by women who were responsible for the daily work librarians needed to do. Some of these women were members of clubs and associations that had initially established free public libraries and were responsible for their maintenance. Because librarianship was seen as a service and a genteel activity that did not threaten male dominance, women were able to enter the profession.

Melvil Dewey, one of the giants in the field, recognizing that women had a role in the success of this relatively new institution, admitted women to his newly established School of Library Economy, which opened at Columbia University in 1886. The university saw this as unauthorized coeducation, and in 1888 Dewey took the school with him to Albany, New York, where he had been named State Librarian. Not until 1927 did the school return to Columbia University. Once it had returned to Columbia University, the School of Library Service, as it was then named, assumed a leadership role in the field.

Librarianship as a career for women has an analogy in the 20th-century growth of many computer and information science careers. When a new career direction opens up and there is no history of male dominance, it is much easier for women to gain responsibility and authority and to be equal partners in the activity. More and more women were admitted to library training programs, and by the beginning of the 20th century were becoming leaders in the field. The impact on society of the opportunities librarianship afforded women at a time when there were very few careers in which women could demonstrate their leadership abilities is often underestimated.

In 1876 the U.S. Bureau of Education published a report including information on approximately 300 public libraries, two-thirds of which were located in the northeast and only 5 percent of which were located in the Southern states. Over the years, libraries increased in the north central states and in the West. This early identification of public libraries provides a valuable benchmark for the study of the growth of the public library movement.

Late in the 19th century several states passed legislation that provided for state-level support for public library development. For example, in 1890 the state of Massachusetts passed a law creating a state Board of Commissioners whose role was to help communities establish and improve public libraries.

New York followed suit in 1892, and Connecticut, Maine, and New Hampshire followed in 1893. More and more states passed similar laws, and the resulting state agencies did much to help communities establish and maintain public libraries. Prior to the establishment of state library agencies, there were few guidelines for establishing libraries or overall plans for their organization. Because of the efforts of the state-level agencies, there was a major expansion in the number of public libraries in many states.

Numerous other landmarks were reached around the turn of the century. The first library to serve African Americans (the Western Branch Library in Louisville, Kentucky) opened in 1905. Though services to children began around 1885, and children were increasingly welcomed to the library, the first branch library for children (Cleveland Public Library) opened in 1908. Once begun, services to children grew rapidly. Children's rooms were a pleasant place, unlike the tenement homes in which many urban children lived. A wide range of activities were available to children and this provided an excellent educational environment. African American children were "barely considered," but those public libraries that had opened "Colored Branches" were heavily used by both children and adults.[8]

Although prior to 1904 service to immigrants was an important part of the activities of some libraries, usually those in major urban areas, after that date services became more organized and widespread. The years before and during World War I (1904–1918) were a high point of public library services to immigrants. Between the two world wars (1918–1939), general interest in services to these groups waned. At the same time, special programs focused on European refugees from dictatorships, Spanish-speaking immigrants, and some immigrants from Asia. This lessening of interest paralleled a recurring national concern that "there are too many of them," and librarians, always necessarily attentive to their communities, were aware of this. They walked a narrow line between providing services to immigrant groups and incurring the displeasure of local groups. Librarians were often asked about their rationale for purchasing foreign- language titles. Despite criticism from some in the community, many librarians in urban areas continued to build foreign-language collections that supported the culture and learning of immigrant groups in their community.[9]

Until the mid-20th century most public libraries in the South excluded African Americans. Though some public libraries opened branch libraries in African American neighborhoods, these were in no way adequate. "The philosophy regarding libraries which prevailed at the end of the last century [19th century] was to make books available to those who could use them to the best advantage, Afro-Americans, particularly in the South were too often considered incapable of using books."[10] Countering this assumption was strong evidence that when libraries were available to African Americans, they were heavily used.

During this period the separate but equal tradition was often applied, but never equally. It was not until the post–World War II era and the civil rights movement that the barriers came down, and it was through a combination of the efforts of many courageous African Americans actively supported by the American Library Association that these barriers were finally removed. An

"Access Study" prepared by ALA in 1963 determined that though some public libraries desegregated voluntarily, some refused and insisted on a federal ruling, some refused and suits were filed, and some closed altogether.[11]

PUBLIC LIBRARY DEVELOPMENT IN THE SECOND HALF OF THE 20TH CENTURY

At the end of World War II, as the country was settling into a new chapter of its history, "library leadership sensed that the time had come to make some big moves—some giant steps toward the development of library services that would require some degree of financial responsibility for libraries at the federal level."[12] It was also recognized that there was a need to develop a benchmark showing where the public library movement was and the directions it should take in the second half of the 20th century to increase service to the country. The ALA was charged with the task of leading the public library into its next phase of growth. One of the first and most important steps was taken in 1946, when ALA approached the Social Sciences Research Council to propose

> that they conduct a thorough and comprehensive study of the American free public library. . . . [T]he proposal further defined the nature of the study as "an appraisal in sociological, cultural and human terms . . . of the extent to which the libraries are achieving their objectives" and of the library's "potential and actual contribution to American society."[13]

The Council agreed to proceed with the project and submitted a proposal to the Carnegie Corporation. This study, based on social science research methodology, would take more than two years to complete and would provide the benchmark for further development of public libraries. The Carnegie Corporation approved the proposal and appropriated $200,000 for the study, a considerable sum of money at that time.

The *Public Library Inquiry* (PLI), as the study was called, did indeed provide an objective understanding of the role of the public library. It "presents a particular justification for library service as a public good by means of a critique."[14] The PLI

> was a professional legitimating project. It proposed professional action on the basis of rational, empirical investigation. Its explicit concern was for the effectiveness of service, the political legitimacy of the library's structural link to the state and public funding, and the intellectual understanding, explanation, and justification of the role of the public library in American society and the assumption that the public library is an instrument of democracy is pervasive throughout the PLI.[15]

Its existence depends on the existence of free, educated citizens to use it and "its proper task" is to develop and nurture the nation's cultural climate.[16]

Using data gathered for the PLI as well as other sources, ALA, with the participation of other agencies including the U.S. Department of Agriculture, developed a legislative program that would address the PLI finding "that nearly 50,000,000 people who lived outside of the cities—in towns, villages, and unincorporated areas- were without access to public libraries. It appeared that public libraries, at least, were serving only from 15 to 25 percent of the population."[17] First introduced in 1946, the Library Services Bill gradually gained support among publishers, educators, and concerned citizens, and was followed by an act to provide libraries in rural areas.

In 1955 the Library Services Act was passed, and it was signed into law in 1956. Federal funds were authorized to be spent to extend public library services to rural areas. To qualify for federal funds, a state would be required to provide matching funds and to submit a plan to the U.S. Office of Education showing how it would spend its allocation. This requirement ensured that each state would have such an agency and also strengthened existing state agencies.

In 1964 the legislation was expanded to become the Library Services and Construction Act (LSCA). It included support for certain services to nonrural areas, specifically for library construction. In the next eight years, with LSCA support, more than 1,800 public library buildings were built or remodeled to serve some 60 million Americans. Federal funds were matched by state and local funds at a ratio of $1.00 to $2.50.[18]

During the 1950s and 1960s, because of the requirements of the federal legislation, state library agencies were strengthened and developed plans for statewide library activities that would maximize the effect of the funds made available to them. Also, the 1957 launching by the Soviet Union of Sputnik was a wakeup call to the public about the need to place more resources in education, particularly in science and mathematics. Passage of legislation— including the National Defense Education Act (1958), which provided support for school library materials in the sciences, mathematics, and foreign languages; the Elementary and Secondary Education Act (1965), which authorized expenditures for school library resources; and the Economic Opportunity Act (1964), which focused on early childhood learning—provided additional funds to the community for the support of library service. Each of these pieces of legislation had provisions that strengthened library services throughout the community and complemented public library resources.

Between 1960 and 1965, public library development had gained a great deal of momentum. The "consciousness-raising" effected on the public by the combination of exposure and demonstration, citizen involvement and publicity, had helped to reinterpret the role of libraries in the light of present-day needs, and helped enormously to raise public expectations (and professional expectations as well) of what public libraries should be able to do for people.[19]

Public libraries developed numerous new and sophisticated reference services, ranging from providing information on health, social services, and other survival information to sophisticated research support. Programs were developed to support vocational education, early childhood education, and opportunities for the aging, the handicapped, and minority citizens.

Also in 1965, the Higher Education Act was passed, Title II of which provided fellowships for PhD study at universities with doctoral programs in library and information science. This marked a turning point in the education of library professionals, from being based almost entirely on practice to also focusing on research-based evidence for decision making and ways of providing service. From 1965 to the present, graduate programs in library and information science have been a valuable source for research-based practice in all types of libraries, which has contributed to a higher level of professionalism. Concurrent with the increased professionalization of library science, other emerging professions, including urban planning, public administration, and other activities associated with local, state, and federal government agencies, were also developing a research base, looking at ways to improve practice through research, and building the planning processes that would provide guidance as they moved forward.

By the late 1970s, planning and accountability were becoming part of the way of life for public libraries. Planning was required of state agencies before they received federal funds, and they were required to account for how the funds were used once a program had been completed. Individual public libraries were expected to submit plans to their state agency and to account for the use of resources. In 1980 ALA published *A Planning Process for Public Libraries*, which gave public librarians a step-by-step means of planning for their services, collecting data, and reporting on their activities. This was the first of several publications by ALA that were to serve as guides for planning and evaluation.

Federal funds were available for demonstration programs that often led to new services and to extending library services to unserved populations, including those in prison and new immigrants who need assistance in transitioning to the American culture. Proposals for new and/or revised services continue to be funded by the Institute of Museum and Library Services (IMLS), which is the successor to the Library Services and Construction Act.

Funding for public libraries continued to be difficult. As has been the case since the founding of public libraries, when the economy is healthy and there are sufficient funds for public services, libraries are supported. When the economy is not as good, public libraries tend to be among the first services to be cut in order to ensure funds for public safety services such as police and fire departments. As has been the case since the founding of public libraries, public support in good and bad times has been crucial to the continuing survival and growth of public libraries.

PUBLIC LIBRARIES INTO THE 21ST CENTURY

The purpose and role of the public library continues to evolve while at the same time holding firmly to its basic responsibility to bring information and people together. In early 2009 the Darien, Connecticut Public Library hosted an event, "In the Foothills: A Not-Quite-Summit on the Future of Libraries," at which participants were instructed to "come prepared to help sketch out the role librarians should play in defining the future of libraries."[20] The discussions at this meeting resulted in *The Darien Statements on the Library and Librarians.* This document captures the purpose and role of the library and librarians for the 21st century. It states:

> The purpose of the library is to preserve the integrity of civilization, that it has a moral obligation to adhere to its purpose despite social, economic, environmental, or political influence, and that purpose will never change. The library is infinite in its capacity to contain, connect and disseminate knowledge; librarians are human and ephemeral, therefore we must work together to ensure the Library's permanence. Individual libraries serve the mission of their parent institution or governing body, but the purpose of the library overrides that mission when the two come into conflict. Why we do things will not change, but how we do them will. A clear understanding of the Library's purpose, its role, and the role of librarians is essential to the preservation of the library.
>
> They define the role of the library by using the words provides, encourages, empowers, facilitates, preserves, expands, and inspires and perpetuates. And they describe the role of the librarians as stewards of the library who connect people with accurate information, assist in the creation of their human and information networks, select, organize and facilitate creation of content, protect access to content and preserve freedom of information and expression; and anticipate, identify and meet the needs of the library's community.

And finally, as librarians,

we must

- promote openness, kindness, and transparency among libraries and users.
- eliminate barriers to cooperation between the library and any person, institution, or entity within or outside the library.
- choose wisely what to stop doing
- preserve and foster the connections between users and the library
- harness distributed expertise to serve the needs of the local and global community

- help individuals to learn and to use new tools to create a more robust path to knowledge
- engage in activism on behalf of the library if its integrity is externally threatened
- endorse procedures only if they guide librarians or users to excellence
- identify and implement the most humane and efficient methods, tools, standards and practices
- be willing to have the expertise to make frequent and radical changes
- hire the best people and let them do their job; remove staff who cannot or will not
- and trust the users.[21]

This well-considered statement from 2009 fulfills the need, as Mathews said of similar documents in the 1960s, to "interpret [the library] in the light of present day needs and raise expectations."[22]

ISSUES FOR THE 21ST CENTURY

Access

Always in the forefront of library activities is the need to provide access to information and to protect intellectual freedom. David Berninghausen, a longtime leader in the continuing effort to protect intellectual freedom, said that "a democracy cannot succeed unless citizens have access to varying views on issues that influence their lives and governance."[23] ALA and its Intellectual Freedom Committee are in the forefront of supporting libraries as they deal with issue of censorship in their communities.

Library as Place

Public librarians understand the library as place, a place in the community where individuals may gather, discuss issues, and enjoy one another's company. McKibben, in discussing the value of local communities, talks about the economics of neighborliness and its value in helping a highly mobile people bond.[24] Although more and more people are building social communities on the Internet, the absence of face-to-face interaction reduces the commitment of participants to each other. In a highly mobile society, individuals and families feel less bonded. His solution is to shift our economy and our social interaction to a more local scale to foster a stronger sense of community, wherein we shift from consumer to participant and where we find "comfort will come less from ownership than from membership."[25] The best of all possible worlds is when one social community enriches and strengthens the other; when on the Internet one can search globally and when in the library one can act locally. Librarians have an important role in fostering both the face-to-face community in the neighborhood and in making individuals aware of the benefits and issues present in social networking communities.

Immigrant Populations

The 1990s saw the highest point in immigration into the United States in nearly a century. The 2000 census reported that "the national foreign born population increased at a faster rate in the 1990s, by 57 percent to over 31 million in 2000, accounting for 11 percent of the U.S. population, up from 8 percent in 1990."[26] Nearly every community has a growing immigrant population, and that population has needs similar to the immigrant populations of a century ago:

- a place to find information about schools, jobs, and classes to learn English

- a place where one feels "less alone"

- an opportunity to connect to the new culture of which one is now a part

- a place to find books, tapes, and other materials for children

- a place to learn how to use the computer and to have access[27]

The public library is the only free access source for any of these. As did earlier immigrants, these new immigrants "perceive the American public library as a helper and a 'passport to a better life. . . . A national study conducted by ALA showed that over a period of twelve months, 58 percent of the Hispanic population and over 72 percent of the Asian/Pacific Islander population used libraries."[28]

Because each immigrant group is unique in its resources and characteristics, librarians need to know what these differences are:

> [T]wo important differences exist between present-day immigration and immigration in the early twentieth century; today's ethnic diversity among immigrants and a more polarized social class demographic pattern . . . with the most educated and wealthy at one extreme and the least educated and most poor at the other extreme. The local public library needs to know about the immigrant groups in their community; the reasons for immigration [voluntary or nonvoluntary], occupational status and social class, nationality and race, gender, generational factors as each of these factors create distinct pathways that new immigrants follow in their adjustment to the United States.[29]

It is important to conduct regular reviews of the immigrants in the community and their information needs and develop and implement a strategic plan that meets those needs.

Internet Services

Public libraries serve as access points to the Internet for the many who do not have access at home or work. In 2007–2008, "98.9 percent of public library branches offer internet access . . . 100 percent of rural, high poverty outlets provided public internet services . . . 72.5 percent of library branches report that they are the only provider of free public computer and internet access in their communities."[30] The increasing demand for public access places heavy financial responsibilities on the library. Library buildings are running out of space for workstations, and many lack the necessary wiring to accommodate additional workstations. As many users of public workstations are new to the Internet, a great deal of staff time is used to provide training.

As more and more Internet services become available—licensed databases, home work resources, information about jobs and about federal programs, and others—more and more individuals need to learn how to access the Internet and how to find the information they need. As reference services become more and more digital, there are opportunities to think creatively. Unless ways are found to meet the expanding public need for services in this area and support is made available to build or rebuild an adequate infrastructure, provide a sufficient number of workstations, and have a sufficient number of staff to work with the public, public libraries will not be able to provide adequate service. Librarians need to continue to explore new technological solutions to at least keep even with the curve.[31]

Financial Issues

Public libraries' growth and prosperity depend on the state of the economy and the funds available. As has always been true, public libraries, despite their proven contribution to the community, the pride with which communities support their libraries, and the increasing need for public libraries, are often the first agencies to suffer cutbacks when the economy is not strong. The economic downturn beginning in 2008 was no exception. The public library must, and should, demonstrate its value to the community daily and show that it is deserving of support.

SUMMARY

Some of these issues, such as access, intellectual freedom, and adequate funding, have been part of library activities since the beginning, whereas others, such as how one adapts to ever-changing technology and the challenges of a virtual and global world, are on the frontier of our experience, and some, such as service to immigrants, appear to be cyclical. New issues for the public library to address will emerge and will require attention. The public library is an institution that has had and continues to have many passionate champions, who have helped it grow and change to meet individual and community needs for information as the path to a better way of life. It is more than an institution or a service. Public libraries are, as Sidney Ditzion titled his seminal study of the public library, *Arsenals of a Democratic Culture*.

NOTES

1. Sidney H. Ditzion, *Arsenals of a Democratic Culture: A Social History of the American Public Library Movement in New England and the Middle States* (Chicago: American Library Association, 1947), 7.

2. Sidney L. Jackson, Eleanor B. Herling, and E. J. Josey, eds., *A Century of Service; Librarianship in the U.S. and Canada* (Chicago: American Library Association, 1976), 1.

3. Quoted in Ditzion, *Arsenals*, 16.

4. Ibid., 7.

5. Ibid.

6. Ibid., 150.

7. Clara O. Jackson, "Service to Urban Children," in Jackson, Herling, and Josey, eds., *A Century of Service*, 25.

8. Ibid.

9. Haynes McMullen, "Service to Ethnic Minorities Other Than Afro-Americans and American Indians," in Jackson, Herling, and Josey, eds., "*A Century of Service*, 42–61.

10. A. P. Marshall, "Service to Afro-Americans," in Jackson, Herling, and Josey, eds., *A Century of Service*, 64.

11. Ibid., 74.

12. Virginia Mathews, *Libraries for Today and Tomorrow* (New York: Octagon Books, 1978), 51.

13. Oliver Garceau, *The Public Library in the Political Process* (New York: Columbia University Press, 1949), v.

14. Douglas Raber, *Librarianship and Legitimacy: The Ideology of the Public Library Inquiry* (Westport, CT: Greenwood Press, 1997), 6.

15. Ibid., 7.

16. Bernard Berelson, *The Library's Public* (New York: Columbia University Press,1949), 134.

17. Mathews, *Libraries for Today*, 53.

18. Ibid., 79.

19. Ibid.,67.

20. *The Darien Statement on the Library and Librarians,* www.blyberg. net/2009/04/03/the-darien-statements-on-the-library (accessed January 2010).

21. Ibid.

22. Mathews, *Libraries for Today*, 67.

23. David K. Berninghausen, *The Flight from Reason; Essays on Intellectual Freedom in the Academy, the Press, First Amendment Rights, and the Library* (Chicago: American Library Association, 1975), xiv.

24. Bill McKibben, *The Wealth of Communities and the Desirable Future* (New York: Henry Holt, 2007), 105.

25. Ibid., 120.

26. Sandra Cuban, *Serving New Immigrant Communities in the Library* (Westport, CT: Libraries Unlimited, 2007), 2–3, 24.

27. Ibid., 5.

28. Ibid., 25.

29. Ibid., 19.

30. John Carlo Bertot and Charles R. McClure, *Public Libraries and the Internet 2008: Study Results and Findings* (Tallahassee: Florida State University, College of Information, Information Institute, 2008), 1–6.

31. Ibid.

ADDITIONAL READINGS

American Library Association, Office of Intellectual Freedom. *Intellectual Freedom Manual.* 7th ed. Chicago: American Library Association, 2006.

Benton Foundation. *Buildings, Books and Bytes: Libraries and Communities in the Digital Age.* Washington, DC: Benton Foundation, 1996.

Borgman, Christine, and Robert Gross. "The Incredible Vanishing Library." *American Libraries* 26. no. 10 (October 1995):904.

McKibben, Bill. *The Wealth of Communities and the Desirable Future.* New York: Henry Holt, 2007.

Palmour, Vernon E., Marcia Bellassai, and Nancy V. DeWath. *A Planning Process for Public Libraries*. Chicago: American Library Association, 1980. (This is the first of several Planning Process titles from ALA, and each is worth reviewing.)

Robbins, Louise S. *Censorship and the American Library: The American Library Association's Response to Threats to Intellectual Freedom, 1939–1969*. Westport, CT: Greenwood Press, 1996.

Sapp, Gregg. *A Brief History of the Future of Libraries*. Lanham, MD: Scarecrow Press, 2002.

Schuchat, Theodor. *The Library Book.* Seattle: Madrona Publishers, 1985.

In addition to these titles, there are many stories of the birth and development of individual public libraries. Each of these libraries has a unique story, and in reading them one gains an understanding of how public libraries came to be and the contribution they have made to society.

Chapter 2

Public Library Governance and the Role of the Trustee

INTRODUCTION

During the 18th and 19th centuries, before the public library became an important component of local government, boards of trustees were regularly used as a governing structure for many institutions. In New England, towns were granted charters by the English government, and members of the township were elected to carry out the provisions of the charter and to supervise the towns. Both Harvard and Yale adopted this form of government, with trustees elected to carry out the provisions of their charters. As public libraries were established, and as social libraries became public libraries, they adopted this now widely accepted form of governance .

Social libraries became popular in America in the 18th century. They were formed when a group of individuals established a club or society and contributed money for the purchase of books, which they would own and use. Two forms of the social library emerged, the proprietary library, in which members owned a share of the library's holdings, and the subscription or association library, to which members paid a fee but did not own its holdings. Association members would elect some of their group to supervise the activities of the library for the group. These elected members were the forerunners of today's public library trustees. In most communities, the public library and its trustees became part of local government; in others the association continued to control the library and contracted with local government to provide library service. These association libraries were managed by the association board of trustees.

Early in the 19th century another type of library for public use was established, the school district library. In 1835 the state of New York passed legislation authorizing school districts to "lay a tax on the district . . . for the purchase of a district library."[1] When coupled with matching funds, school district libraries became popular in New York for several years. These libraries were governed by trustees who reported to the Board of Education. Because of a lack of planning, supervision, and trained personnel, the school district library declined, and by 1892 any remaining school district libraries became school libraries. Other states, for example Michigan, adopted the format used in New York, and they were successful in organizing and maintaining the school district library. School district libraries in Michigan derive from this base, although they also have become building-level school libraries and are for public use by children and young adults attending those schools.

Salisbury, Connecticut, was the first community to provide funds for a local library, an activity that began in 1803. The first community to establish a tax-supported library was Peterborough, New Hampshire, in 1833. A free circulating library with a library committee to manage it and funds appropriated from the state literary fund to support it was established. The literary fund was obtained from a tax on banks and was divided among the towns in New Hampshire for the use of schools or other educational purposes.

The first state law enabling a community to tax its inhabitants to support public libraries was enacted in Massachusetts in 1851 and is directly related to the efforts of the founders of the Boston Public Library. They saw the public library as an essential component of public education and therefore worthy of tax support. Although the General Library Law of 1851 allowed the establishment of public libraries and the use of tax monies to support them, it set up no mechanism for library governance. The Boston Public Library, the first municipal public library, established a board of trustees made up of one alderman, one councilman, and five citizens elected by the city council. The Board of Trustees had the power to control expenditures and to make rules and regulations for library activities. After a period of conflict between the city council and the trustees, the board gained its independence in 1879 to run the library as it saw fit. It had the power to appoint its executive head and set library policy.

The municipal public library movement grew rapidly after 1851, with states passing enabling legislation allowing libraries to use tax monies for the library. The governance model developed by the Boston Public Library, in which libraries were governed by a board of trustees selected by the mayor and city council, was adopted by most municipal libraries.

These three types of libraries—the social library, which developed into the subscription or association library, with its governing trustees elected by members of the association; the school district library, whose trustees are responsible to the board of education; and the municipal public library, with trustees selected by the mayor and city council—are the source of the major variations in modern public library governance. All three types of libraries are "public" in that they receive tax support and are responsible for providing service to the public. Though the funding arrangements differ for each of these types of library, the primary source is the same, tax revenue.

The municipal library is a department of city government, and its budget is part of the overall city budget. School district libraries are supported through the education budget, although in some communities the library budget is voted on separately by the public, and the association library contracts with the municipality to provide library service and receives a sum of money to provide the service. Numerous variations on the above exist; libraries that are part of county government, libraries that combine service to the public and school libraries, libraries that serve a university and a municipality. The Hyde Park (NY) Free Library serves the town's fire and water district. This association library was given to the town in honor of Franklin D. Roosevelt's father James. The Roosevelts were also patrons of the fire and water district. Though there are variations of the above, all public libraries fit into three categories—association library, school district library, municipal/library—and all are primarily tax supported.

TYPES OF BOARDS OF TRUSTEES

Boards of trustees may be either administrative or advisory. Administrative boards are responsible for setting library policy, approving the library budget as it goes forward to the funding agency, hiring the library director, and being an advocate for the library. Advisory boards make recommendations on the above, budget, hiring, and advocacy, but do not have the authority to carry them out. Their major role is to serve as an advocate for library service and as a means of keeping the library informed of community concerns and interests. During the early years of public library development, administrative boards were the norm. Over time, as local government became more professional, an administrative board for a government agency was often seen as an anachronism, and administrative boards have gradually been transformed into advisory boards. The focus of their activities moved from making policy for libraries to library advocacy.

An exception is the role of the association library. One finds this type of library in those states where the public library movement began and where the energy of community groups was behind the organization of the public library. In these cases, an association was formed, trustees were elected from the association, and the library then contracted with local government to provide service for an agreed upon annual amount. As a quasi-public institution, the association library trustees are responsible for the library.

In some instances, the library has no board of trustees but is a department of local government and is no different from other departments. Although this may simplify lines of authority, there is a downside in that government departments cannot advocate for the activity they are responsible for providing. They cannot go directly to the community to ask for support, and there may also be provisions in the law preventing donors from giving funds or other support to the library.

BOARD COMPOSITION

The board of trustees is "an organized group of people collectively controlling and assisting an agency or association which is usually administered by a qualified executive."[2] The citizen representatives who make up the board are the link between the library and the school district board, the library association, or the municipal government. Boards of trustees have also been organized to oversee the activities of other community activities, including public parks, schools, hospitals, museums, and even fire and police departments. In recent years the trend has been away from the use of boards as governing units, particularly in areas such as police and fire departments. Other activities such as hospitals, museums, schools, and libraries continue to rely on citizen leadership. Many specialized not-for-profit agencies continue to rely on the board form of governance.

Trustees should not be selected because of their social standing in the community or because they have been active in the political campaigns of the current mayor or city council members, but for their leadership qualities, their belief in the importance of the public library, and their willingness to work and take their position seriously. Trustees should not overstay their value as trustees. New ideas and new ways of doing things energize a board, and those who have served more than five or six years on the board have had their opportunity to contribute. Those boards that are self-perpetuating also run the risk of selecting new trustees who think like the existing trustees and represent the same elements of the community as the old trustees.

Benefits of board leadership include the input by board members of their particular expertise and their knowledge of local government as well as their knowledge of the community. They can and often do provide a link between community expectations and the programs the library provides. Critics of leadership by a board of trustees say that rather than bringing to the library a range of perspectives on the community, if it is controlled by individuals with a specific bias, it can serve as a barrier to the kinds of service libraries are expected to provide. Others say that rather than serving as a communication channel between the municipal authority or school board, it can serve as a barrier between the two. And others say that boards tend to be fiscally conservative and unwilling to support the kinds of library budgets necessary to ensure quality service and in this way are barriers to service.

Who should serve on a board of trustees? The board should include representatives of all elements of the community: demographic, educational levels, ethnic, cultural, and other elements unique to that specific community. The board should be reflective of the community it serves and at the same time should include individuals with specific areas of expertise that will assist the board in its decision making. As a trustee, the board member should place library interests above personal interests, political interests, or other interests that detract from the kind of service the board is charged to provide. As a board member, the trustee is expected to be involved in board activities and to make fair decisions based on the facts. Studies of public library trustees show that trustees for larger public libraries tend to be well-educated males in their fifties, who tend to serve for ten years or more. Women tend to be better represented as trustees in smaller public libraries. It was also found that trustees were often reluctant to involve themselves as advocates for the library, and that this was often the reason why libraries did not receive the budgets or public support necessary for them to achieve their goals.[3]

BOARD RESPONSIBILITIES

The board of trustees is responsible for "holding and administering library property and funds to formulate policies and guide the direction of library affairs."[4] The specific duties and responsibilities of the library board and the trustees are spelled out in state legislation and in the requirements specified by the government of which the board is a part, for example, part of municipal law or school district law. Typically the duties of library trustees include

- participation in the development and continuous revision of a long range plan;

- reviewing and making decisions on library policy as presented by the director;

- the selection of a competent and qualified library director who is charged with carrying out the policies and directives of the board;

- an awareness of the functions of the library and the qualifications staff need to carry out those functions;

- ensuring that the library is operated efficiently and that funds are used wisely;

- reviewing goals and objectives, determining financial need to carry out goals and objectives, and presenting the case for funds to the public and to the funding agencies; and

- maintaining good relations with local government agencies and ensuring that the importance and role of the library is part of the planning activities.

In addition, board members are expected to be strong advocates for the library and to participate in community activities that further the library's role in the community. They are expected to be active not only on the local level but also in the regional, state, and national trustee association activities. Trustees are also expected to support library activities, report on those activities, and keep the governing body and the public aware of how the library is contributing to the quality of the community they serve. They are responsible for both short-term decision making and long-range planning for the library. The American Library Association (ALA) has published numerous titles on the role of the public library trustee that outline and discuss the role of the trustee.

It is often written into the law describing the governance of the public library that the board is responsible for selection of materials. This responsibility is delegated to the library director and staff who have the expertise to select materials. Trustees must be informed about ALA' s *Library Bill of Rights*, "formulated on the U.S. Constitution's concept of freedom." They should also be knowledgeable about and be strongly committed to the tenets of intellectual freedom that support the individual's right to know.

Librarians select materials that provide a balanced view of timely subjects that does not favor one perspective over another. When there are criticisms about a selection, the board consults the director about the title in question for review and the director's recommendation. This review should include the basis on which the title was selected, the nature of the complaint, and specific reasons why the title should or should not be retained in the collection. A director who handles the situation fairly and who neither bends to those with a particular perspective nor follows his or her own personal views provides the trustees with the best possible advice. Sometimes, despite the best professional advice, trustees bend to local pressure and overrule that advice, even when general public opinion supports the director's position.

The board also has an important role in public relations and in knowing how the library is seen by the community it serves. A library that is well managed and that serves the needs of the community with excellence will have the support of the community. The library that appears to be poorly managed, does not respect and support its community, and does not provide appropriate services of high quality does not deserve community support. It is a responsibility of the board to see that the library serves its community well, and if there are reasons why the library does not or cannot provide quality service, it is the responsibility of the board to do something about it. If there are concerns about the extent to which the library understands any changing demographics that would require new services and new approaches, or if there are concerns about quality of service, the board may find it useful to commission a study of the community. This shows a willingness to look at the community and at library activities and to collect data that will influence library planning. It is also an opportunity to involve the community in discussing library issues.

Board members may find it useful to speak to community groups about library programs and the ways in which they enrich the community. The board is also often involved in direct fund-raising activities. They may be acquainted with community members who would be willing to contribute to the library through gifts or endowments. They may also have connections with other community groups willing to support library programs, either financially or by informing their members and the larger community of their support. In these and other ways, trustees are advocates for the library as they work to build and maintain connections between the library and the community it serves.

TRUSTEE ORGANIZATIONS

Library trustees have been active in state and national trustee organizations since the end of the 19th century. The American Library Trustee Association (ALTA) was founded in 1890 and in one way or another has been affiliated with

ALA since then. In addition to trustees and trustee associations, many libraries have Friends of the Library groups. These volunteer associations are made up of community members who support the library and its programs. They have no role in library government and no relationship to local government. Friends of the Library elect their own officers and maintain their funds separately. Their objective is to support the library and help it serve the community by providing funds for special projects, volunteering to support library programs in the community, and being advocates for the library. Recently, at the national level trustees and Friends have come together to form a new organization that includes both.

In 2008 ALTA received a new name, its membership was expanded to include the Friends of the Library USA (FOLUSA), and it was renamed the Association for Library Trustees, Advocates, Friends and Foundations (ALTAFF). Though its administrative relationship to ALA and the association has become more inclusive, its primary role as advocate has continued to grow. This new division works with trustees and Friends at the local, state, and national levels to promote and advocate for libraries. ALTAFF provides workshops and other opportunities for trustees and Friends to meet other trustees and Friends, discuss common issues, and become informed advocates for public libraries.

Working with trustees from other libraries provides an opportunity for trustees to visit those other libraries and learn about the ways in which they function. As trustees review their own library's programs as part of the periodic evaluation program, they have examples of how other libraries function. Trustees may also discuss with other trustees issues of quality of service, reasonable cost of service, whether library services are growing to include more members of the community in new ways, and how the library is making a difference in its community. The kinds of information available from the trustee and Friends associations provides an overview of these and other issues of importance to libraries and suggests ways in which trustees can incorporate this information into their planning and actions as they work for their public library. Strong working relationships between Friends and trustees can only benefit libraries.

THE LIBRARY DIRECTOR AND THE TRUSTEE

The most important single responsibility of the board is to select a competent director who has the judgment, initiative, and experience to manage the library. The library director is either hired by an administrative board or recommended to the local government agency by an advisory board. The director shares with the board the responsibility for supporting long-range planning activities, managing the library's activities, and providing quality service. The director provides trustees with the information they need to be advocates for the library during budget hearings, but also on a daily basis. The director is also responsible for keeping trustees informed of library issues and alerting them to possible issues that may arise.

A very specific demarcation should exist between the board's decision-making authority and that of the director. Once the director has been hired, that person is responsible for managing the library without interference from the board. However, the balance of responsibility for decision making between board and director is to a degree dependent on the size of the library. In small communities in which the director may not have the education and experience to make some decisions, the board is more involved in decision making than it is in a large library that has professional staff. When hiring a new director, there should be discussion between the director and the board about this balance so there will be no misunderstandings about who has the authority to make decisions. And in return, the director must keep board members fully informed.

It is the responsibility of the library director to get to know board members and to ensure that they are informed about library activities, meet library staff, and are informed about library operations. The director keeps the board president informed of ongoing activities and alerts the president about possible problems. In this way, trustees are aware of what the library does and how it serves the community. When questions arise about library operations, trustees have a context within which to place them. Typically, the director anticipates the need for a new policy or for a decision on a particular issue, collects data to present to the board, and answers all questions. The trustees may then make a decision or request additional information. Board members represent different aspects of the community and also bring to their role extensive experience that is valuable to the director. Not only are they a sounding board, they also bring specific skills and interests to the table.

Typically a dynamic director brings out the best qualities in trustees as they are provided with the information they need to lead the library, and dynamic trustees support the director's efforts. Conversely, an uncertain director who is unsure of what the job entails does not motivate trustees to support library activities. A director who lacks enthusiasm and the willingness to work to make the library a center of community activities and who relies unduly on trustees for guidance will not succeed and should be replaced. A good relationship between the board and the director is essential.

Whenever serious issues arise or there is a pattern of small disagreements, there should be immediate discussion to determine any differences and how to deal with them. Once the area of disagreement is identified, both the board and the director are responsible for finding a solution. When the board and the director have worked together on library issues, and there is good communication, most issues can be resolved. If they cannot be resolved, the director has no choice but to resign.

BOARD MANAGEMENT

The board of trustees, whether it is administrative or advisory, is responsible to a large degree for representing library interests to local government and for acting as spokespersons to the community. This requires that the board's time be used wisely and that it has regular meetings that are well attended.

Library boards typically have five to seven members, but there may be as few as three or more than twelve. If the board has fewer than five members, there may be a heavy workload for each member; if it is too large, it is difficult to arrange regularly scheduled meetings.

Boards should have by-laws that describe their organization, their responsibilities, and how they function. Board structure is determined by the by-laws. Boards typically elect a president, vice president, secretary, and treasurer. They also identify specific board members to be in charge of specific activities. In many instances, the library director, rather than a board member, is responsible for secretarial duties.

Meetings should have an agenda, which is typically prepared by the director and the board president. It includes a current financial statement, a report from the director of library activities, reports from committees, special issues such as building plans, complaints about service, and new legislation and its potential ramifications, all presented along with supporting information provided by the director. Time is allocated for each item so that the agenda moves forward. The director attends all meetings and serves as the internal information source for items discussed. The board members bring their external perspectives to the issue, and in this way a balanced decision is usually reached. Boards of trustees are typically subject to open meeting laws. This means that members of the public are welcome to attend all meetings except for those meetings or portions of meetings dealing with personnel issues. Board agendas often provide time at the beginning of the meeting for community comment so that individuals may make brief presentations to the board.

Boards often name standing committees, which have specific responsibilities, such as personnel, finance, building, etc. Each committee is responsible for being knowledgeable about its charge and for being the initial group to consider issues relevant to it. If the board membership is fewer than seven individuals, board members may find themselves serving on multiple committees, and if they are not careful, the structure may become unduly complex. Another difficulty with standing committees is that when board members become very involved in a particular area, they may forget the line between trustee responsibilities and the responsibilities of the director. This is not a good thing. A larger board may have an executive committee that deals with finance, personnel, and building, and when this is the case, that group can be of considerable value in advising the director and serving as a sounding board.

For smaller boards in particular, there is an advantage to naming ad hoc committees to deal with a particular issue, report to the board, and dissolve. This has the advantage of simplifying the board structure and providing board members the opportunity to deal with more than one issue, as might be the case with standing committees.

SUMMARY

Public libraries typically have either an advisory or an administrative board of trustees, whose members serve as an important link to the community and also serve as advocates for the library. The library director and the board of trustees work together to ensure that the library meets the needs of the community, tax funds are spent wisely, and the public library attains its goal of being an important center for ideas and information available to all members of the community.

NOTES

1. Carleton B. Joeckel, *Government of the American Public Library* (Chicago: American Library Association, 1935), 9.

2. Cyril Houle, *The Effective Board* (New York: The Association Press, 1960), 12.

3. Ann E. Prentice, *The Public Library Trustee: Image and Performance in Funding* (Metuchen, NJ: Scarecrow Press, 1973), 38–63.

4. Joseph L. Wheeler and Herbert Goldhor, *Wheeler and Goldhor's Practical Administration of Public Libraries* (New York: Harper & Row, 1981), 32.

ADDITIONAL READINGS

Baughman, James C. *Trustees, Trusteeship, and the Public Good: Issues of Accountability for Hospitals, Museums, Universities and Libraries* (New York: Quorum Books, 1987).

Miller, Ellen G., and Patricia H. Fisher. *Library Board Strategic Guide: Going to the Next Level.* Lanham, MD: Scarecrow Press, 2007.

Mina, Eli, and Keith Michael Fiels. *101 Boardroom Problems and How to Solve Them.* New York: American Management Association, 2008.

Prentice, Ann E. *The Public Library Trustee: Image and Performance on Funding.* Metuchen, NJ: Scarecrow Press, 1973.

Young, Virginia, ed. *The Library Trustee.* Chicago: American Library Association, 1988.

Chapter 3

Public Library Laws and Policy

INTRODUCTION

The public library is governed by laws enacted at the federal, state, and local levels by elected bodies at each. Policies are developed and/or adopted by the library to provide guidance to staff in carrying out library responsibilities. Laws and policies cannot be in conflict, and if conflict occurs, law takes precedence over policy, state law takes precedence over municipal law, and federal law takes precedence over all of the above.

LEGISLATION

Federal Funding

From the beginnings of public library development, its legal basis has resided in state law. Most federal legislation specifically affecting public libraries began with the Library Services Act in 1956, which enacted into law the decision to grant federal aid to public libraries. This decision and the resulting legislation were directly related to data developed by the *Public Library Inquiry*, data from the Department of Agriculture and others, and advocacy by library associations. The Library Services Act provided funding based on the percentage of rural residents in the state. Matching funds were required from the state, and the federal legislation mandated that a plan for dissemination of funds be provided prior to the allocation of any funds. This requirement spurred state library agencies to move ahead with plans and activities to support public libraries at the state and local levels. The

Library Services and Construction Act (1962) expanded the Library Services Act to include nonrural areas and provided funding on a matching basis for construction or renovation of libraries.

During the decade from the mid-1950s to the mid-1960s the United States saw the Soviet Union launch the first rocket into space, and Americans became concerned about the quality of education, particularly science education, and our ability to be competitive in what became known as the Sputnik era. One outcome of this concern was that funding for education and libraries flourished.

Additional legislation, the Elementary and Secondary Education Act (1965), provided federal funds to public schools with one part, Title II, specified for school libraries. The Higher Education Act (1964) provided funding to colleges and universities, and funding was provided to specific groups and their libraries through other legislation.

In an effort to consolidate cultural and programs at the federal level, the Museum and Library Services Act, enacted in 1996, combined the Institute of Museum Services, established in 1976, with the Library Programs Office, which had been part of the Department of Education since the enactment of the Library Services Act in 1956.

According to the Library Services and Technology Act (LSTA), which is a part of the Museum and Library Services Act:

It is the purpose of this subtitle:

1. to consolidate Federal library service programs:

2. to stimulate excellence and promote access to learning and information resources in all types of libraries for individuals of all ages;

3. to promote library services that provide all users access to information through State, regional, national and international electronic networks;

4. to provide linkages among and between libraries; and

5. to promote targeted library services to people of diverse geographic, cultural and socioeconomic backgrounds, to individuals with disabilities, and to people with limited functional literacy or information skills.

Activities to be awarded grants included education and training in areas in library and information science education, particularly new technologies and other critical needs, research and demonstration projects, preservation or digitization of library materials and resources, and model programs demonstrating cooperative efforts between libraries and museums.[1] Since its enactment, this legislation has been the primary source of federal funds for public library demonstration programs.

Privacy Legislation

Another component of federal legislation relates to privacy issues. The U.S.A. Patriot Act (2001) extended the ability of federal, state, and local law enforcement agencies to demand usage records about individuals thought to be involved in terrorism or clandestine activities. This legislation affected all libraries and library users.[2] The original legislation included the use of a National Security Letter (NSL) issued by the FBI. This was an administrative subpoena, not reviewed by a judge or jury, which allowed the FBI to collect personal data in areas including books checked out of the library or medical records. The librarian or anyone in another organization receiving a NSL could not disclose that it had received such a letter and could not inform the individuals under suspicion that their records were under review.

Because of the negative reactions by those concerned with this violation of civil rights, the 2006 reauthorization of the bill was rewritten. It states that "libraries, businesses, and other targets were given the legal standing to challenge 'gag orders,' but the challenge had to be handled through secret court proceedings."[3]

The Children's Internet Protection Act (CIPA), enacted in 2001, required that public and school libraries certify that they have an Internet safety policy that includes safety protection measures to block or filter Internet access to pictures that are obscene, child pornography, or harmful to minors. This would apply to computers that are accessible to minors. Schools and libraries must certify that they have safety policies and technology in place before they can participate in the E-rate program, which under the Telecommunications Act of 1996 provides cost discounts to schools and libraries when they purchase telecommunications equipment other than telephone service. Public librarians dealt with this legislation in a variety of ways. Some filtered all public access terminals; others filtered those terminals available to children. The conflict between free access to information and filtering to protect a particular group continues to be a topic of discussion.

Other federal legislation includes components that apply to public libraries, such as the Americans with Disabilities Act (1990), which sets out requirements for access to public buildings, including libraries. Other legislation, such as that dealing with building construction, education, and training; hiring requirements; and workplace safety has components that affect the library.

The American Library Association's Washington office monitors all legislation affecting libraries and is the best resource for information about pending and existing legislation, including copyright issues, which affects or could affect libraries. Its Web site provides up-to-date information and is a regular "go to" place for trustees and librarians. ALA and its Legislative Committee sponsor a day each spring, and librarians and trustees meet with their legislators to discuss libraries and their importance and the need for adequate library support to the country. As stated by Sidney Ditzion in his 1947 study of the American public library, "Libraries are the Arsenal of a Democratic Culture."[4] The American Library Association continues to be a strong advocate nationally for libraries and library support.

State Library Legislation

The library's legal status derives primarily from state law. It may be part of education law or part of general municipal law. Although state law enables the creation of public libraries, it does not mandate them. "Cities and other municipal corporations as well as townships and counties, are creatures of the state. The state creates them and can dissolve them, subject of course to constitutional limitations."[5]

Every general library law has three provisions:

1. Power is granted by the legislature to a municipality; a city, county, village, or township;

2. It authorizes "the corporate authority of the local government unit to levy taxes for library purposes for the public library"; and

3. The governance structure of the public library is described, usually a board of trustees that may be appointed or elected. The power of the board and its duties are listed.[6] If the library does not have a board of trustees, it is a department of local government, and like all other departments of local government, it reports to the executive who is responsible for the management of the municipality.

In addition to enabling legislation, there is a body of case law that modifies or clarifies state legislation. Legislation that relates to social issues such as dealing with equal access and diversity affects public libraries along with all other governmental units.

Each state has an agency that is usually part of the state's Department of Education, or it may be stand-alone. Because the state agency has the force of law, it can mandate planning, developing, advising, and evaluation of public libraries statewide, and because federal legislation requires that a state agency have the authority to allocate federal and state aid based on criteria established at the state and federal levels, the state agency has considerable control over individual libraries. This includes the development of statewide plans for service.

Though most public libraries are chartered to serve municipalities, there is research showing that larger units of service such as the county or counties generate a better basis for funding. Planning data for determining optimum public library units is available through GeoLib. "A nationwide public library data base system, GEOLIB is funded by IMLS and linked to a digital base map which includes data sets from the U.S. Census and the National Center for Educational Statistics. The database provides consolidated information on public libraries nationwide and is available over the Internet."[7]

State law sets requirements for accountability, with the expectation that there will be accountability for how funds are spent. It also sets requirements that meetings and records of public agencies be open to the public. The definition of "meeting" has expanded over time to include online meetings, including teleconferencing. Record keeping now includes maintaining electronic records as well as hard copy records.

State law also limits the authority of individual members of boards of trustees by stating that trustees are responsible for governing the library within the parameters set forth by law and regulations. Only the board as a whole has the legal authority to make decisions. Individual board members do not, and all board members and library staff are required to avoid any conflict of interest or appearance of conflict of interest.

Until 1983 the American Library Association compiled library law. Library law, state by state for most states, is now available on the Web site of the Chief Officers of State Library Agencies (COSLA, www.cosla.org), which profiles each state library agency and has links to the legislation for libraries currently in force. Some states prepare and keep current documents that cover their own library law. One example is the state of New York, which produces the document titled *Public Library Law in New York State*, which includes "all statutes and regulations that pertain to public libraries."[8] This includes court decisions, administrative opinions, and occasionally memoranda to aid in their interpretation. In its more than 200 pages, this document deals with issues ranging from the apportionment of state aid, to how to organize interstate compacts, to how to deal with conflict of interest, to the right to have "love your library" license plates on one's car. This compilation, prepared by the New York Library Association and the State of N.Y. Education Department, is revised regularly and provides an example of how extensive public library legislation is. It, too, is on the Web and easily accessible (www.nysl.nysed. gov/libdev/fundlaw2htm).

Local Legislation

In addition to state and federal legislation, local bodies may enact statutes and regulations. So long as these statutes and regulations do not conflict with existing state and federal law, they are part of the legal requirements the local public library must follow. Examples of local legislation include the requirement that the trustees file an annual report to the municipality and laws relating to the theft or misuse of books and other materials in the library. Most materials in the library are purchased with local tax funds, and because they are property of the community, the municipality can enact legislation to protect them. Local building codes, regulations covering bans on smoking in public buildings, and codes related to signage and building occupancy are locally established, and the library is required to conform.

Because of the many laws and ordinances that apply to public libraries, it is often the case that an attorney is selected as a member of the board of trustees. In larger municipal libraries, the library board of trustees often retains the services of an attorney to advise them on legislation and to deal with the possibility of someone in the community bringing suit against the library over an issue.

POLICY

Though legislation is imposed on the library from external bodies, it determines its own policy. Its purpose is to create and implement procedures that will support achieving the goals and objectives of the library. Library by-laws provide guidance for the trustees to organize and record their activities. Except for the very new library, most libraries will have by-laws and policies, and it is the responsibility of the trustees and the director to review them and keep them current. The director and staff will recommend new policies or policy revisions and prepare the document, and the trustees will review the document to see if it provides direction for an activity and is in the best interest of the community. In this activity, the trustees are the voice of the community the library is chartered to serve. Should the library find itself sued, it is most likely that the suit will be the result of a policy that causes a member of the community to be concerned about the way in which a policy has been written or has been applied. The trustees and, if needed, an attorney should take care to ensure that the policy is not in conflict with the law and to understand how that policy will relate to the cultural and other interests of the community. In some communities, policies dealing with intellectual freedom have been at issue, and trustees have had to take a stand. Once a policy has been approved, implementing the policy is the responsibility of the library director and staff. The board of trustees reviews the policy and the director implements it.

Developing Policies

The number and range of policies relative to public library activities is extensive. Before creating or revising a policy, it is useful to go to the Internet and visit the Web sites of public libraries that have demographics similar to those of one's own library. Librarians look at policies that cover the issue they are considering and use them as a guide for their own efforts.

Policies describe the way in which the social contact between the library and the public will be carried out. A policy will typically include the following information: title of policy; the date approved by the board of trustees; the purpose of the policy; who is affected by the policy; how the library staff will carry out the policy; and how the policy relates to local, state, and federal law. If there is objection to the policy, how can a member of the community request reconsideration? The policy may also include information about the community or special situations that may influence it. It is important that policies follow a standard format, as their content is easier to follow. They must be well written so that they are easily understood and there is no question about what they mean, they should be reviewed regularly by the board, the library director, and the attorney. Maintaining up-to-date policies reduces the possibility of complaints, grievances, and lawsuits, and if a member of the community should object to a policy, a well-written, current policy that is specific to an issue is important evidence that the library is well managed.

Types of Policies

Every library needs certain basic policies. These include collection development and those dealing with customer relations, minors, and the use of meeting rooms. These are particularly important, "because they address major parts of the implied social contract between the library and its funders, especially taxpayers. In return for the latter's dollars, the library provides resources, facilities and services that improve the community."[9] Policies cover each of these areas and indicate how that contract will be carried out.

Policies that affect all libraries are the concern of the American Library Association, and its committees have prepared policies that many public libraries have adopted. This includes the *Library Bill of Rights*, the *Freedom to Read Statement*, and the *Freedom to View Statement*.

In introductory statements concerning library policy, adherence to these policies is stated. Other introductory statements support the right of each family to decide what their children will read or view and that the parents and/or guardians are responsible for the child's use of library materials.

Every library should have an up-to-date policy in the following areas:

1. *Collection development.* Every community is unique, and its librarians need to know whom the community serves and the kind of collection that best serves the community. How will it best serve the literary, cultural, educational, informational, and recreational needs of the community? How will it best address people of all ages and interests? What materials of local history and local interest will it include? What formats will it collect: print materials, audiovisual media, electronic media, Internet resources, devices for the visually impaired, games, and other formats?

   The policy needs to state the general criteria for selecting materials: public demand or interest; significance; recommendations by critics and reviewers; importance of the author; timeliness; how it fits into the existing collection; alternatives point of view; and authenticity of regional, social, or historical setting. In selecting electronic formats, how accessible are they to multiple users?

   If the library has a Web site, does it link to the online catalog and other online resources? Has professional staff recommended subject-focused Web sites? Does the library endorse links from the library's Web site to others?

   Who is responsible for selection of materials? How does the library deal with suggestions for additions to the collection by library users? What procedures take place to ensure that the collection is reviewed and weeded to make sure it meets user needs? Gifts are part of the collection policy. What does the library accept? If the title is not included in the collection, how does the librarian dispose of that title? If members of the community have opinions about materials purchased, what is their recourse?

2. *Confidentiality of library records.* Does the library maintain confidentiality of all records that connect users to materials and/or services? Nearly all libraries guarantee confidentiality, and this should be supported by a policy to protect both the library and the user. What are the exceptions to confidentiality: staff needing information for library management, an individual or individuals authorized by the borrower, parents of children under age 16, an agency or individual having a subpoena or court order? In this latter instance, will the library seek legal counsel?

3. *Meeting rooms.* What are the purposes for which community meeting rooms are available? Who is eligible to use the meeting room: locally based organizations, local government, other? What proof that the requester is locally based is required? What permits are needed? Who issues them? What are the conditions of use of the facility requested? What uses are prohibited: fees to attendees for use of the facility, sale or advertisement of items or services, smoking? What responsibilities for the condition of the meeting room or other space do those using it have? On what grounds can the library refuse to issue or revoke an application?

4. *Policies relating to minors, including the following issues:*

   - What is the library's responsibility for unattended children?
   - Under what age should a child be accompanied by a caregiver? If an unattended child is in the library, what is the responsibility of the library?
   - At what age may children be issued a library card?
   - How is the Children's Internet Protection Act applied?

Public librarians may wish to develop numerous other policies. The following list identifies some of those issues most likely to be addressed by the public library's policy book:

- Disruptive behavior and patron suspension
- Use of video monitoring equipment
- Internet use
- Naming of library buildings
- Library volunteers
- Exhibits policy
- Gifts
- Local history

SUMMARY

As new forms and formats of information become available and new programs are developed in the community, existing policies need revision on a regular basis and new policies may be needed. For example, what policies relating to social networking and the library's role should be developed? Maintaining and managing up-to-date policies is key to an efficient and well-managed public library. It also provides a platform on which one builds quality service to the community. And it provides a means of evaluating that service.

NOTES

1. Museum and Library Services Act (Title II of P.L. 94-462), Ch. 2, Sec. 231, "Library Programs."

2. Ellen G. Miller and Patricia H. Fisher, *Library Board Strategies Guide: Going to the Next Level* (Lanham, MD: Scarecrow Press, 2007), 12.

3. Ibid., 13.

4. Sidney H. Ditzion, *Arsenals of a Democratic Culture: A Social History of the American Public Library Movement in New England and the Middle States* (Chicago: American Library Association, 1947).

5. Alex Ladenson, *Library Laws and Legislation in the United States* (Metuchen, NJ: Scarecrow Press, 1983), 13.

6. Ibid., 17.

7. Kathleen de la Peña McCook, *Introduction to Public Librarianship* (New York: Neal Schuman, 2004), 109.

8. Robert Carter, *Public Library Law in New York State,* rev. ed. (Albany: New York Division of Library and the New York Library Association, 2006).

9. Miller and Fisher, *Library Board Strategic Guide,* 20.

ADDITIONAL READINGS

American Library Association, Public Library Association. *The Public Library Mission Statement and its Imperatives for Service.* Chicago: American Library Association, 1979.

Futas, Elizabeth. *Collection Development Policies and Procedures.* 3rd ed. Phoenix, AZ: Oryx Press, 1995.

Molz, Redmond Kathleen, and Phyllis Dain. *Civic Space/Cyberspace: The American Public Library in the Information Age.* Cambridge, MA: MIT Press, 1999.

National Board Governance Survey for Not-for-Profit Organizations. Chicago: Grant Thornton LLP, 2005.

Chapter 4

Leadership

INTRODUCTION

Leadership is an important, if not the most important, skill in managing libraries or any other type of organization. In one way or another it affects everything we do in the library. It has been of great interest to scholars and researchers, who want to know how one becomes a leader. Is it a skill to learn, or is one born a leader? Much of the research conducted about leadership has focused on individuals who are seen as leaders. What they believe, how they interact with others, and what they accomplish is analyzed to see if a pattern of behavior emerges that may be called leadership. The modern study of leadership began with Machiavelli's *The Prince*,[1] and much of what he said is still relevant: that leadership is not a talent; rather, it can be taught and it can be practiced. His definition of a leader was one who treated others with respect, avoided bad company, and maintained order in an appropriate way.

For many years, the study of leadership was the study of great men, and biographies appeared regularly, many of which can be considered case studies in leadership. Many biographies and autobiographies continue to be published, each of which in some way is a study in leadership, and library leaders are among those who have had their stories told. Most of these biographies were of giants in the then emerging library profession, who lived in the late 19th and early 20th centuries, including individuals such as Melvil Dewey, John Cotton Dana, and Justin Winsor. Unfortunately, many early library leaders were often better known for their brilliance, contrariness, and difficult personalities rather than for their ability to instill respect and a feeling of worth in those they managed.

Scientific study of leadership began in the 20th century and can be divided into three periods. Early studies focused on the idea that leaders were somehow different from others, and if one could identify the traits that made them different, one would be able to identify leaders. Then the focus changed to a study of behavior and the idea that leaders behaved in a certain way, and if one could identify the behaviors, one could identify leaders. The idea was to look at situations in which people found themselves, look for common responses, and identify these responses as indications of leadership.

One group of researchers studied approximately 100 individuals who held responsible positions to see if they demonstrated common ways of dealing with issues. Despite these studies, no common definition of leadership emerged. What was found was that leadership is culture dependent, in that each culture has its norms, and an individual very successful in leading an organization in one culture cannot always transfer this ability to another culture.[2] We can also look at different professions as cultures and may well find that leadership in one profession does not transfer easily to another profession. A military officer may be very successful in that environment, but those skills may not transfer easily to the management of a library staff, who expect a more participatory style.

WHAT IS LEADERSHIP?

Cribbin defined leadership as "the ability to gain consensus and commitment to common objectives which are attained through the effort and experience of others."[3] The workforce has changed since the 1970s, and most individuals no longer expect or want to be treated as parts of a machine but insist on being respected for their abilities and their performance. Leaders must respect those they lead and demonstrate that respect. Warren Bennis, one of the most prolific researchers in the field of leadership studies, looked at leadership in a changing society to provide new insights. A study he conducted with Burt Nanus in 1985 is a benchmark in the area of leadership studies.[4] They defined leadership "as the pivotal force behind successful organizations and, that to create vital and visible organizations, leadership is necessary to help organizations develop a new vision of what they can be, then mobilize the organizational change toward the new vision."[5]

Although there are some 350 definitions of leadership, some of which conflict with others, there is no way to differentiate effective leadership from ineffective leadership or an effective organization from an ineffective one. Bennis and Nanus point out that the world we live in has changed and continues to change. As we move from an industrial society to an information society, as the workforce is better educated, as technology and networking have changed the ways in which we interact, there is a new awareness of the role of leaders and leadership. Because information is much more available to staff and the public, the person responsible for an organization cannot maintain control by withholding information. Leaders no longer have the privacy to act without interacting with others. We need new leaders who will move our organizations forward and who, rather than hiding information, use it as a means of enriching social and professional interaction.

To identify today's and tomorrow's leadership, Bennis located CEOs from both the public and private sectors who were successful in leading their organizations and asked them three questions:

- What are your strengths and weaknesses?

- Was there any particular experience or event in your life that influenced your management philosophy or style?

- What were the major decision points in your career, and how do you feel about your choices now?

Bennis also interviewed each individual and observed each at work as he or she interacted with staff and the public. Nearly all those interviewed were white males; the first study of women as leaders was done by Sally Helgesen in 1990.[6]

From his interviews, Bennis identified four types of leadership skills:

1. Attention through vision. The leader creates a focus and an agenda, and has a vision that leads to an outcome. Staff knows that the leader has a vision, understands what that vision is and where it will lead the organization; and buy into the vision. The leader is willing to work to achieve the vision, and staff supports the vision. Where does one find a vision? It may come from ideas discussed with staff or with other leaders, opportunities in the environment, current trends, or past experience.

2. Meaning through communication. If an individual is unable to articulate the vision so that others understand it, they cannot buy into the vision. The leader defines the vision through an agenda and shows the steps needed to achieve the vision. Staff members, who are expected to participate in the vision to make it fact, need to understand what is expected and where it will lead.

3. Trust through positioning. Bennis says that trust implies accountability, predictability, and reliability. The leader needs to point the direction in which the organization will move and to stick with that course of action unless there is a very good reason to change course.

4. Deployment of self through positive self-regard. Leaders know their strengths and weaknesses and their personal worth. The leader has positive self-regard and positive regard for others and treats everyone with respect. How individuals see themselves often determines the success or failure of a situation.

Bennis summarized his study by saying that the leader is a catalyst. He also debunked five myths of leadership: that leaders are born, not made; that leadership is a rare skill; that leaders are charismatic; that leadership occurs only at the top of the organization; and that the leader controls, directs, prods, and manipulates the organization. Leadership is a skill one can learn through trial and error, and it occurs at all levels of the organization. "The leader does not lead by force but by the quality of the vision and the ability to make it work."[7]

How does the work done by Bennis and Nanus relate to library leaders? In 1991 Brooke Sheldon, a past president of ALA, former dean, faculty member, and widely respected library consultant, replicated their study by interviewing 60 library leaders. She expected to find that library leaders' responses would be essentially the same as those of the leaders Bennis and Nanus had studied. She asked library leaders the same questions plus these two additional questions:

1. What, if any, has been the influence of mentors on your career?

2. How do you feel about the future of the profession?

She learned that library leaders have strong visions. One interviewee said that vision is "setting your sights on what would be the best possible thing, not under the naive assumption you'll ever get there, but to make certain that if you do certain things, you go in that direction rather than some other direction."[8] Library leaders are results oriented, and many have the personal drive to capture attention, draw people in, and move forward to a common goal. Librarians believe in what they are doing and have a deep commitment to the importance of librarianship and its role in society.

Library leaders communicate their vision well. They have a global view of their community and the world at large and see the library within that context. They develop networks and coalitions because they know that working together is critical to achieving the vision. Within the library, they are proactive in working with staff members so that they understand the vision and their role in achieving it. They build consensus for innovation and lead the effort. They emphasize simply stated ideas and develop one or two directions. For example, if the goal is to put the library user first, they look at the library's organizational structure, its staff, and the arrangement and look of the facilities to see if each of these and other elements are focused on the user.

Library leaders have a talent for working with staff to achieve goals. They respect staff members, listen to staff concerns, and communicate what they expect from staff. They have a healthy self-image. They are willing to mentor others. The only difference between Bennis and Nanus's findings and Sheldon's findings was that library leaders have a stronger service orientation.

PUBLIC LIBRARY DEMOGRAPHICS

What does today's public library workforce look like? Where are the public library leaders? How will we ensure that today's leaders are preparing the next generation of public library leaders? During the first decade of the 21st century, the Institute for Museum and Library Services funded *A National Research Study on the Future of Librarians in the Workforce.*[9] This "once in a decade" study, conducted by Dr. José Marie Griffiths and Donald King, set out to look at the anticipated labor shortages in the library/information science field due to retirements, to assess the number and types of jobs that will become available in the United States, either because of retirement or new job creation; determine the skills that will be required to fill such vacancies; and look at ways to recruit and retain workers. The researchers also reviewed the importance and value of libraries, particularly from the perspective of funders, users, and potential recruits into the LIS workforce.

This study has a 10-year time line and makes projections about the library/information work force until 2015 and 2016. Also, the data acquired for this study and recommendations for ongoing data collection and workforce monitoring will serve as the basis for continuing review of the library/information science workforce. Although the study looked at the entire library/ information science workforce, one major section of this monumental task dealt specifically with public libraries and public librarians. Data on public libraries were collected over a three-year period, and a full report became available in late 2008.

All 9,763 public libraries in the United States were sampled, and 3,127 responded, thus providing a sufficient number of responses to analyze productively. It was found that demand for MLS public librarians for the decade from 2008 to 2017 would be 22,449. It was also noted that the demand for MLS librarians would decline from 3,245 in 2008 to 1,385 in 2017. When one adds in the unmet demand from previous years, the figures are very different. Adding the unmet demand from the previous year to the projected demand minus the supply, one gets the effective demand, which shows that, for all types of libraries, the effective demand will rise from 7,464 in 2009 to 18,789 in 2018.

Although this figure is for all types of libraries, a substantial percentage of the demand comes from public libraries. The current age range of public librarians shows that nearly half are over 46 years of age, and nearly half of this group is over 56. Most of today's leaders are in that grouping, and most of tomorrow's leaders are in the 40 percent who are under 40. Other data from this study appear elsewhere in the book and may be found in discussions of staffing and organization.

And What Does This Have to Do with Leadership?

As the information professions change, tomorrow's leaders need to be conversant with staffing changes. Two of the issues identified by panels working with the IMLS study deal directly with leadership:

- What will leadership mean in an environment with
  - new and perhaps different positions;
  - differing interrelationships among professional, technical, and support staff;
  - changing expectations for staff learning and renewal (the expectation that staff will be in a continuous learning mode);

- changing management structures; and

- a new emphasis on collaboration, both external and internal.

- (This is just the beginning of the changes that are, might, will occur.)

- How does one ensure that leaders will be available to lead the new generation of information professionals?

    - What is the role of continuous education and courses in preparing leaders?

    - How do we ensure that mentors are available?

    - Will LIS leaders come from other professional situations? Are they socialized to the values of librarianship and, if not, how do we socialize them?

- How do we help more library leaders develop a public voice about the importance of libraries and library service to a healthy society?

This latter concern ties in with discussions of the role of the public intellectual. Who would be better than a librarian who is well-versed in the ways in which information is organized and used, interacts daily with the public, and has the characteristics of curiosity, desire to investigate, and skill in expressing one's self to become a public intellectual in the best sense of the term? Though the IMLS study focuses on leadership within the information professions, the public librarian is also a community leader and has an important role in using the library's resources to lead or at least support discussions important to the community. This responsibility goes back to the beginning of the public library movement in the United States, when Ben Franklin saw the public library as a valuable source of education and information that would improve the lives of all.

ON BEING A LEADER

The ways in which we look at the role of the leader have changed. Leadership today comes less from the person at the top of the organizational chart than it once did. Leadership can come from anywhere in the library. There may be several leaders, each with special information, responsibilities, and/or skills. The leader is part of the community and leads not just from a position of authority but also as a result of consensus of those being led. Historically, there was an informal contract between the employer and employee, between the leader and the led. If the individual being led was loyal to the leader, that individual's job was secure. That contract no longer exists, largely because employees are unwilling to give loyalty as easily as was once true. If a contract between a staff member and a leader still exists, it has become one in which mutual respect and appreciation have replaced the earlier, more paternalistic model. "Leadership has become a reciprocal relationship between those who choose to lead and those who decide to follow."[10]

Technology has changed the nature of leadership. The leader is no longer the sole owner of information. Information is now available throughout the library and empowers the entire staff, not just the director. Ease of communication, combined with the availability of information, means that information is a shared tool. Today's leader is a servant/leader. The leader helps staff members become what they need to become to achieve objectives. The old carrot/stick approach has been replaced by expecting the best efforts of others and by helping them achieve their goals.

Today's workforce is better educated because information jobs require a higher level of competence. Staff members with higher levels of education and expertise have higher expectations of how they are to be treated. They expect to have access to needed information and to be able to grow and prosper in their work.

What has not changed is that the leader sets the tone of the organization. Is it a well-run, efficient operation? Do staff members work well together for the benefit of the operation and to provide the best possible service? Do they staff support one another's efforts? Is there a spirit of innovation and change? Is it a good place in which to grow and prosper and from which those the library serves gain the maximum levels of support? If this is the tone, the leadership is working.

Several types of leaders and leadership emerge, depending on the individual's skills and talents. Some work well and others have limited value. For example, narcissistic leaders are so convinced of the rightness of their ideas and abilities that they are unwilling to listen to others. This type of leader would be willing to die for the vision rather than to compromise what he or she thinks is right. Such leaders are risk takers, hate criticism, don't listen, lack empathy, hate to mentor others, and are highly competitive. They want everything to go their way, and if things go wrong, it's someone else's fault. Media love this type of leader, and the leader loves the media. This type of leader is not aware of the interests of those who follow, or even if anyone is following.

At the other end of the spectrum are the quiet leaders, who move patiently and incrementally. "They do what is right—for their organizations, for the people around them, and for themselves - inconspicuously and without casualties."[11] Because many big problems can be resolved only by numerous small efforts, quiet leadership, although seemingly slow, may be the quickest way to achieve success. Success is the cumulative effort of many people and not the activities of someone who sees herself or himself as a hero. Quiet leadership is a way of thinking about people, organizations, action, and the flow of events. Quiet leaders are realists and see the world as it is rather than how they want it to be. They are aware of the limits and subtleties of power. Quiet leaders are successful because they do their homework, take many factors into consideration, and then act in the best interests of all. They are rarely recognized or rewarded, but they are the ones who move the world forward. Most leadership styles fall between these two types and reflect the strengths and personalities of the individual responsible for leading.

Do the leadership styles of men and women differ? A definitive answer to this question was not available until Sally Helgesen published her research in 1991.[12] She followed four women leaders through their daily activities to see how they spent their time and then compared her findings to a similar study of male leaders done earlier. She found that women and men differed from one another as leaders in several ways:

- Male executives tended to work at a rapid pace all day with no breaks, whereas women worked at a steady pace with brief scheduled breaks during the day. Both scheduled about 60 percent of their time in formal meetings, but the women were less stressed because of built-in short breaks that allowed them to "catch their breath."

- For men, days were heavily scheduled and then interrupted by subordinates asking questions or by other interruptions. Secretaries were used as a shield against interruptions, which were seen as a negative element in their planned daily activities because they were hard to control. Women made an effort to be accessible, particularly to subordinates, so that they would be seen as part of the daily work activities rather than interruptions. Women saw secretaries as a link to others rather than a protection from others, both inside and outside the organization.

- Men left little time for activities not directly related to their work, whereas women made time for activities outside their work lives. For women, family was the first priority and work came second. Women also read widely in professional journals, management books, history, politics, fiction, and anything else that would broaden their knowledge of the world around them.

- Men preferred phone calls or face-to-face meetings as the primary way to gain information. They were impatient with written information and saw mail as an annoyance. They rarely set aside time to deal with mail, skimmed any professional magazines in minutes, and usually delegated handling mail to their secretaries. Although women preferred live action encounters, they scheduled time to attend to mail and other external communication because they saw it as a means "of keeping relationships in good repair by being polite, thoughtful, and personal."

- Both men and women maintained a complex network of relationships with people outside their organization because they saw representing their organization as a primary role and as a major way of gaining information.

- Men immersed themselves in the day-to-day needs of their organization, leaving little time for reflection. They were so involved in daily tasks that they didn't have time to look at long-range issues. While men focused on daily tasks to the extent that they had little time to think about long-range issues, women also focused on big picture issues and the way that their organization would be affected by social, educational, economic, and other issues.

- Men identified with their jobs and tended to feel that the job defined them. They derived personal benefit from being in charge and enjoyed playing the role of leader/director. They had access to a great deal of information, which they identified with power and were reluctant to share, because it meant sharing power, which they would not do. Women viewed their jobs as just one element of their identity and tended not to see their leadership role as a way to exert their power. And women scheduled time for information sharing because they wished to give others in the organization the tools to problem solve. In summary, women were more concerned with relationships and more willing to reach out to others; men were concerned with maintaining power and dictating to others.

Since Helgesen's study, more women have assumed leadership positions and more studies have been conducted. A study published in 2009 looked at "Women and the Vision Thing"[13] to see if there were differences in perception of women as leaders by men and women. Ten dimensions of leadership were identified, and both men and women were asked to rate men and women on each of these dimensions. On the dimensions of empowering, energizing, designing and aligning, rewarding and feedback, team building, outside orientation, global mind set, tenacity, and emotional intelligence, there was either no difference, or women received a higher rating.

On one dimension, envisioning, men received a higher rating. Because having vision is key to leadership, women managers and leaders participating in executive education programs were asked to interpret this finding. They suggested that women are equally visionary, but in a different way. They are more collaborative in forming the vision, bringing in diverse inputs from many sources, and thus may be seen as less involved in building the vision because they didn't do it all by themselves and needed help. Rather than collaboration being seen as a means of inclusion, some saw it as a sign of weakness and an inability by women to think through a process to reach a vision by themselves. Another suggestion was that women are pragmatic and take a pragmatic approach to achieving a vision. They value substance over talk. They also want to get the job done, and this is more important than self-promotion by presenting a unilateral vision.

Among many styles of leadership, men and women tend to have different styles. Women tend to be transformative leaders. They transform the library by identifying objectives, providing support, rewarding positive behavior, and serving as role models. Men tend to be transactional leaders. They establish give-and-take relationships, clarify objectives, and reward good behavior. Women's leadership style is to say "let's do" rather than "do." They can make progress without ruffling feathers. Because their style is not as attention getting as the "do" style, they may not be seen as active leaders.

WHO IS RESPONSIBLE FOR TOMORROW'S LEADERS?

Many individuals and organizations have a role in preparing tomorrow's library leaders: the staff of the library where the individual works, professional organizations, schools that prepare library/information science professionals, community groups, and most important, the individual. Each individual who interacts with other staff has a role in preparing tomorrow's leaders. It is not just the director or department head of the library who is responsible for working with staff members to help them add to their academic preparation to become successful librarians. Every member of the staff has a role. The technical specialist who can provide specific skills is a leader. The staff member who has worked in the library for many years and knows its history and how the community and library demographics have changed is a leader in his or her area. The staff member at any level and any place in the library who can help another become more competent in dealing with the many complexities of human interaction is a leader. It was once said that it takes a village to raise a child. It also takes a whole staff to bring out the best in others and to give them the confidence and skills to lead.

Professional organizations at all levels are actively involved in workshops, seminars, in-service training, research, and publications intended to prepare tomorrow's leaders. These efforts have been underway for some time, and the number of programs available continues to grow. Leslie Burger, ALA president in 2007, said:

> We are busy thinking about the ways that we should educate 21st century librarians both in formal MLIS curricula and through our various certification programs. We are seeking ways to recruit a more diverse workforce that reflects the communities we serve and [we] are searching for people who can assume the positions of longtime professional leaders. The challenges faced in libraries today are changing at a rapid pace and require an agile workforce of problem-solvers, team players, leaders, and articulate spokes persons. . . .
>
> ALA has a key role to play in developing formal and informal professional leadership opportunities throughout all stages of our careers. I like to think of it as a situational leadership training—wherever you may be in your career, ALA will have a leadership program that enables you to move to the next step. . . . And finally, for those ready to go off to our next adventure, I would like to see training that enables us to lead during the transition in both our organizational and personal life.[14]

One of the centerpieces of her presidency was the establishment of a program for emerging leaders to which new librarians with an MLIS degree or working on the degree could apply. Those accepted would agree to serve on an ALA Division, Chapter, or Round Table committee, task force, or work group once they had completed the program. This not only provides leadership training to representatives of today's workforce but also provides ALA with emerging leaders and provides the emerging leaders with experience in working with others in professional organizations.

State library associations are also involved in leadership activities that cover both general information on how to develop leadership skills and information specific to the demographics of their state. As an example, the

Maryland Library Association has sponsored the Maryland Library Leadership Institute, which "is the place for you so long as you have the necessary spark to lead the Maryland Libraries of tomorrow!" The institute, held every two years, is a week-long experience aimed at helping participants develop their own leadership skills, and at the same time it is a way to build a network of leaders for Maryland's libraries. Similar programs are available in nearly every state or region. Not only do they teach leadership skills, these regional programs also serve as an important means of networking among librarians in that region.

Schools and colleges of library and information studies often offer courses, workshops, or seminars focused on leadership, which are open to librarians. Not only do these activities provide an opportunity to develop an understanding of leadership, they also provide a means for tomorrow's leaders to meet and interact with others interested in playing a role in tomorrow's libraries.

Librarians receive a continuous stream of advertisements for opportunities to attend institutes and other educational formats that promise that they will

- develop skills for team leadership,

- unleash and empower their staff,

- learn to inspire and lead through better communication,

- adopt a leadership style that generates heightened performance, and

- lead with emotional intelligence.

These are sponsored by groups such as the American Management Association. They may be advertised by consulting firms that specialize in continuing education, by individual consultants. Some may be face-to-face, whereas others are online. There is seemingly no end to the opportunities to explore leadership issues. The problem is to find those that meet one's needs and the needs of staff and to match one's objectives with the objectives of the sponsor of the learning experience.

Mentoring

Mentoring is one of those activities that is difficult to define in a few words, but as has often been said, "I know it when I see it." There is agreement that mentoring is based on a relationship of trust. Leaders are "the keepers of the big picture," and they have a responsibility to develop leaders who will carry the vision forward. They do this by creating an environment in which individuals can take charge of their activities. As individuals gain confidence, they can lead others. Leadership development takes time and is a conscious process. It is done by putting people at risk working on projects that matter, thus stretching their awareness of what they can do when they are expected to perform. The leader leads by example. Leaders must be learners who entertain new ideas, ask for feedback, and are able to admit mistakes. The leader must have a personalized, teachable view of what leadership is, how it contributes to the health of the organization, and how it is used to create change. Leaders must look toward the future, develop a shared and compelling vision of the future, and "embrace what the future may hold." If leaders are not future oriented, how can they mentor tomorrow's leaders? Leaders who are in the comfort zone of believing that "all is well and we can coast for a while" are out of touch with reality and are not competent mentors of tomorrow's leaders.

Each organization has its distinct culture, which is "an invisible guidebook for employees." It serves as a compass for making decisions when the policy manual doesn't work. This culture may be a mentoring one, in which employees are encouraged to look at things from new perspectives, try new things, and transform mistakes into learning experiences. Bennis says that the organization itself can often be a better mentor than an individual, as turnover in many organizations limits the continuity in mentorship that an individual may find useful. He also says that the organization as mentor in areas including organizational behavior, tone, pace, and values may be either a positive or a negative mentoring experience.[15]

Everyone in the organization can benefit from mentoring or from being a mentor. In our increasingly global economy, mentoring is particularly important as cultural issues play an ever-increasing role in the workplace. Not only must one understand the job assignment, one must also be aware of how to interact with coworkers who may represent different cultures and how to interact with those they serve who may also represent different cultures.

Studies of mentoring[16] have indicated that there are four criteria for being a good mentor:

1. *Mentoring is personal.* There is no organized format for the activity. The person being mentored wants to know how well he or she is doing. The mentor pays attention, listens, asks, shows interest, and provides suggestions. The mentor is also interested in the individual's personal goals, perceived strengths, and interests. There is a fine line between mentoring to enhance performance and getting too personal. Most individuals understand this and maintain the appropriate balance.

2. *Not everyone is an A player.* The majority of staff members are B players: those "solid citizens" who aren't seeking the top positions in the field, stay in the organization for a fairly long time, hold the institutional memory, have a longer term perspective of the organization, and appreciate stability. They are the solid, reliable backbone of the organization. Often the A employees look down on the B employees and underestimate their competence. The wise leader understands both A and B employees and provides appropriate mentoring for both.

3. *The number of choice assignments in which one can grow and learn are limited.* To provide opportunities for more individuals, the leader could place a more experienced individual in the choice position and then assign a new staff member to shadow that person. Another way to provide experience is to give the new staff member a research

assignment or pose a problem that needs to be solved. This gives individuals a chance to show what they can do. The mentor should look for opportunities that truly contribute to the organization or to the individual's experience to learn and grow. Make-work assignments are an insult to the staff member's intelligence.

4. *Mentoring is a two-way activity.* If a staff member wants a mentor, he or she should act accordingly and seek out individuals who can help. The new staff member may be invaluable to senior staff, as that individual brings a different perspective, and perhaps new skills, to the organization.

Criteria for being a good mentor were summarized from interviews with successful professionals. They stressed the following attributes. The successful mentor is someone who

- is absolutely credible, whose integrity transcends the message, be it positive or negative;

- tells you things you may not want to hear but leaves you feeling that you have been heard;

- interacts with you in a way that makes you want to become better;

- makes you feel secure enough to take risks;

- gives you confidence to rise above your inner doubts and fears;

- supports your attempts to set stretch goals for yourself; and

- presents opportunities and highlights challenges you might not have seen on your own.

A mentor can be a teacher, a parent, an older sibling, a senior associate, or others individuals have met who "demanded more from them than they knew they had to give." Others find that reading biographies or the classics can be a mentoring experience. Friends and friendship can have a strong mentoring element. Mentoring need not be tied to professional activities. Friends can teach values, how to deal with adversity, and many other lessons we can use throughout our personal and professional lives. It is often stressed that one cannot mentor or be mentored unless there is a personal link such as friendship or respect. Mentoring is a two-way relationship, and each must be interested in the other as a whole person.

Many leaders have had mentors who have changed their lives. The best mentoring interactions are those that spark mutual learning and explore similar values. It is important that the individuals being mentored are wise enough to avoid a mentor who wants to mold them into that mentor's image. This does not work. Neither does allowing oneself to be pushed into daily activities that are neither enriching nor of personal interest. Saying no to a mentor's suggestions, as long as it is done carefully and with options, helps the mentor better understand what the needs and interests of the mentee are.

Individuals being mentored must not assume that a mentor will look out for them and guide them to the next steps in their career. That is the responsibility of the individual, who is the one most responsible for personal success.

Role Models

A role model is an individual we may select because he or she is someone we wish to emulate. A role model can be a mentor or someone we respect for his or her values, integrity, and the way in which he or she leads. Barbara McClintock, the Nobel Prize–winning scientist who worked in genetics and was ridiculed for years by male colleagues and had difficulty obtaining research funds, but kept working on her theory of "jumping genes" in corn, persevered. In doing so, she changed the face of her science. She was a role model to other molecular biologists because she would not quit, she fairly quietly persevered in what was seen as a man's world, and she won. We may find role models in every facet of our lives and professions. They are the ones who dared, who persevered, who succeeded despite adversity, and who did it with class and integrity.

Tomorrow's Leaders

The primary purpose of mentoring is to prepare tomorrow's leaders. Although leaders do not follow the path laid out by others but rather find their own way, those who have a worldview and who have the confidence to shape their own direction have often benefited from mentoring relationships. New realities require new ideas and new ways of looking at what we do and what we need to do. The leader fosters an environment that encourages others to look at things from different perspectives, try new approaches, learn from these activities, and continuously reshape what we do in light of what has been learned. Although the vision remains essentially the same, the way in which it is carried out is modified by changing circumstances. Successful organizations of all types are future oriented, and their leaders are willing to look at different futures. Whereas the manager's comfort zone is determined by what is known and what is familiar, the leader tends to see the comfort zone as a complacency zone that can quickly insulate the organization and put it out of touch with reality.

Today's workforce is different from the past in that it is better educated. Today's jobs are different in that they require a higher level of education. The hierarchical structure of the industrial age organization does not fit well with these new jobs and the more educated, more independent workforce. The workforce is also more varied demographically (e.g. gender, ethnicity, age, cultural background), which further differentiates it from previous years. "The time is ripe to redefine leadership in the 21st century . . . . People are too well informed to adhere to a set of rules or simply follow a leader over a distant hill. They want to be inspired to a greater purpose."[17] The 21st-century leader is authentic, and authentic leaders are "good in their skin," so good they don't feel a need to impress or please others. They not only inspire those around them, they bring people together around a shared purpose and a common set of values and motivate them to create value for everyone involved. "[Authentic] leaders are more concerned about serving others than they are about their own success or recognition. Which is not to say that authentic leaders are perfect. Every leader has weaknesses, and all are subject to human frailties and mistakes. Yet by acknowledging failings and admitting error, they connect with people and empower them to take risks."[18]

Leadership is about going somewhere and about having a vision to guide that journey. Leadership is a journey, and we never reach the vision. As we close in on our goals, we renew the vision and set new goals, always keeping the vision ahead of us. We continuously examine the vision and adjust as needed. Leaders of the future need the ability to teach others and to maintain a climate of continuous learning so that those being led have the tools to move forward.

Tomorrow's leader has multiple perspectives and is "consciously connecting [them] and applying a variety of skills to establish new directions, options, and solutions for the organization."[19]

SUMMARY

Today's librarians have thought about their profession and their future in that profession, and they understand where libraries are today and the direction in which they are moving. They see themselves as leaders and are anxious to be leaders in training from their first work experience. They do not want to wait until some later time to take responsibility, learn new things, and be part of the vision for the library.

NOTES

1. Niccolo Machiavelli, *The Prince* (London: Penguin, 1999).
2. Bill George, Peter Sims, Andrew N. McLean, and Diane Mayer, "Discovering Your Authentic Leadership," *Harvard Business Review* 85, no. 3 (2007): 129–38.
3. James J. Cribbin, *Leadership Strategies for Organizational Effectiveness* (New York: American Management Association, 1981).
4. Warren Bennis and Burt Nanus, *Leaders: The Strategies for Taking Charge* (New York: Harper & Row, 1985).
5. Ibid., 2.
6. Sally Helgesen, *The Female Advantage: Women's Ways of Leadership* (New York: Currency Doubleday, 1990).
7. Bennis and Nanus, *Leaders*, 222–24.
8. Brooke E. Sheldon, *Leaders in Libraries: Styles and Strategies for Success* (Chicago: American Library Association, 1991).
9. Institute of Museum and Library Services, *A National Research Study on the Future of Librarians in the Workforce* (Washington, DC: IMLS, 2009).
10. James M. Kouzes and Barry Z. Posnedr, *Credibility: How Leaders Gain It*

and Lose It, Why People Demand It (San Francisco: Jossey-Bass, 1993), 1.

   11. Joseph L. Badaracco, Jr., *Leading Quietly, An Unorthodox Guide to Doing the Right Thing* (Boston: Harvard Business School Press, 2002), 2.

   12. Sally Helgesen, *Female Advantage.*

   13. Hermina Ibarra and Otillia Obodaru, "Women and the Vision Thing," *Harvard Business Review* 87, no. 1 (January 2009): 62–70.

   14. Leslie Burger, "President's Message," *American Libraries* 36, no. 1 (November 2006): 3.

   15. Bennis and Nanus, *Leaders*, 180.

   16. Thomas Delong Jr., John J. Gabarro, and Robert J. Lees, "Why Mentoring Matters in a Hypercompetitive world," *Harvard Business Review* 86, no. 1 (January 2008): 115–21.

   17. Ibid.

   18. Bill George, "Special Report on America's Best Leaders," *U.S. News and World Report* 141, no. 16 (October 30, 2006): 52–95.

   19. Ibid.

ADDITIONAL READINGS

Badaracco, Joseph L., Jr. *Questions of Character: Illuminating the Heart of Leadership Through Literature.* Boston: Harvard Business School Press, 2006.

Eagly, Alice H., and Linda L. Carli. *Through the Labyrinth: The Truth About How Women Become Leaders.* Boston: Harvard Business School Press, 2007.

Hesselbein, Frances, and Marshall Goldsmith, eds. *The Leader of the Future 2*. San Francisco: Jossey Bass, 2006.

Horrocks, Norman, ed. *Perspectives, Insights, and Priorities: 17 Leaders Speak Freely of Librarianship.* Lanham, MD: Scarecrow Press, 2005.

Peters, Thomas J., and Robert H. Waterman. *In Search of Excellence.* New York: Harper & Row, 1983.

Rosen, Robert H. *Leading People: Transforming Business from the Inside Out.* New York: Viking, 1996.

Snyder, Kirk. *The G Quotient: Why Gay Executives Are Winning the Leadership Race . . . What Every Manager Needs to Know.* San Francisco: Jossey Bass, 2006.

5

Public Library Demographics

INTRODUCTION

From the beginning of the public library movement in the late 17th century, there has been a great deal of interest and concern about who should benefit from free access to information. In the early days, the desire to spread Christian knowledge was paramount. In 18th-century America, Benjamin Franklin's view of the ideal library user was the young man seeking to improve himself through self-education. Wealthy businessmen saw the public library as a means of educating the workforce. They provided resources in its early days as an inexpensive means of providing continuing education to young men, who would then be able to contribute to a new country in need of educated workers and individuals capable of fulfilling their responsibilities as citizens of a democratic republic.

Many public libraries, great and small, from the Enoch Pratt Free Library in Baltimore, Maryland, and the New York Public Library to the Troy, New York, Public Library and libraries in even smaller cities and towns, were responses by philanthropic businessmen to the need to support the growth of an educated workforce. As science and technology became increasingly important to the growth of industry, the public library served as an inexpensive means of self-education. Those worried about the rhetoric and reality of revolution in Europe during the 19th century maintained that if one was well educated, that individual was less susceptible to being led by any particular theory or group. And this was one more reason to support the public library.

Women as library users became more visible in the latter half of the 19th century, and they too needed information, to be more efficient managers in their homes and family activities. Although there was an impression by some that all women wanted to read were fluffy romances, in fact many were as interested in bettering their lives in a growing country as were the men. They may not have had the same opportunities in the workforce as the men, but they were no less interested in their communities. It has been suggested that the struggle for women's rights has a direct link to the public library. Certainly the assumption that the public library was a place where genteel ladies could safely work served as an opportunity for women to work outside the home in nondomestic roles. And thus were sown the seeds of one of the first waves of the information professions.

In the last decade or so of the 19th century and early into the 20th century, the public library began to include children among its users. Once the public library welcomed children, services to children grew rapidly and became increasingly important. Also at the turn of the 20th century, the first library to serve African Americans was established in Louisville, Kentucky. Although service to immigrants was common in urban areas throughout the late 19th century, it was after 1904 and through the end of World War I (1918) that the public library was a particular friend to immigrants. This was the place immigrants could learn English, build a bridge between the culture of the home country and America, find free reading material, better themselves economically, and begin to become a part of their new country. Interest in working with immigrant groups tended, and continues to tend, to wax and wane depending on economic and political priorities at the time.

It wasn't until the *Public Library Inquiry*, conducted after the end of World War II (1941–1945), that there was a concerted effort, through research, to define the role of the public library and learn who the public library served and why. Bernard Berelson's *The Library's Public* focused on this aspect of the public library. He reinforced the longstanding purpose of the public library: "Its existence depends upon the existence of free, educated citizes to use it and 'its proper task' is to develop and nurture the nation's cultural climate."[1] And Berelson's study, for the first time, provided research-based evidence of who uses the library. It, like the other volumes of the *Public Library Inquiry* (PLI), provides a benchmark from which other studies have been conducted.

Data from the PLI and other sources were used to develop a legislative program to address the PLI finding "that nearly 50,000,000 people who lived outside of the cities in towns, villages, and unincorporated areas were without access to public libraries. It appeared that public libraries, at least, were serving only from 15 to 25 percent of the population."[2] The Library Services Act (1956) was a response to the limited number of individuals in rural areas with access to public libraries. The Library Services and Construction Act (1964) extended support of library services to nonrural areas with the particular purpose of building public libraries. This legislation was responsible for supporting the construction or remodeling of more than 1,800 public libraries. It was estimated that these efforts provided service to some 60,000,000 Americans. "The 'consciousness raising' effected on the public by the combination of exposure and demonstration, citizen involvement and publicity, has helped enormously to raise public expectations (and professional expectations as well) of what public libraries should be able to do for people."[3]

This consciousness raising and funding to encourage the development of new services to groups not always well served by the public library further increased the range of services available to the public. Public librarians developed business information services for the small business community. They provide health information for those wishing to be more sophisticated consumers or who need to know where to go in the social support system to get help. Job information centers, support of early childhood education and vocational education, opportunities for those with disabilities to access information and programs, and opportunities for minority and immigrant populations and many other services have become part of the activities of many public libraries. The public library has become an important access point for Internet services and assistance in using other information technology. For many, it is the only access to the world of online information.

AND HOW DO WE KNOW WHO OUR USERS ARE?

All public librarians have the responsibility to know whom they serve, whom they do not serve, and how the community they serve is changing demographically so that they can provide the best possible service. Without this information, librarians cannot plan for the future. They do not know which groups in the community are on the increase and which are declining. What is the average age of those being served? Is the community aging? What about the number of young families with young children? Is it increasing or decreasing? What immigrant communities exist within the library service area? How are they changing? What are their needs? What is the level of unemployment in the community? What is the library's role in supporting those looking for work? These and many more questions require answers as the library staff assesses its present programs and plans for the future.

When librarians plan for services and programs both in the short and long term, when they make their budget requests for the next year and look to the future years, when they look at the building and the extent to which it meets today and tomorrow's needs, they need to be aware of the demographics of the community they serve today and will serve tomorrow.

STEPS IN BUILDING THE DEMOGRAPHIC PROFILE

The first step in reviewing the demographics of the library's service area is to know what the boundaries of the service area are. A public library is chartered to serve a municipality, a county, a town, or another defined area. Because the largest component of public library funding comes from the local tax base, property tax in particular, it is necessary to use the area defined as eligible for local funding as the basis of any demographic study. In many areas, individuals who live outside the primary service area have the opportunity to pay a fee and use the resources of another library. If an individual lives in a rural area near a city with a large public library, or if a public library is close to the individual's workplace, that individual often pays the fee to access resources more conveniently Also, several states have instituted statewide borrowers' cards, which allow an individual to borrow materials from any public library in the state. In any demographic study, it is important to recognize these borrowers, but as they typically count for less than 5 percent of borrowers, they do not greatly alter the demographic profile of the community served.

In larger libraries, it is important to break down the demographic information to focus on branch libraries, as each branch may have a different profile of library users. A standard rule of thumb in siting branch libraries is that they should be a mile and a half from other branches. This assumes that a mile and a half is the distance users will be willing to walk to the branch library.[4] As one can see, it is easier to determine the service area of a public library and its branches in a smaller city or community than in a large one. Regardless of the number of branches, each branch will serve a group that is in some way unique, and a major strength of branch libraries is that they take into consideration the different needs and interests of those they serve.

The second step in building a demographic profile is to identify reports prepared by other agencies. The U.S. Census provides information on the total population, broken down by a number of factors including age, occupation, number of households, number of children per family, and level of education. Because it is conducted once every 10 years, its value recedes as the census data age. But in the years between the decennial censuses, other censuses are conducted by the federal government and provide data that are useful in providing information on specific elements in the community. Because there is a political aspect to census data, it is important to use locally accepted figures. If this important step is not taken, the data used by the library may not be accepted by local government officials.

School districts conduct a regular census of their student body and projections for increase or decrease. This provides very useful information. Because the school district and public library service areas are often not the same, it is important to review their areas of coverage so that one knows what information from this type of census is useful to the library.

The local Chamber of Commerce is useful in identifying groups in the community, their interests, and how the library supports their interests. One can also get a listing of business and industry in the community so that it is possible to match their needs and interests to the programs of the public library. They can also provide a listing of agencies in the community and their services: social agencies, educational institutions, health services, and other agencies, both private and public.

The public library director needs to look at each of these resources to see what information they provide and to cast a wide net in the community to identify any other demographic studies that may be useful.

In the third step, the library committee responsible for demographic information identifies the information they can use from these studies and determines which types of information the librarians should collect to provide a complete picture of the community the library serves. Larger public libraries often have one or two staff members whose sole responsibility is to gather, analyze, and present demographic data for the entire library system. We are a society well known for its mobility and also a society that includes numerous immigrant groups. The Library Research Service Community Analysis Scan Form (http://www.lrs.org/public/ca_form.php) is an excellent form for recording the information collected, or it can be used at the outset of data collection to identify the types of information to gather. Not only does it ask questions such as "How many people speak a language other than English at home in your community?," it also provides a Web site source where it is possible to find the answers.

Numerous other Community Analysis Community Survey Forms are available on the Web. Many of these forms were funded under the Library Services and Technology Act, which is a component of the Institute of Museum and Library Services (1996). Search the Web under Public Library Community Analysis to see which form(s) are most appropriate to your size library.

In the fourth step, many community analyses include the use of focus groups. Community members representing various groups in the community, library users, and those who do no use libraries are asked to identify those programs they find useful and those they do not use. They are also asked to recommend new directions and services. These focus groups may or may not include library staff. Interviews with selected community members provide yet another way to collect information useful to planning. The public librarian may identify a core group of community members who use the library regularly and will ask them to respond to online questionnaires that address specific issues. One could call this a continuous virtual focus group.

In the fifth step, in addition to data collection, it is important to get a "feel" for the community, which can best be done by participating in community activities and going out into the community to meet people. This will provide a sense of the cultural richness of the community and how the librarian can respond to their needs and interests. It is a way to identify issues in the community that concern residents (e.g., transportation problems, the need to bring new industry to the community, renewable energy). It will also show that library trustees and staff are interested in the community, are approachable, and welcome community input.

Another important way to learn about the community is to stay informed of the local issues that appear in newspapers. What are the political issues? Are new industries planning to come into the community? Are existing industries expanding, contracting, planning to leave the community? What information on sports and entertainment is available? In addition to the major newspaper for the community, are there local newsletters from communities and clubs that discuss community interests and needs? This information is much more qualitative than census data, and it has the benefit of providing a view of what really concerns and interests members of the community and filling out the community's profile.

In the sixth step, librarians may wish to develop a database of community data that can be updated easily. Having the latest data easily accessible is an asset to both long-range and short-term planning. It is also available when staff members wish to evaluate a particular program to make sure that it is in sync with the community group or groups it is intended to serve, and that it is available when questions are asked by members of the community about the extent to which particular groups or interests are being served.

WHY DO A COMMUNITY ANALYSIS?

A community analysis is more than data. It is a point in time in an ever-changing environment that allows librarians to assess their programs in relation to the community they serve. It is a means of collecting data so that they can build a profile of the community and to use this information to design programs and services that best meet community needs and interests. It is a way to ensure that library service is inclusive, for example, that it serves those with disabilities, those living below the poverty line, and those who are foreign born. It is a way to determine if the programs we now have fit the profile of need and interest, and it provides building blocks for new or revised programs and services.

The data will show those areas in which basic information should be provided and those in which a much more comprehensive level of information is needed. For example, in a public library serving a farming community, a comprehensive level of agriculture-related information is useful. In an urban library, only basic information on the topic would be maintained.

The data will also provide guidance in selection of materials for branch libraries so that available materials meet the needs and interests of each community. A study conducted by the American Library Association in 2007 and made public in March 2008 profiled the range of library services and programs developed for non-English speakers.[5] The study reported that about 21 million people in the United States speak limited or no English. The most frequently used services they used were special-language collections (68.9 %) and special programming (39.6%), including language-specific story hours and cultural programming. The study also found that Spanish is the most supported non-English language (78%), with Asian languages ranking second (29). Barriers to library use included language (76%), a lack of awareness of the availability of programs (74.7%), and a lack of discretionary time (73.1%). As stated by Sandra Cuban, "once a community understands the totality of its residents' needs and culture and decides that service to all is truly the library's mission, a plan can be put in place to implement services."[6]

SUMMARY

"A public library is by definition a people's library. The bedrock of planning for urban library service is therefore the people of the city, how many there are, who they are, and where they are."[7] This is as true of the small community as it is of the large urban area, and the task of identifying those we serve is continuous as communities change in age, ethnic composition, and interests. The public librarian needs to be well connected to the community at all levels so that there is an easy flow of information and interest between the library and the community. "Public libraries that recognize the importance of sustaining the public sphere will respond to their community's desire for a place to address critical issues in their lives."[8] And public libraries keep the connection with the community fresh by continuously updating their demographic information in order to provide the best possible service.

NOTES

1. Bernard Berelson, *The Library's Public* (New York: Columbia University Press, 1949), 15.

2. Virginia Mathews, *Libraries for Today and Tomorrow* (New York: Octagon Books, 1978), 51.

3. Ibid., 67.

4. Robert A Cronenberger and Carolyn Luck, "Analyzing Community Human Information Needs: A Case Study," *Library Trends* 24, no. 2 (June 1976): 57.

5. "ALA Unveils Study on Library Service to New Americans," *American Libraries* 39, no. 5 (May 2008): 12.

6. Sandra Cuban, *Serving New Immigrant Communities in the Library* (Westport, CT: Libraries Unlimited, 2007), xi.

7. Lowell Martin, *Library Response to Urban Change* (Chicago: American Library Association, 1969), 1.

8. Kathleen de la Pena McCook, *Introduction to Public Librarianship* (New York: Neal-Schuman, 2004), 300.

ADDITIONAL READINGS

Greer, Roger C., and Martha L. Hale. "The Community Analysis Process." In *Public Librarianship: Reader*, ed. Jane Robbins Carter, 358–66. Littleton, CO: Libraries Unlimited, 1982.

Jaggers, Damon, Shana Smith Jaggers, and Jocelyn Duffy. "Comparing Service Priorities Between Staff and Users in ARL Member Libraries." *portal: Libraries and the Academy* 9, no. 4 (2009): 441–52.

Chapter 6

The Library as Place

INTRODUCTION

The public library as place has three major components: the vision the community has of what the public library should be and do, the public library as virtual place, and the public library as physical place. Each of these elements is intertwined with the other two so that the public library can serve the community, meet user expectations, and provide the best possible professional approach to bringing information to all segments of the community in ways most useful to them. Each component is discussed separately here and then brought together to show how each supports the other.

THE PUBLIC LIBRARY IN THE COMMUNITY

Approximately 9,000 public libraries exist in the United States, over 17 percent of which have branches, which add approximately 7,000 additional outlets, a figure that has not changed appreciably in some time.[1] Each library and branch is part of a community, some large and some small, and each public library and branch has the responsibility to reflect the needs and interests of the community it serves.

"Libraries' unique characteristics take on special meaning today, when thoughtful people worry about the fragmentation of contemporary life and the apparent decline of the local activities that bound people together in the past."[2] Libraries are seen as stable institutions that are welcoming, provide a setting for individual activities, and meet the need to be part of a community. Molz and Dain commented that "public libraries are a visual affirmation of metropolitan vigor."[3] Libraries, along with museums and art centers, draw people back to the center of the city and in many communities have served a central role in the redevelopment of the city center. Examples of these are the state-of-the-art Fairfax County, Virginia, Public Library, built as part of the downtown redevelopment. Montgomery County, Maryland's, library is the centerpiece of Rockville Town Square, "a public private partnership including 650 residences and more than 170,000 square feet of retail."[4]

Vartan Gregorian, a former president of the New York Public Library, recognized that "the library always has provided and always will provide a *place elsewhere*—an imaginative retreat, an imaginative recreation, an imaginative rebirth."[5] It is both a community and a personal asset. McKibben describes the "gulf between the individual and the community"[6] and stresses the value to the individual of being part of a community. He discusses the economics of neighborliness and says that using the Internet allows us to access information locally and that the community's mix of resources and tradition give it a strong base on which to build. This is an excellent definition of what the public library is and does.

The public library, because it serves the entire community and creates an environment that welcomes everyone, is a natural meeting place. As community concerns and interests change, the public library changes as well. It is the place to go for information about the community, and if that information is online, it is the place to go to become computer literate. In smaller communities it is often the source of information on what to do in an emergency. For parents who homeschool their children, it is a primary information source. It brings the world to the community by providing access to the ideas and concerns of other cultures, and it has the community's trust because it is a neutral meeting place to which everyone is welcome.

Many members of the community the public library serves have specific ideas about the role the public library should play in the community. Most are very proud of their library and see it as an essential part of their community. Many see it as a community resource for information, education, and enjoyment, if not for themselves then for their children and other community groups. During difficult financial times, the public library is among the hardest hit tax-supported agencies, because when it is in competition with fire and police services, the community leaders tend to support safety first and learning second. At the same time, during financially difficult times, it is the public library that offers information on jobs and job seeking and that provides information essential to solving daily problems. Most communities have a strong public library advocacy group consisting of those who use the library regularly and who see the value of its services. Library trustees and Friends of the Library groups often lead the charge when public library funding is at risk. When public library funds are cut more sharply than those for other services, they speak out in support of the library. And the news media have published numerous articles indicating that this advocacy has often lessened the cuts to public library service. Financially difficult times are hard for everyone, but with the support of advocacy groups who help the community understand the importance of the public library particularly in difficult times, budget cuts to library services may be less severe, and the library budget may be less apt to take an unduly heavy hit.

Some say that in the information age, no one needs a library because we can find everything we want on the Internet. But where does the individual without a computer, or one who is unfamiliar with using a computer, go to be introduced to the wealth of information that is available? Where does an individual go to get specific information about a job search, to look for local information not available online; will we ever want to borrow, rent, or buy *Goodnight Moon* on Kindle to read to our child at bedtime?

For every new information advance, someone has said that it would displace what had come before. Television was expected to replace the radio, but it didn't. The telephone was expected to replace letter writing, but it hasn't, and the Internet was supposed to replace print resources, but it hasn't. What has happened is that each medium has found the niche in which it functions best and continues to thrive in that area. When driving to work or at work, the radio and not television is where one goes for information or entertainment. If someone wants to see a football game, it is more interesting to do so on television. Writing a letter is more personal and at the same time more formal than corresponding by e-mail. We are still working on the relationship between hard copy to electronic copy and will be doing so for some time. Each of these areas is continuously changing as new delivery systems are devised, as library users find new ways to use their virtual library, and as the popularity of different social networking activities changes.

During the first decade of the 21st century, the popularization of social science research; the Gates Foundation's investment in public libraries, which assured that public access computing is a core service; and the popularity of social networking have raised questions "about what the library does, how we should be doing it, where we should be doing it, and for whom."[7] During this same period, researchers have noted that public engagement has declined because of commuting long distances, increasing work demands, and technology. Community building has been in decline. Public librarians "were grappling with what may prove to be the most critical change impacting library service in the past century; the emergence of computing as 'standard fare' service to libraries."[8] Since 1996 the percentage of public library outlets in the United States has increased from 44.6 to nearly 100 percent, and more than 14 million people regularly use public library computers to access the Internet. "By facilitating collaboration and communication with other users, the social Web is pushing everyone, not just libraries, to determine and articulate their place in a new media world."[9]

THE PUBLIC LIBRARY AS VIRTUAL PLACE

As our lives change to accommodate the information-rich world in which we live, the printed word has become only one of many ways to find information. In response, librarians have created a virtual presence for the public library through the development of Web sites, blogs, and attention to the various forms of social networking. Library users can access their public library at any time and from any electronic communication device. Not only does the public library provide access, it provides training in the use of the Internet so that members of the community can extend that access to the virtual library.

The virtual library presence requires careful planning and continuing maintenance to provide essential information in an easy-to-use format that is both pleasing to the eye and enjoyable and productive to use. Libraries that are departments of local government are usually expected to follow the template established by the local government Webmaster, so that there is uniformity throughout local government in the way information is presented. Public libraries, not a department of local government, often have their own Webmaster, who is responsible for selecting appropriate software, implementing policies about what will be on the Web site, and maintaining the information on the Web site so that it is always up to date. Some public librarians have also created the position of "Virtual Branch Manager," who works in tandem with the Webmaster to create, add, and delete content as appropriate. The Virtual Branch Manager deals with content and services, while the Webmaster is responsible for technical aspects of virtual access. A committee representing different departments and services of the library is often a part of the virtual library organization, and its role is to decide what will go on the Web site so that it is always up to date. Through the use of frequent queries to the user community, the ideal Web site reflects both the services and resources of the library and the needs and preferences of the community.

What skills should the Virtual Branch Manager and the Webmaster bring to their roles? The Virtual Branch Manager is a librarian who combines expertise in virtual reference services and readers' advisory services and is sensitive to the interests of the community about what kinds of information are most important to the community. This includes not just location, hours open, contacts, access to the library's catalog, and how to reserve or renew a book online, but also which links to specific resources are of interest to the community. It is helpful if the Webmaster is a librarian, but it is essential that the Webmaster be technically proficient and understand the role of the Web site in the overall library structure. Experience with Web site design is particularly important because the Web site is the "library place" and should be a pleasing place for the virtual library visitor. For many, the Web site is the first introduction to the library, and the Web site, through its design, information, and continuous maintenance to ensure that it represents the latest information, provides the expectation that the physical library will also be a pleasant and efficient place to visit, should they wish to do so. Conversely, a poorly designed, managed, and maintained Web site may lead the user to suspect that the physical library may have similar shortcomings.

The Web Site as Part of the Virtual Library

As defined by WordIQ.com, "A website is a collection of web pages, that is HTML/XHTML documents accessible via HTTP on the Internet. All publicly accessible web sites in existence comprise the World Wide Web."[10] Web sites may be dedicated to a particular topic or represent an organization or business. In the case of the public library, the Web site provides the community with information about their library and often allows them to interact with the library, for example, ask a reference question or reserve or renew a book.

The amount of information on a public library Web site varies. Typically one can find information on location, hours open, a calendar of events, and other information relevant to the library and its branches. It often includes information about the community: demographics, location of hospitals, police and fire stations, government agencies, important events, and a link to local history archives. Catalog access so that the user can search for particular titles is usually available; if the title is available, it is possible to put a reserve on it. Information on availability of newspapers, magazines, e-books, and videos is also provided. Librarians often include information on new titles and access to readers' advisory services. One may also be able to download audio or e-books, watch videos, or use Utube. Many Web sites also provide pages directed toward teen interests and activities and pages for children's activities. Web pages for these groups usually have their own design that appeals to these age groups.

Public libraries that serve a multi cultural community often provide information in more than one language. For example, using a Google translation link, the Queensborough Public Library in New York offers its Web site in six different languages. Information and/or services available are limited only by the decisions of the committee and Webmaster about what to include.

Ease of use by all levels of users is essential. A Web site that welcomes a general audience should be easy to navigate, and there should be a limited number of links. It should have a clean rather than cluttered appearance, and the design should be consistent. Each page should be balanced so the flow of the information is pleasing. For many users, visual presentation may either add or detract from the Web site. Therefore it is important for the Web designer to carefully consider each component and presentation that appears on the site.

What one is looking for is a Web site that is intuitive, streamlined, and efficient and is free of library terminology users might not understand. Most Web sites also include information on "How to use the website," and when the user still has questions, there is a link to a librarian. Site visitors are asked to comment on the Web site so that it can continue to be responsive to its users.

Numerous techniques are used to tie the virtual library to the physical library. The homepage may include a picture of the library so that one relates the building to the Web site. Activities that occur in the physical library may also be provided online. Programs that take place in the library may be recorded and made available on the Web site through podcasts. Users may browse the collection through the readers' advisory service or ask a reference question. For those whose ability to visit the physical library is limited by distance, time, or physical limitations, the virtual library may be the primary connection they have.

The key to a successful Web site is that it is identified as a library place and the user feels comfortable while in that virtual space. Within a library system, each branch should have its own virtual space tailored to the needs and interests of that branch. Although it is important to keep the design and content current, it is also important to avoid radical design change when possible. If radical change is necessary, explain to users why the change is necessary and how they will benefit, and show them how to use the new space. There are hundreds of public library Web sites, and you can browse them to see what other librarians are doing and if a particular approach and/or design would meet your library's needs. Of primary importance is that the Web site should always reflect current, correct information.

Blogs

As defined by Wikipedia, "a blog is a type of website, usually maintained by an individual with regular entries of commentary, descriptions of events, or other materials such as graphics or video. Entries are commonly displayed in reverse order."[11] Blogs may be a means of communication within an organization or between an organization and an outside constituency, or a statement of personal activities. Many blogs focus on a particular topic and invite others interested in that topic to participate. They have also become a vehicle for individuals with a common interest to build a virtual, interactive community. Since their inception in the 1990s, blogs have become an increasingly popular means of communication and in many cases expressions of personal opinion. Blogs have become a popular means of outreach in the public library world, and one can find hundreds of examples on the Web of library-based blogs

Librarians have found that blogs are most useful when they are designed with a specific audience in mind. For example, a blog developed by the Corvallis-Benton County Public Library in Oregon focused on the child from "Birth to 6,"[12] and the intended audience includes parents, caregivers, and educators of very young children. Included on the blog are reading recommendations, activity ideas, and book reviews of interest to this group. Library activities relevant to this group are announced. Sidebars link the blog to the library homepage and other useful resources. Parents may subscribe to the blog or follow it on Facebook. A review committee reported that this one-stop destination for literacy information or ideas while keeping up to date on events happening at the library "extends the exchange that happens between a children's librarian and a parent into the virtual world, where parents are free to explore and learn at their leisure."[13]

The successful blog is well designed and well organized. The posts are relevant to the topic and are well written. New voices and numerous participants keep the blog fresh and avoid the possibility of a few individuals taking over the discussion and imposing their particular views on a multifaceted subject. Some suggest a moderator to ensure that posts are on topic. For some subjects, there are sub-blogs for particular categories. Teens often have their own blogs. For libraries serving a multicultural community, a Google translation link may be helpful.

Blogs that are linked to the library's Web site expand their usefulness because information on programs and services is readily available. Blogs build community as library users and others have the opportunity to comment and ask questions on the topic under discussion. As does the library Web site, blogs provide an opportunity to participate in the community without going to a physical place, thus providing opportunity for more individuals to be heard and to discuss issues of interest to the community. Blogs must extend the library's reach in a substantive way. Those blogs that do not have a specific purpose or that become opinion pieces detract from the library's purpose.

Many public libraries also have blogs used by staff as a means of internal communication. This is in some ways the Web-based version of the water cooler or the coffee break of earlier years. It gives staff a place to comment in real time on issues that concern them. Blogs can be an important component of informal communication within the library, both as a means of sharing ideas and as a social connection. These blogs are not for access by the public.

Social Networking

Social networking sites are

web based social services that allow individuals to

1. construct a public or semi-public within a bounded system

2. articulate a list of other users with whom they share a connection, and

3. view and traverse their list of connections and those made by others within the system.[14]

Those who join a social network, such as Facebook, MySpace, and LinkedIn, submit a personal profile. In some networks, such as MySpace, individuals can decide whether they want their profiles to be shared with a small group or to be widely available. Users are asked to identify others in the system with whom they have a relationship. Individuals with similar interests often form groups. Since the onset of social networking in the late 1990s, this communication mechanism has grown rapidly, particularly among students. By 2005 Facebook had expanded its membership to include anyone who wished to join. Other sites limit membership to individuals with specific interests. What is distinctive about social networks is that they are centered around people rather than around an idea or interest, with the result that a new organizational structure for online communities has emerged. Anyone who belongs to a social network can participate in the network. However, in some instances, if one wishes to participate in more than a very basic way, a fee may be assessed.

It is important that the library have a presence on social networks, and librarians must find innovative ways in which to interact with their users. Social networking can be a means of finding or creating groups with similar interests and creating online dialogs. It can be a means of providing up-to-date information on a topic or an event. It is also important to be aware that there may be limitations in this means of communication. In a research study issued in 2010,[15] it was found that 73 percent of wired American teens use social networking, a significant increase from a year or two earlier. Seventy-two percent of 18- to 29-year-olds use social networking, and 40 percent of those over 40 participate in social networking.

Different age groups tend to use different social networking sites; for example, teens do not use Twitter but use MySpace and Facebook, with Facebook the most-used network. Although online use is increasing at every age level, "over the past ten years, teens and young adults have been consistently the two groups most likely to go online."[16] As social networking becomes increasingly common, it is important that the public library keep current with the ways in which it can utilize this as a means of enhancing the services of the virtual library. As the early generations of social networkers continue to grow older, the public library needs to take into consideration the social networking interests of these long-term social networkers.

Maintaining the several aspects of the virtual library requires planning, coordination, and a means of evaluating the success of each of these media. A great deal of time may be spent in producing and maintaining a Web site, a blog, and social networking connections. As the community changes and interests change, these also need to change. Librarians need to evaluate success on a regular basis and place their emphasis on those activities that are the most productive.

THE PUBLIC LIBRARY AS PHYSICAL PLACE

The third component of the library as place is its physical space. Each of these perspectives and their components combine to provide an overall view of the pubic library today. In many ways, the public library as a physical space is the most important, because it is how members of the community first think about their library. "The public library has always been a place to be with others, yet alone, to fill in time purposely or not; to reflect, relax, or react. It is a place that is different from other kinds of place, with its own conventions of public behavior."[17]

The Public Library as Center of the Community

The public library has been part of the community for more than 150 years and has built up a reputation of being a place where everyone in the community is welcome. The public library has a tradition of service and inclusiveness, and this tradition brings the community together. Those who have lived in the community for most or all of their lives remember their experience with the library as children, young adults, and parents bringing their children to the library. It is a safe place, a friendly place that brings people together. There is no requirement that one must join a club to be welcome.

The public library is actually many communities; children who see the public library as a place to read or watch videos, curl up in a special spot and imagine other worlds, learn about the world, and envision an unlimited future; teens who find it a place to work together on school projects, search the Internet, play the games they enjoy, and do so in a place they can call their own. It is a place for the adult looking to find a new job and learn new skills in order to get a better job and work toward a better life, for immigrants wishing to learn about this new country and how to move from one culture to the one in which they now live. Many are looking for information on social services and health care, some are interested in local history, and some are looking for a good read. Each of these and many more communities find their own physical space in the library and use it in their own way.

In an era in which individuals move from place to place more often than in the past, and in which they often work outside the community in which they live, the sense of community has become increasingly fragile. Many individuals and families become isolated from one another. Our American culture continues to champion individuals who can succeed by their individual efforts, yet our world increasingly recognizes the importance of the group, of community. Other cultures built more firmly on the family, the clan, and the community do not understand this lack of awareness by many Americans of the importance of community. McKibben suggests that by shifting to economies that are more local in scale, "they would be better able to weather coming shocks; they would allow us to find a better balance between the individual and the community, and hence find extra satisfaction."[18]

Where better to build community than to look to the public library as a cornerstone for that effort? The public library has a history in the community, is respected because it is a neutral environment, and has access to information to help us address the problems we face. Some may ask if the library is open to all, and although at some times and in some places certain groups were not welcome, in recent decades public librarians have worked very hard to show that it is an inclusive environment where all are welcome.

The public library is more than just a good thing, something that every community needs. It is a symbol of the community and a source of pride. It is also an important communication center for the mobile community we have become. This is one of the intersections between the physical and the virtual library. One can come to the physical library for information and interaction with others, or the library can come to the individual via its Web sites, social networking, and related communication.

Library Location

For more than a century there has been discussion about the best location in the community for the public library. In the 19th century the public library was often built in the newly emerging center of the town or in an elite neighborhood. In the 1920s Joseph Wheeler, legendary director of the Enoch Pratt Free Library in Baltimore, Maryland, insisted that the main library be located "in a prime retail location in the central business district."[19] His approach was based on opinion rather than substantive data, and for many years his viewpoint was generally accepted as fact. As we look at the history of libraries, it was often the case that they were placed in a particular location because of political pressure or because a donor provided land and resources and thus decided where the library would be located. Quite often, that location was central to community activities.

We must pay tribute to Andrew Carnegie, who in the late 19th and early 20th centuries provided millions of dollars to build public libraries in the

United States, the United Kingdom, and the then British colonies. Communities receiving funding for a Carnegie Library were required to contribute funds and to agree that they would staff those libraries. Many of the Carnegie libraries had a similar look, and this was not by accident, as Andrew Carnegie and the staff who carried out this program had specific ideas about library construction.[20]

Branch Libraries

By the early 20th century, branch libraries became necessary outlets for public library services. A rule of thumb for branch location was that they should be approximately a mile from other branches and the central library. They should also not be in a dangerous location, such as near railroad tracks or other barriers to access. They should be near public transportation or be in walking distance for many users. After World War II, when family cars became the norm, there was more freedom in branch location as many people no longer had to rely on public transportation or walking to the library.

As more and more libraries were constructed to meet the needs of a growing and increasingly suburban population, library planners gained experience in understanding the best locations for the public library and its branches. Though some continued to insist on Wheeler's assertion that the library be built in the center of the business district, there was general consensus that the three most important factors in library location and presence were

- accessibility by car and public transportation,

- image and visual quality of the building, and

- visibility of the location.

Branches are important, not only because they make it possible to serve more individuals, but also because they can be tailored to the interests and needs of specific communities. A library serving the business community could be located in the center of the city or in the main library. A branch could serve the Polish community or Italian community, and these branches would include materials in both the immigrant's language and English and would provide programs important to the lives of particular groups, such as classes in English as a Second Language. With the growth of suburbia since the 1950s, branches were built to serve newly emergent communities and were often tailored to their demographics. For example, a new community with young families would need an emphasis on children's services.

Library building activities increased in the first half of the 20th century. In 1909 John Cotton Dana cautioned that no building and no location was permanent. "Do not imagine your structure for all time, or even for a hundred years when twenty five will probably find it out of date, out of place, and a burden."[21] A survey of public library buildings after World War II found that 60 percent of central library buildings were more than 30 years old and that only half were adequate. The Library Services and Construction Act (1962) provided funding for construction of new or renovation of existing public library buildings and was the beginning of a new era in library construction.

Today's public libraries continue to provide public spaces accessible to all in the heart of our urban and suburban communities. "Unlike their turn-of-the-twentieth century and mid century predecessors, today's libraries do not fit a mold. In fact, many of them don't even look like libraries.' In rejecting an obligation to conform to an architectural type, today's public librarians are free to choose shapes and styles that speak to the cities and populations they serve."[22] These new libraries reflect the communities in which they were built and the information-rich technological world in which we live. Here again we see the coming together of the community vision of the library, the library as virtual place, and the library as physical space.

Inside the Library

The library is much more than books. For many years it has been moving toward being a place that includes all information in all formats, a place that responds to the public's demand for information; popular materials; and programs that educate, entertain, and enhance the community and its residents.

"Libraries need to be good, not just look good,"[23] said Aaron Cohen and Elaine Cohen, noted library space planners. The Cohens began working with libraries in the 1970s and were noted for their design of innovative library spaces. Their aim was to provide functional, comfortable, and attractive spaces that would provide individuals and groups with their own personal space. Robert Sommer's *Personal Space*[24] is a classic in the study and application of human behavior to the space in which one lives. It sensitizes the reader to the influence of elements including color, light, noise, and placement of furnishings on the way individuals view and use their environment.

Different age groups view and use space differently. For example, children tend to work in groups and like to spread out, while adults are more apt to work alone and have their materials close at hand. Children are often noisy when they work, while adults prefer a quiet space. Color may be used to create a calming atmosphere in some areas or to signal that noise is welcome in others. Cool colors tend to calm and bright colors to encourage activity. Lighting is also a means of defining spaces within the library so that individuals are led toward certain areas.

It is important to have space that is flexible and can be reconfigured to meet changing needs. As more and more information is available electronically and there is decreasing use of print reference materials, space planning should accommodate the need to add terminals and reduce shelving. As the demographics of the community change, it should be possible to enlarge or decrease the size of the children's area.

Placement of library departments is also very important. Where are the children's room and the young adult area in relation to quiet study areas? Where is the reference department in relation to the entrance to the library? Where are circulation services in relation to the entry and the exit? What is the workflow of the staff? Are the traffic patterns anticipated by the planners those that the public uses ? How can the designers guide the public to use particular traffic patterns through lighting, color, and carpet design?

The literature is filled with examples of excellent design. One can review the richly illustrated annual issues of *American Libraries* and *Library Journal* to see photographs of the most interesting buildings of the year. The architect is listed along with information on the size of the building, its cost, and features of particular interest. With the increasing interest in building libraries that are sustainable, there has been an increasing emphasis on green buildings.

One of the first things a library construction planning committee typically does is to visit other public libraries to see how they have built a space that meets community needs for beauty, comfort, and ease of use This provides an opportunity to become acquainted with the work of various architects, see new solutions to the use of space, and gain a sense of the range and cost of the many alternatives. In this way, they can begin to develop a building plan that best meets the needs of the community they serve.

Maintaining the Library's Space

The daily tasks of maintaining the library keep the library a clean, pleasant place in which to work and learn. A building that is clean and well cared for sends a message to the community that its staff takes pride in the building. This includes not just the building itself but also its grounds and parking areas. The community takes pride in well cared for public spaces and responds with a positive attitude.

Another aspect of library space is to ensure that the environment is secure. Often library management will conduct a security audit to determine the physical safety within the building. It may be conducted by fire or police officers or by an insurance agent. The auditors may suggest better lighting in parking areas and ways to address potential hazards of use for those with disabilities and to ensure both staff and public that the library environment is safe. Numerous books are published annually that inform library staff about current trends in library architecture, space planning, and ways to maintain a safe and efficient library. They provide up-to-date information on how to maintain and enhance the public library as physical space.

SUMMARY

A public library is many things. "It is its contents and their containers, its publics and their activities, perhaps even its city and that city's character. It is information and knowledge; it is multiple epistemologies. It is multiple pedagogies. It is a collection of atmospheres and auras."[25] It holds information that tells the story of the history and current concerns of the community and provides spaces in which the future of the community is discussed. It is the many different people of all ages, cultures, and interests who use the library to participate in community interests, find information to meet personal needs, or just be.

For an increasing number of libraries, the use of the virtual library is outpacing the use of the physical library. The virtual public library provides the opportunity to locate information and to communicate from any place at any time. If it is not convenient to visit the library, one can visit the Web site, the blogs, and participate in social networking from any location. Limitations of time, space, and disability no longer prevent one from being an active user of library resources and services.

The physical library continues to serve as a place where individuals can come together and participate as part of a community. Whereas the virtual library provides convenience, the physical library provides face-to-face interaction. Ever-expanding applications of technology provide new opportunities for service. The combination of physical and virtual access fulfills the library's promise to provide information and communication to the community.

NOTES

1. National Center for Educational Statistics, *Public Libraries in the US: Fiscal Year 2003* (Institute of Educational Sciences, NCIS 2006-363, September, 2005).

2. Redmond K. Molz and Phyllis Dain, *Civic Space/Cyberspace; The American Public Library in the Information Age* (Cambridge, MA: MIT Press, 1999), 205.

3. Ibid., 208.

4. Marc Fisher, "D.C. Libraries Mired in Political Dithering," *Washington Post*, July 10, 2008.

5. Vartan Gregorian, "A Place Elsewhere; Reading in the Age of the Computer," *Bulletin of the American Academy of Arts and Sciences* 59, no. 1 (January 1996): 62.

6. Bill McKibben, *Deep Economy: The Wealth of Communities and the Desirable Future* (New York: Henry Holt, 2007), 106.

7. Christie Hill, "Inside, Outside, and Online," *American Libraries* 40, no. 3 (March 2009): 38–41.

8. Ibid.

9. Ibid.

10. Word iQ.com.

11. Wikipedia.

12. www.corvallislibrarybirthtosix.blogspot.com/

13. Ibid.

14. danah m. boyd and Nicole B. Ellison, " Social Network Sites: Definition, History, and Scholarship," *Journal of Computer Mediated Communication* 13, no. 1 (2007), jcmc.indiana.edu/vol13/issue1/boyd.ellison.html

15. Amanda Leinhart, Kristin Purcell, Aaron Smith, and Kathy Zickuhr, "Social Media and Mobile Internet Use Among Teens and Young Adults," *Pew Internet and American Life Project*, February 3, 2010, pewinternet.org

16. Ibid.

17. Michael Dewe, *Planning Public Library Buildings: Concepts and Issues for the Librarian* (Hants, UK: Aldershot, 2006), 21.

18. Bill McKibben, *Deep Economy: The Wealth of Communities and the Durable Future* (New York: Henry Holt, 2007), 105.

19. Christine M. Koontz, *Library Facility Siting and Location Handbook* (Westport, CT: Greenwood Press, 1997), 10.

20. Abigail VanSlyck, *Free to All: Carnegie Libraries and American Culture 1890–1920* (Chicago: University of Chicago Press, 1995).

21. John Cotton Dana, *Libraries, Addresses, and Essays* (White Plains, NY: H.W. Wilson, 1916), 54.

22. Aaron Cohen and Elaine Cohen, *Designing and Space Planning for Libraries, A Behavioral Guide* (New York: Bowker, 1979), 3.

23. Ibid.

24. Robert Sommer, *Personal Space, the Behavioral Basis of Design* (Englewood Cliffs, NJ: Prentice Hall, 1969).

25. Shannon Mattern, *The New Downtown Library* (Minneapolis: University of Minnesota Press, 2007), 145.

ADDITIONAL READINGS

Aabo, Svanhild, Ragnar Audunson, and Andreas Varheim. "How Do Public Libraries Function as Meeting Places?" *Library and Information Science Research* 32, no. 1 (January 2010): 16–26.

Jeng, H. L. "The Future of Public Libraries is in the Community." *Texas Library Journal* 84, no. 4 (Winter 2008): 132–35

McCabe, Gerard B. *Planning for a New Generation of Public Library Buildings*. Westport, CT: Greenwood Press, 2000.

Trotta, Carmine J., and Marcia Trotta. *The Librarian's Facility Management Handbook*. New York: Neal-Schuman Publishers, 2001.

Chapter 7

Innovation and Planning

INTRODUCTION

Public libraries are not what they used to be. They are not even what they were two or three years ago. As is true of information professionals, information services, information users, and any other group that benefits from information, if we wish to thrive in the present environment, we must reinvent ourselves and our workplace. And this reinventing is part of our daily activities. For some, continuous change is exciting, and these individuals thrive on being part of an environment in which there is always a new idea, a new process, or new and different individuals to whom one can provide a new service. For others, this dynamic environment poses a threat. They find it difficult to deal with an ever-changing environment and are much more comfortable doing what they know they do well rather than learning new ways of doing. Unfortunately, for those uncomfortable with this environment of continuous change, the world we live in requires that to remain relevant, we must reinvent who we are and what we do. Although the basic role of the public library, which is to bring people and information together, does not change, nearly every way in which we do so has changed, is changing, or will change. Our responsibility is to stay informed about changes that affect the public library world, evaluate them, and adopt those that will make our library more responsive to the needs and interests of those who rely on the library as a source of information and cultural enrichment.

FINDING THE NEXT NEW THING

Where do we start looking to find the next new idea, the enhanced technology that allows us to find information easier and faster, a new way to collect data that will help us manage our resources more efficiently, or a new communication medium? One of the most useful ways of doing this is to be part of the numerous social networks that surround us. A social network is defined as "a set of relationships between a group of 'actors' (the 'actors' could be individuals, departments, and others" who usually have similar interests.[1]

Social networks may be large or small. Professional associations are large social networks that provide valuable connections to others with similar interests. Personal knowledge networks include online communities that focus on a particular area of interest, discussion groups that can be both face to face and/or virtual, and cross-functional work teams that approach the same issue from different directions.

Technical presentations by those responsible for developing hardware and software and for making them available to the public provide additional information on their "next new thing," and for particularly exciting information on what's out there in technology land, librarians can watch the new ideas being tested in places such as MIT's Media Lab or other research groups whose role is to look far ahead to see what may be an important trend.

As individuals, we need to look about and conduct investigations to see what others have learned about a particular new thing, and then within our social groups we may think about what we have learned and brainstorm to see if a new use that is of particular interest to us can become a part of our lives. If a new idea or application results, we can test it and determine whether it improves our products and/or services. Once we have new information, then transfer it through our social networks and thus share with others. This requires a paradigm shift from the old ways of keeping new information close to our organization to new ways that encourage knowledge sharing. Again, for some sharing is a part of the culture in which we work and live, whereas for others sharing may be seen as giving up power and therefore a dangerous activity.

How do we operationalize innovation? In order to have an organization whose members are creative and willing to suggest new directions, it is necessary to have a leader who welcomes interaction. Staff members will be more likely to contribute new ideas when they know that those ideas will be welcomed, will be discussed, and if appropriate, may be implemented. In addition to cultivating an environment of innovation and motivating others to do their best work, leaders/managers have several additional responsibilities.[2] They need to build a staff that includes individuals representing various disciplines, backgrounds, and areas of expertise so that they can share their diverse approaches to a problem.

As has been regularly demonstrated, diversity enhances creativity. Those who have similar backgrounds tend to think alike and often settle on a common solution to a problem, whereas those with diverse backgrounds and thought patterns will usually come up with a variety of potential solutions.

In addition to encouraging staff creativity, the leader/manager will often look outside the organization for individuals who may contribute new ideas and/or new perspectives. These may be consultants, technical experts, researchers who have new insights to offer, or members of the community who envision new approaches to service. Of particular importance is the ability to "provide paths through the bureaucracy" so that new ideas or directions have a chance to be implemented. The leader/manager provides staff with an intellectual challenge; allows people to pursue their passion; appreciates their efforts through encouragement when needed; and makes it clear that not all innovative ideas will work, that failure is possible, and that failure is acceptable if something useful is learned.[3]

How does one turn into action the creative forces from which innovation comes? The following enabling conditions within the organization are necessary to support innovation. As with any problem-solving task, the first step is to identify the question. Exactly what is the problem, and what are we asking about it? When describing the problem, it is important to avoid getting bogged down in things that don't help us. This includes what happened in the past, attempts to solve the problem that were only partially successful, attitudes of individuals who dealt with the problem earlier, and other no longer relevant information. Are the stakeholders those who have an interest in solving the problem? What can they contribute to the discussion? Do they have a bias that may skew their objective thinking? What information is needed, and how will it be gathered?

Five enabling conditions that support innovation within the organization, outlined by Nonaka and Takeochi, provide a guide to moving forward:[4]

1. Organizational intention. The organization needs to decide what kinds of knowledge will be most valuable to it and "apply this vision as the principal yardstick for judging the usefulness of new knowledge."

2. Members of the organization, either individually or in self-organizing teams, should have the autonomy to explore new areas.

3. The organization may introduce a change in an existing process to see what new ways of dealing with that process will emerge.

4. Information, beyond just what an individual knows to do the job, should be made available.

5. Members of the organization should have access to a wide range of information so that they can do their jobs.

Much of the information needed to look at one's activities and propose new and different ways of getting things done is already in the library. The tacit information, what people know about their work life but rarely write down, is a rich resource for thinking of new services and new ways to serve. The innovative workplace is enriched by this type of information, and it is enriched further when individuals in different areas of the library work together to solve a problem, as this provides different perspectives.

Who are the innovators? An innovator is an individual who is curious about the world and how it works. That individual is aware of his or her surroundings and regularly asks why we do a certain thing or why we haven't tried another approach. This person doesn't rely on "how we did it in the past" but is looking at how we might improve on past performance. These individuals are always looking for new ideas and how they can recombine old ideas to meet new challenges, and they don't get bogged down in details but are able to tease out the new idea, the new opportunity, and then suggest ways to take advantage of it. Innovators may be found throughout the organization. They are the individuals who not only do their assigned tasks but also see opportunities for doing those tasks in new and different ways.

The leader who supports innovative thinking and action needs to seek out innovators in the organization and build ways in which those individuals can share their ideas, get feedback on their ideas, and when possible test those ideas to see if they should be incorporated into daily activities. The leader/manager needs to be accepted and trusted as an individual who appreciates innovation as well as the individual who often has new and perhaps controversial ideas. It is not always easy to include innovators on the staff, as they are more apt to question procedures than to just do something. These are often the individuals who do not conform, are always doing something different, and often disrupt daily activities. But if one wants a healthy organization, one needs to hire innovators and give them the opportunity to question, try, and be change agents.

Support of innovators throughout the organization complements the vision of the leader, as do staff members who are knowledgeable about current activities. Although the leader provides direction for the library and is constantly looking toward the new ideas that may appear on the horizon, staff members who are experienced in particular tasks can help move those tasks forward in ways that support the vision. Leaders need to go beyond their vision for the library and its services to envision what is new. What is the next thing? Is there a better way to provide service? Without innovators within the library who can make that vision real in the many things they do to move activities forward, the leader would find it difficult to promote a viable vision for the future.

The most difficult task of the leader is to communicate "an image of the future that draws others in that speaks to what others see and feel."[5] It is essential to connect in the present, listen to others, and bring them to the future. Some think that the way in which to lead the library to a new future is to hire a new director who will singlehandedly drag that organization into a new way of doing things. The board of trustees may think that they have assured the library's future by hiring a new and energetic director who will take care of things. This may appear like change, but change comes from an attitude throughout the library, from the trustees to the clerical support system, an attitude of innovation and a willingness to try new things. "Future trends and directions first become visible through problems, difficulties, conflicts, and dysfunctions, making it essential for organizations to listen non-hierarchically to everyone who has an idea or problem, whether they are part of management or not."[6]

CHANGE

Probably the most difficult thing to do in a stable environment is to initiate change. People like to work within their comfort zone and know that they have the expertise to do a good job and to feel positive about what they are doing. In our fast-moving world, if one wishes to survive, there are few places where we can always be within our comfort zone. Every day there is a new regulation, a new product or service, a new group of individuals to serve in new ways, and something new to learn. Every member of the library team is affected by these changes and needs to be involved in decisions made to move forward. Some individuals will be excited by the fact that each day provides a new opportunity to try new things; others will dread going to work and having to do something different. These different reactions to change result in different ways individuals function. Some use passive resistance; others actively resist change, and still others are excited by it.

One major reason people resist change is that they fear they will lose something of importance to them if changes are made. They may be assigned new tasks that will take them away from the activities they really enjoy. They may be asked to learn new skills and fear that they will not be successful in the new environment. They may fear that reorganization will put them in contact with a staff member they don't want to work with. Any changing situation has winners and losers. The 2005 Nobel Prize winner for medicine had for several years conducted research on the causes of stomach ulcers and established that in many cases they were caused by a bacteria or virus and could be cured using antibiotics. The drug industry, which had invested millions in medication which was used on the assumption that ulcers had other causes, did all it could to downplay his findings, as they feared losing the profits from their now largely outmoded drugs. This is not an isolated incident of resistance to change for economic reasons.

In the not-for-profit world, numerous objections to change can be cited. Perhaps a job will no longer be needed, or a program will be replaced by one more relevant to the need. In some communities, there has been a move to eliminate the public library "because technology has made it irrelevant." When there appears to be a strong objection to a proposed change, it is important to check to see who thinks they may lose something important.

Resistance to change may also be the result of insufficient information. Staff members may not understand the reasons for a needed change. In some environments, staff members do not have a high level of trust in the supervisor, and it is easy for misunderstandings to grow either because of insufficient information or because the supervisor has in the past made decisions the staff didn't see as an improvement. In other instances the supervisor may recommend change, and staff members do not agree. A reorganization of reference services to accommodate a new online service may appear to be a positive step to the supervisor, but staff may have other ideas. In an era of reduced resources, with the accompanying downsizing or reorganization, there is great stress on the library and its staff to continue to provide excellent service with less. The key to moving ahead is to communicate with all staff, discuss the reasons why changes are desirable and/or needed, and involve them in the decision-making process. And the supervisor will also involve them in reviewing the changes once they are made, so that they can be part of fine tuning the change.

In leading change, there are a number of things to keep in mind:

1. Making changes for the sake of change doesn't work. It upsets the organization for no good reason and causes the manager to be seen as incompetent or perhaps a manipulator. Some managers appear to think that change is a way of shaking up a department or other unit in order to "keep staff on their toes." The result, rather than keeping staff alert, is that staff spend time wondering what the supervisor will do next, making them do something different when they would otherwise spend time more efficiently doing the things that need to be done. It may make them more resistant to needed changes because they don't trust the supervisor to have their best interests in mind.

2. Don't rush into adopting the latest new thing until you know that it will improve the situation. Enthusiasm for a new project or new tech solution is good, but it is important to involve staff in the discussions to determine whether it will be a positive step forward.

3. Innovation can have unintended consequences. Building road systems around major cities and making it possible for individuals to live in the suburbs was seen by many planners as a step toward a more comfortable life. An unintended consequence was the near death of the central city, which created a whole new set of problems. Fixing problem A may exacerbate problem B or create a new problem. So be aware of possible consequences.

4. Technology is not the only change agent. Demographics of the community change, and they change the kinds of services we provide. Economic difficulties reduce the resources available to the library and require hard choices between what we can do and what we must no longer do. Other change agents both large and small affect how we serve.

5. In a changing environment, staff members will live up to your expectations if given a chance. If you expect growth, change, enthusiasm, and a job well done, and if you are a fair, responsible supervisor, you will nearly always get them.

Change is not an option. In many instances, neither is the rate of change. In paleontology, the term *punctuated rhythm* describes how living things move ahead slowly and then events occur that cause major changes in the flora and fauna in a very short time. Events move more slowly, and change again comes more slowly, often with little or no ability to predict how fast change will occur.

Our only protection is to create an innovation/change environment in which we are always looking at external forces, internal forces, and new ways of doing things so that we have the habit of looking toward the future and keeping the library, its objectives, and its staff always ready to move ahead rather than being too comfortable with today or looking longingly at the past, which rarely was as wonderful as some may remember. Periods of rapid change are times when the democratic leadership style may for a time become authoritative and perhaps even pace setting. Once the need for rapid change becomes less, the leader will ease back into a democratic style. The leader's role is to say that "this is where we must go, so let's go together and I'll lead the charge."

We live in a changing world. We each have comfort zones, which provide us with a physical and/or emotional resting place. We have no choice about whether or not to deal with change as life and work change each day. Where we do have a choice is how we deal with our changing world and the workplace. It is more productive to look at the world around us, identify problems and opportunities, and set a course of action knowing that it will require adjustments along the way. In that way, we are using change as a positive asset and managing it to some extent, rather than allowing it to be a disruptive force.

PLANNING

Planning is the process by which the mission, goals, and objectives of the library are turned into a action. Based on both internal and external factors, priorities are set. Tasks and activities are identified and are assigned to appropriate units. Allocation of resources follows the plan. Staff members are assigned tasks in order of their priority, budgets are allocated based on priorities, and space and equipment are allocated in a similar fashion. The organization is evaluated based on its success in meeting stated goals and objectives. Throughout the process of planning, setting objectives, assigning priorities, and evaluating success, staff and users of services should be involved.

Staff members must be involved, as they are the ones who do the work. They need to have a role in assigning priorities and determining how the tasks should be carried out. They are the individuals closest to the customer and may serve as informed advocates for those who use the services. Users know what services they want/need and how they would like them to be provided. A good plan will take staff and user concerns, wants, and needs and add a forward-thinking element. Usually wants/needs are based on "what we now do or get that we like." Staff and users may or may not be aware of new services, new approaches that could enhance their satisfaction. Or they may have ideas about innovative approaches to an existing service or the development of a new service. Such additions help make the plan become more than "this is what we did last year, so let's continue it."

A plan should be realistic, be based on good management practices and use of resources, have quantifiable elements, and be a statement of what the library sees as its role in the community. The plan is a kind of promise that "we will provide these services if we are allocated the requested resources." That promise contains the understanding that we will deliver. Being able to show that that promise has been kept is the role of performance appraisal and program review.

Long-Range Planning

Public libraries, as part of larger municipal or regional government agencies, are usually required to prepare long-range plans for the library. The larger governing unit will have developed a process for planning that needs to be followed. Its purpose is to understand how the library fits into the larger picture; what programs and activities the librarian wishes to add, delete, or change; and what the projected costs will be. It should be recognized that this level of planning over the longer term tends to be inflexible and data driven. Despite this, it serves as an important component of the librarian's own planning activities.

Librarians often begin their planning activities by looking several years into the future to project where they want library programs and services to be in three years or in five years. When the rate of change was not as rapid as it now is, planners could assume that there would be relatively little change in the economic situation, the demographics of the library service area would change slowly, and the technology and other supporting factors of the library's programs and services would also change at a leisurely rate. They would regularly review the library's mission, goals, and objectives; make any desired changes; and develop an updated long-range plan. Most of the data to support long-range planning activities are internal and based on statistics that are regularly collected. The data are analyzed, models are built, and future decisions are extrapolated from existing data.[7] Planners will also use external data as they build their long-term forecasts. This information informs areas including economic growth and demographic changes.

Short-Term Planning

As part of the planning process, the long-range plan will be organized in annual increments, with each year's plan building toward activities in the following year. The annual plan is a more useful working document, as it covers a shorter period of time and is responsive to what is actually happening now. Library planners can build a working budget for the following year. They can assess program growth over the shorter period of time and make adjustments as needed. Whereas the long-range budget provides direction, the annual budget provides day-to-day opportunities to make corrections as one moves ahead. Data that are collected on a regular basis can be used to make those corrections. Budgeted funds can be redirected as needs change. It is the combination of the long-range (directional) plan and the short-term (operational plan) that shows a road ahead for the library.

In most situations, planning is the responsibility of a small group within the library, which includes the director, department heads, the budget officer, and other decision makers. It may include a member of the board of trustees and/or a member of the municipal or county government. This group determines the external and internal data that will be used for planning. They also work with planning process requirements of the larger government agency, add elements specific to library needs, and may adapt or adopt an existing planning process such as *A Planning Process for Public Libraries*,[8] developed by the Public Library Association of ALA to guide them in their activities. A problem with this form of planning, despite its many useful elements, is that it is slow to respond to the increasingly rapid rate of change. It also carries the false promise that if one has an organized means of using appropriate data to plan for the library's future, the resulting plan will work. We cannot accurately predict the future. What we can do is provide our best guess.

Strategic Planning

The strategic planning process was developed to compensate for the shortcomings of the planning processes discussed previously. It builds on many elements of the long-range planning process but is more dynamic and therefore more responsive to the changing environment. The strategic planning process focuses on identifying issues, collecting both internal and external data, and exploring external strategies to respond to current situations. The process assumes a dynamic rather than a static situation. It collects qualitative and quantitative information from both internal and external sources. Current and future trends are examined to make current decisions.[9] It has been said that long-range planning is the science of planning, and strategic planning is the art of planning.

Strategic planning emerged in the 1970s and 1980s from several disciplines: policy, marketing, effectiveness research, geopolitical theory, systems theory, and interdisciplinary research conducted in many business schools. Peter Drucker, who was one of the first (1954), if not the first, advocate of strategic planning said: "First determine what your business is and what it should be and then set objectives and allocate resources."[10] Drucker stressed that strategic planning looked at doing the right things (effectiveness) over doing things right (efficiency), and that rather than focusing on individual parts of the organization, it is necessary to look at the whole organization to see how its parts interrelate. He also urged that planners look at the context within which the organization exists to determine their effect on the organization.

Components of Strategic Planning

Strategic planning focuses on identifying issues and resolving them and recognizes that there are many constituencies with an interest in the process and who wish to participate. To be successful, strategic planning must have an individual in the organization who is of sufficient stature to conduct the process and to ensure that after its planning stages, the process will continue and action steps identified in the strategic planning process will be taken. Ideally, strategic planning takes place as a result of discussions among staff, supervisors, and other stakeholders. In fact, it is often initiated because of a crisis situation: the loss of a key staff member, a budget crisis, or another emergency situation. Strategic planners look at the external conditions within which the library functions. What is the economic situation? Are there political issues that affect the library? Are the demographics of the library service area changing? What other internal and external environmental conditions currently affect the library?

The strategic planner examines and reexamines issues and conditions and in this process identifies the important issues that need to be resolved. Strategic planners look at the changing conditions and see the need to take advantage of shifting situations and opportunities. They look at the special competence of the library and its unique mission. This is a continuous process and is fueled by internal and external data and stakeholder concerns, all of which are based on an understanding of the library's mission. Strategic planning is the art and the act of selecting the right decision or decisions from the several possible ones that will best further the mission and objectives of the library.

"Strategic planning sets an institution's movement in a direction to travel."[11] It deals with the important issues of how to utilize resources to maximize opportunity. Strategic planning provides a methodology to help an organization think through what it is doing and identify the changes necessary to meet new circumstances and opportunities.[12] It can facilitate communication and participation, accommodate divergent values and interests, and foster orderly decision making.[13] All stakeholders come together in the planning process to discuss the library's mission and goals and come to an agreement on what they are and what they should be. In this way, there is agreement on the direction the library should take to meet its responsibilities to serve the community.

When the stakeholders agree on the mission and goals of the library and the direction it should take to achieve them, the library's image is strengthened, as it is shown that the library knows what its role is and agrees on how to fulfill its promise. Until there is agreement on mission and goals, planning does not go forward. When there is a lack of agreement, it appears that the library does not have a common purpose; if this is true, the library will not prosper.

Strategic planning supports the library as it helps librarians to

1. think strategically and develop effective strategies,

2. clarify future direction,

3. establish priorities,

4. make today's decisions with a view to future consequences,

5. develop a coherent and defensible basis for decision making,

6. exercise maximum direction in the areas under the library's control,

7. make decisions across levels and functions,

8. solve major problems,

9. improve organizational performance,

10. deal effectively with rapidly changing circumstances, and

11. build teamwork and expertise.[14]

Strategic Planning Models

A model developed by the Harvard Business School faculty focused on the identification and analysis of internal strengths and weaknesses by asking senior managers to discuss these issues. External threats and opportunities were identified, as were the social role and obligations of the organization. This SWOT analysis focuses on

S (strengths),

W (weaknesses)

O (opportunities, and)

T (threats)

and is intended to provide a structure for asking the right questions about the role and activities of the organization. One can conduct a cursory SWOT analysis and identify the more obvious issues, or go into greater depth and learn about more fundamental issues that may affect the way the organization functions or does not function.

Competitive analysis is another planning model, in which planners look at the five forces that shape an organization: relative power of customers, relative power of suppliers, threats of substitute products and/or services, threats of new entrants, and the amount of rivalry among the players in the field. Planners then analyze these forces against the propositions that

1. the stronger the forces that shape an organization, the lower the general level of return; and

2. the stronger the forces that affect a unit, the lower the profit of the unit.

The relevance of this type of analysis to public libraries and other nonprofit organizations is that any organization, profit or nonprofit, competes for resources, and it is essential to understand the forces that drive competition.

The Planning Approach

Everyone in the library is involved in planning, as are representatives of those who use library services, sell products and services to the library, or otherwise interact with it. The reason for this is that full participation promotes understanding of what the library does and that everyone involved with the library has a common purpose: to serve the community as a freely available information resource. Although the library director is given the responsibility by the board of trustees to take charge of the planning process, the director usually names individuals respected by the library staff and the community to chair the planning process. Sometimes the director and/or board of trustees hire an outside consultant to lead the planning process. The consultant will have worked with other public libraries to build their plans, and this individual has the experience and broad view of public libraries that comes from working with a variety of institutions.

The planning committee usually consists of department heads, because they know an area of the library well and will have both the expertise to contribute to the study and responsibility for implementing the plan in their units. The committee also needs representation from technical and clerical staff, the board of trustees, and any advisory groups such as the Friends of the Library. Staff will be named to the committee and will include both technical experts to act as advisors and support staff, who will collect and organize data and prepare reports. Too large a committee will be unwieldy, but too small a committee will not be sufficiently representative of those who need to be heard. One solution is to have a large representative planning committee from which a smaller steering committee of eight to ten individuals is selected.

This steering committee will organize the study in accordance with its purpose and use, which will have been agreed on by the larger committee. The steering committee will manage daily activities, appoint ad hoc committees to investigate specific topics when appropriate, and produce documents for discussion by the larger committee. If a consultant is hired, that individual will work with the steering committee to help design the process, develop gathering tools when needed, and provide advice as appropriate. Because the study should be conducted within an appropriate time frame, a timeline for completing the study should be agreed upon in advance.

As soon as the committee structure is in place, an orientation session to inform committee members about the planning process and their role and responsibilities is held. Not only does the steering committee provide information to the larger planning committee, it also provides an orientation session for the entire library staff so that each member knows about the study, what it is, its purpose, and what they may be asked to contribute. The best way to do this is to have a full staff meeting or for each department to hold a staff meeting outlining the process. Continuous follow-up would be through the use of a Web site describing the process, providing regular updates, and giving everyone the opportunity to ask questions and receive prompt answers. The use of a Web site allows for real-time, two-way communication among all parties.

Concurrent with orientation and the naming of ad hoc committees to study specific areas, staff on the committee will be collect both internal and external data. Clarifying organizational mandates underlie all subsequent activities and are the first thing to investigate. These mandates include legislation, administrative roles, policies, charters, contracts, or other documents defining roles and responsibilities.[15] These formal documents specify what the library can and cannot do under present regulations.

The committee's first task is to look at its existing mission and the values that are expressed in the mission. In many instances, that mission may need to be revised or completely rewritten. Committee members will seek information from a number of sources. A stakeholder's analysis will be conducted to identify the stakeholders, what they expect from the library, and what the library needs from the stakeholders. Not all stakeholders are equal in power, and it is important to identify those who are most able to influence the library's role in the community. A user analysis will tell planners how satisfied the users (who are also stakeholders) are with library services. In addition to stakeholder input, the library's mission is influenced by the values it holds. These include personal values, professional values, and community values, and as the library's mission is reviewed, it is important to see how it reflects these values. The mission statement itself develops from the discussion of the following elements:

1. Who are we as an organization?

2. What are the basic social or political needs we fill or problems we address?

3. What do we do both actively and passively to address these?

4. How should we respond to our key stakeholders?

5. What is our philosophy; what are our core values?

6. What is it that we do that makes us unique?[16]

A variety of responses will emerge, and with open and honest discussion, a mission will emerge that all can support. It is important that there be full discussion of difficult issues and agreement reached, because otherwise the mission does not reflect the thoughts and ideas of the library, and a mission statement that is not representative of the entire library will not have the needed stature to serve as the basis for planning.

External Review

Once the library's mission is agreed upon, the next step is to review the external environment. Many community organizations and local government agencies regularly conduct economic, demographic, and other reviews of the community and when available, these reviews provide needed input. If there is no acceptable environmental scan available, the steering committee may wish to name a committee or task force that will develop a process for collecting external data. This process will provide input to planning activities and may also become a regular component of the library's data-gathering activities. Even when environmental scanning is conducted by organizations outside the library, there are specific questions the library planners need to ask that are not of interest to those other organizations, and library staff will need to develop a means of asking these questions.

In recent decades environmental scanning has become a basic component of the planning process. "The role of environmental assessment in strategic planning is to identify environmental factors relevant to the mission of the institution; to assess favorable or unfavorable impacts of events, conditions, and trends or priorities; to develop scenarios; and to devise realistic strategies for creating viable futures for the institution."[17]

Though we all informally scan the world around us on a daily basis, this informal view is not sufficiently rigorous to allow us to use it in our planning decisions. A formal scanning process is more structured and well organized and follows from the identification of issues critical to the library. Planners look at the external environment to identify information related to those issues and look for trends that will allow the library to position itself to meet future opportunities. In addition to its role in supporting more proactive decision making, environmental scanning also allows planners to assess the extent to which their organization was socially responsible, how it supported community needs and interests. Scanning focuses on emerging issues and trends that may affect the library and its services.

When compiling a list of trends to monitor, each member of the planning committee will suggest different issues that need attention. The list will include demographic issues that may influence the types and levels of services provided, economic trends that may influence levels of funding for the library, changes in technology that may influence services and programs, and social and political trends that may affect attitudes toward the library.

The list will also include a review of legislation affecting the public library and how this may influence library activities. Issues unique to a specific library may also be included in the list. Standard environmental scanning taxonomy is available[18] that addresses social/lifestyle, political, economic, technology, and demographics/manpower topics, and it is usually easier to adapt it to one's planning needs than it is to build a new taxonomy. When one uses an existing taxonomy, it is easier to locate data that fit into the categories identified for study. When one collects data, it is relatively easy to collect information on demographic and economic trends, as these data reside in regularly issued reports; when these reports provide projections they are based on reliable statistics. It is relatively easy to follow trends in technology because information is widely disseminated by the industry. Information on social trends is softer data and open to many interpretations, and is therefore more difficult to quantify. The librarian will identify those trends most important to its operation and track their development. As the library's interests and concerns change, the list of trends will change as well.

Scanning data come not only from reports provided by government agencies, business organizations, social agencies, and other formal and quasi-formal organizations, but also from selected national, regional, and local newspapers and magazines. Journals from relevant professional associations, databases that track areas of interest, and blogs that may provide contrarian ideas are all relevant resources .It is very easy to identify too long a list of this type of resources, so one should select them with care. One should review them as necessary to remove less useful resources and add new ones that may be helpful. One may also conduct interviews with key decision makers and use questionnaires to elicit information from specific groups. It is important to scan the media to see what they say about one's library. How many articles appear? How frequently is the library mentioned? What topics seem to be of interest to the community?

Depending on the sources selected, it is possible to skew the scan in different directions. One may interview individuals with a particular point of view, or scan select newspapers and magazines that support a particular perspective. The scanning process should be free of bias and should reflect a range of views; otherwise, conducting the process has no value for planning.

It is important to build a database at the beginning of the scanning process so that over time, the data collected in the scanning process reflect trends and patterns. This information provides an ongoing source, describing external trends and issues of importance to the library. Then planners can look at current programs and ask if those programs should be revised to meet future interests. They can look at financial data to get a sense of the economic climate for the next year and of how difficult it will be to request additional funding. They can also conduct a SWOT analysis to identify strengths, weaknesses, opportunities, and threats. Environmental scanning provides us with the information to make good guesses about what will happen in the future, but it does not tell us what will actually happen.

Environmental scanning is a means of conducting a continuous review of information from the media, available data, and other sources. It assists in identifying trends and allows us to review our activities in relation to that information and those trends. It is a continuous process, not an occasional activity. Its value is in the gradual accumulation of data that gives us a sense of the direction different areas of society are taking so that we can plan our strategy. The quality of our planning is directly related to the care with which the scanning process takes place and the currency of its data.

Internal Data

The internal data needed for planning are collected on a regular basis by each unit of the library, and reports are available. The municipality or county of which the library is a part usually sets standards for data collection, so that not only are data available for the library, the information is in a format that makes any applicable comparisons with other units possible. In addition to purely financial data, data on library use, library collection management, and other program information are used in planning. How the library evaluates performance and the results of the evaluations are also a part of the planning process.

Setting Direction

Once both external information and internal information have been analyzed, planners have a good idea of the strengths and weaknesses, opportunities and threats that face the library, and using the mission statement of the library, they identify issues that the library can influence and act upon. They ask:

1. What factors make the issue important to the library?

2. What goals can be identified?

3. How does one define success?

4. How do the data relate to SWOTs?

5. What consequences emerge from not dealing with the issue?

If there are few if any consequences of not dealing with the issue, that issue can be set aside. For those issues that are of importance to the library, goals will be set, objectives that focus on specific activities will be developed, and strategies will be proposed. Through this process, goals, objectives, and strategies selected must meet the criteria of being realistic and measurable.[19]

Once critical issues have been identified, the next step is to develop strategies to manage the issues. This combines the issues individuals have identified with what they are willing to do to act upon them. Bryson proposes a five-part management strategy:

1. Identify practical alternative solutions, ideal solutions, and so forth. This is an opportunity to think broadly and be both creative and practical.

2. Identify barriers to each of the solutions proposed. Are there political, legal, technical, social, or economic barriers?

3. Develop proposals for achieving the most promising alternatives. These proposals will address the steps to be taken, intended results, time frame, who is responsible for actions, resources required, costs, possible cost savings, flexibility, implications for other organizations or other individuals, and external effects. Is the strategy acceptable to stakeholders, decision makers, and the general public? Is it technically feasible?[20]

4. Identify actions to be taken in the next one to two years.

5. Develop a six- to twelve-month working plan to guide actions. The strategy selected "must be technically workable, politically acceptable to key stakeholders, and must accord with the organization's

philosophy and core values."[21] It must also address the issue it is supposed to address.

The last step in developing the plan is to build an organizational vision for the future. This brings together the mission and actions to achieve the mission and provides a guide to future decision making. It tells everyone what the library will do and will not do. The planning committee prepares a written plan for future action and makes it available to all constituencies. Many libraries put their planning document or a summary of that document on their public Web site so that the community knows what the library's plans for the future are. The plan is not to be seen as a statement of "where the library is" but a set of actions that show "where the library is going."

SUMMARY

Planning is the hard work of turning innovation into action through the process of data collection and analysis, evaluation, and decision making. Innovation suggests what can be, and planning sets the path on which we travel to achieve it.

NOTES

1. Jay Liebowitz, *Social Networking: The Essence of Innovation* (Lanham, MD: Scarecrow Press,2007), 3.

2. Teresa M. Amabile and Mukti Khaire, "Creativity and the Role of the Leader," *Harvard Business Review*86, no. 10 (October 2008): 103.

3. Ibid.

4. I. Nonaka and H.Takeuchi, *The Knowledge Creating Company: How Japanese Companies Create the Dynamics of Innovation* (New York: Oxford University Press, 1995).

5. James M. Kouzes and Barry Z. Posner, "To Lead, Create a Shared Vision," *Harvard Business Review* 87, no. 1 (January 2009): 21.

6. Kenneth Clark, *The End of Management and the Rise of Organizational Democracy* (New York: Jossey-Bass, 2002), 69.

7. Robert G. Cope, *Strategic Planning, Management, and Decision Making* (Washington, DC: American Association for Higher Education, 1981), 1.

8. Vernon Palmour, Marcia Bellassai, and Nancy DeWath, *A Planning Process for Public Libraries* (Chicago: American Library Association, 1980).

9. John M. Bryson, *Strategic Planning for Public and Nonprofit Organizations* (San Francisco, Jossey-Bass, 1989), xii.

10. Cope, *Strategic Planning and Decision Making*, 1.

11. Ibid., 20

12. Bryson, *Strategic Planning for Public and Nonprofit Organizations*, 14.

13. Ibid., 5.

14. Ibid., 11.

15. Ibid., 49.

16. Ibid., 50.

17. Ibid., 52-53.

18. Chun Wei Choo, *Information Management for the Intelligent Organization,* 3rd ed. (Medford, NJ: Information Today, 2002).

19. Robert H. Glover and Jeffrey Holmes, "Assessing the External Environment," in *Using Research for Strategic Planning,* ed. Norman P. Uhl (San Francisco: Jossey-Bass, 1983).

20. Bryson, *Strategic Planning for Public and Nonprofit Organizations,* 59.

21. Ibid., 179.

ADDITIONAL READINGS

Innovation and Change

Bolman, Lee G., and Terrence E. Deal. *Reframing Organizations: Artistry, Choice, and Leadership.* San Francisco: Jossey-Bass, 1991.

Cash, James I., Jr., Michael J. Earl, and Robert Morison. "Teaming up to Crack Innovation Enterprise Integration." *Harvard Business Review* 86, no. 11 (November 2008): 130–39.

Christiensen, Clayton M., Max Marx, and Howard Stevenson. "The Tools of Co-operation and Change." *Harvard Business Review* 84, no. 10 (October 2006): 73–80.

Kotter, John P., and Leonard A. Schlesinger. "Choosing Strategies for Change." *Harvard Business Review* 87, nos. 7/8 (July/August, 2008): 130–39.

Planning

Martin, Allie Beth. *A Strategy for Public Library Change.* Chicago: American Library Association, 1972.

Martin, Lowell. *Library Response to Urban Change.* Chicago: American Library Association, 1969.

Mintzenberg, Henry. *The Rise and Fall of Strategic Planning.* New York: Prentice Hall, 1994.

Slater, David C. *Management for Local Planning.* Washington, DC: International City Management Association, 1984.

Tregoe, Benjamin B., and John W. Zimmerman. *Top Management Strategy: What It Is and How to Make It Work.* New York: Simon & Schuster, 1980.

Chapter 8

Decision Making

INTRODUCTION

We make decisions every day to guide our professional activities and our personal lives. Decision making is not a special activity, but is integral to our daily lives. The kinds of decisions we make depend on our role and status in the organization and society in which we live. They also depend on the amount of information available to us, when it is available to us, and the ways we use that information. The public library uses information to make sense of the external environment: whom it serves, how it serves its several publics, the resources available to provide service, and the anticipated outcomes. It also uses information gathered internally to make decisions about how to allocate resources to meet its service and operational objectives. The organizational culture within which decision making takes place is continually fed by the flow of information, both internal and external. And information, not whim, political bias, or other subjective input, is the necessary basis for good decision making.

Although we would like to think that decision making is a rational activity that looks at the library's goals and objectives and its plans for the future, analyzes available information, and makes informed decisions, the reality is less clear cut. In fact, decision making is not the simple task one might assume. In many situations there are competing interests. One department head may make a case for additional computer terminals, while another insists that the demographics tell us that we need more support services to deal with the influx of immigrants into the community. Individuals may wish to support particular areas for personal reasons, their own or those of a community group. Negotiations take place among the competing interests until a solution (decision) that is acceptable to everyone, or nearly everyone, is reached.

WHO MAKES DECISIONS?

Who makes the decisions depends in large part on the way in which the library is structured. Traditional libraries were very hierarchical, and all decisions came from the top and filtered down to the lowest level. The library director, who might or might not have an understanding of daily operations, would make decisions based on his or her assessment of the community, the wishes of the board of trustees, the objectives to be met, and the resources available. Library directors might listen to their department heads or even include them in the decision-making process. Studies of decision making conducted in the 1960s and 1970s provide a benchmark of how decisions were made and the extent to which decision making has changed or not changed since that time. A study of 165 top executives found that although decision makers said that they had positive attitudes toward discussing new ideas and taking new directions, they were actually more interested in conforming to standard procedures and following what had been done before.[1] They were more interested in getting the job done than in looking at alternate ways of doing things that had the potential of improving the quality of the work to be done. To get the job done, one controlled from the top and told others in the library organization what they were to do. As one might expect, staff working in such an environment had very negative attitudes toward those who were making decisions that might or might not have relevance to the actual operation of the library. Those at higher levels in the organization saw their managers as conforming to the status quo and unwilling to listen to any information that might disagree with the status quo. This perception by staff that their managers were unwilling to listen to the ideas of others or to deal with uncomfortable information meant that staff did not trust the decisions of their superiors. It also meant that they were unwilling to present uncomfortable information to their managers, which in turn led to a misalignment between the decision makers and their decisions and the reality of day-to-day activities. The sad aspect of this situation was that the decision makers thought everything was going well. They were unwilling to hear bad news and therefore assumed that it did not exist. Because staff input was unwelcome, decision makers assumed that everything was fine.

This author recently asked a representative group of library staff members how their supervisors made decisions. They reported that some supervisors were particularly sensitive to the political environment, others were reluctant to do anything that had not been done before, and others made decisions that seemed to be based on the enthusiasm of the moment. In each of these instances, decisions were made with little or no input from staff. Other supervisors involved staff in the discussion of issues and then made decisions based on the best information available. When staff members did not know the reason for a decision, had not been consulted about the decision, and could see that the decision did not follow from the information available, the result was low morale and high staff turnover. When staff members were involved in the decision making and were able to contribute their skills and knowledge to the solution, morale was high.

The majority of decisions were made by the director or others in top management positions. Input from staff in some instances was minimal, while in other instances staff were encouraged to provide information. Communication with staff by those making decisions ranged from very poor to excellent. In those cases where input was encouraged and communication was open, staff members felt that their concerns had been heard and were willing to support the decision. When they had little or no input in the decision-making activity, they had little or no stake in the decision or in carrying it out. For staff, the most positive decision-making process was when they were involved in providing information, discussing the issue, and participating in the decision. They then had a stake in carrying out the decisions.

Things have changed over the years, and organizational structures, including those of the library, are less hierarchical. Fewer and fewer decisions are made from the top with little or no input from those who carry out the programs and activities of the library. Changes in our social interactions have resulted in less willingness by staff members to go along with the often arbitrary decisions of others and a greater expectation that they will be included in the decision-making process. One management consultant described the new approach to decision making thus: "Innovation and creative problem solving are stimulated by teamwork, dialogue, experimentation, play, and curiosity and weakened by working in isolation, listening to lectures."[2]

The team approach to decision making is becoming more and more accepted as the way to accomplish the task. When one looks at other cultures and other countries, it is evident that they are team oriented. In the United States there is a celebration of the individual who goes it alone or dominates others. This may result from our being only a few generations away from the pioneering spirit so important to the early days of our country. Only in the past two or three decades have we come to appreciate the fact that everyone has good ideas and should be included in the discussions and decision-making activities that affect their workplace. The world is too complicated for one person to think he or she knows enough to make unilateral decisions. Today's approach to decision making is to recognize that the greater the number of people involved, the more opportunity exists for looking at all facets of a decision, inclusion of more relevant information, and a wiser decision. Those who conduct research on diversity often note that the best decisions are made when individuals who do not come from the same educational, ethnic, or other background discuss a decision. One researcher calls this "the wisdom of crowds." Given this move toward decisions made through group discussion, some staff members may wish to opt out of participating in decision making because they do not wish to take responsibility for the decision and prefer to be given a task determined by someone else. In any situation there will be a range of individuals who are more or less interested in participating in decision making. Regardless of the degree to which decisions are made by teams or groups, one person who is at the top of the organization has final responsibility for the decision. When it is made using a participatory process, it is a stronger decision than the unilateral decision, and there may be greater organizational comfort with the decision, but there is still one person who is ultimately responsible.

INFORMATION FOR DECISION MAKING

Prior to the advent of the development of information systems to collect, organize, store, and provide information about library activities, the larger governmental organization of which the library is a part, and the larger world, information to support decision making was largely paper based and limited in its scope. Today we benefit from several decades of the development of databases designed to make information easily accessible to decision makers. Internally, we now have easily accessible financial data, circulation and other use statistics, demographic information on borrowers, and many more useful kinds of data. And is the data are available for several years so that we can see patterns and trends. Externally, we have demographic information and financial information for both the larger organization of which we are a part and the community at large. We can access information from similar organizations to compare their costs and services to our own.

Information systems within the library are designed to meet specific objectives. Their major purpose is to collect data to be used for internal decision making. For some routine decisions, such as how to staff the circulation desk, the data can be used directly for decision making. Circulation statistics will indicate increases or decreases in borrowing, borrowing patterns by time of day, time of week, month, or year, and these data can be used directly by those assigning staff to circulation to meet the need. In other situations, where information from several databases is needed for decision making, they provide indirect support. Information systems are also a means of monitoring performance over time. They are also a means of maintaining necessary records. The information systems provide a much speedier way of collecting and organizing data than was possible previously. They also make it possible for more people in the library to have access to the information. How library directors share the information has an important effect on how decisions are made. Even though technology allows us to collect and manage data to make decisions, a study of decision making by Bonabeau showed that nearly half of the administrators studied preferred to follow their intuition rather than to follow the data available. They tended to use the data to support what their gut instinct told them.[3] Many managers still base their decisions on experience rather than on the advice of others or the data. This approach tends to support the status quo, which in an era of rapid change may be more dangerous than stepping out of one's comfort zone. And if the manager picks and chooses the information to be used for decision making, the decision is at best faulty and at its worst, misleading and perhaps dangerous.

Because of easy access to the Internet, more individuals may participate in decision making. The process is no longer limited to the number of individuals who can fit around a conference table. We can include as many staff members as desired and access information from our library, other libraries, local government, and consultants, in real time. Although there is no substitute for face-to-face communication, we can mix this with electronic access and include as much information and as many people in the process as needed to reach a good decision. One advantage of this environment that is more open than in the past is that information at the lower levels of the library can move upward more easily, and information from the department and director level can move downward, thus allowing for a much faster means of responding to situations that require decisions. Also, decisions that reflect the input of more librarians and staff are easier to implement, as more individuals have been part of the process and have bought into the decisions as they were being discussed. Strategic decisions are still made at the upper levels of library management, but they benefit from the information and ideas that are produced at lower levels.

When we design information systems to conduct the business of the library, it is important that we structure the system so that it collects all relevant information and that the format used is easy to read. We need to be as careful to keep extraneous data out of the system as we are to include all relevant data. We need to look at external databases we use for decision making to be certain that they collect the data we need. It is also important to know the purpose of each external database used. Often a database is designed to collect a certain type of information in a certain way. Although that may be useful for its primary purpose, when put to other uses, it may skew the output because it has not included the kinds of information the library needs for decision making. It is also important to review any external databases that are used to be sure that their coverage has not changed; they may no longer be useful to the library, or the library may have found a different way to access the information and no longer needs a particular database. Information overload is always a problem, and decision makers need to focus on those databases or other information formats that are most useful.

Other types of information for decision making include environmental scans, marketing studies, community analyses, demographics, and similar studies. These may be collected by the library or by other agencies. They may be part of long-range plans or may be stand-alone studies. Each of these resources is an important source for decision making. These and related information sources for decision making are discussed in chapter 7.

TYPES OF DECISIONS AND ELEMENTS OF DECISION MAKING

Regardless of the type of decision or the way in which the decision is made, decision making follows from the mission and goals of the library. The public library serves the residents of an area defined by local and/or state government, and its mission is to provide the residents with information and ways to access information that will serve their daily needs and interests as well as to meet their recreational interests. Each member of the library staff understands that his or her role is to serve the community and its information needs, and this knowledge informs staff members' attitudes toward work and the decisions they make. Though different decisions are made at different levels of the library, everyone supports the mission. The clerk who checks out materials or the member of the maintenance crew who keeps the building and grounds in excellent condition supports the mission just as much as the department head or the director who determines the services to be provided.

The first step in decision making is to identify the customer. The primary customer of the public library consists of residents of the governmental unit served by the library. Substantial information is available to describe these residents: census data, economic data, studies conducted by local and state government, studies conducted by organizations including the Chamber of Commerce, the United Way, and other community groups. In addition to local residents, the library has other customers: members of the library staff, other libraries in the region with which they interact, those who supply information materials and services to the library, and others who may in some way be affected by the services the library provides.

We include these groups in decision making for the library in several ways, the most important of which is to listen to their positive comments and their complaints about services; interactions with staff; and by actively asking for feedback. When the various stakeholders in the library believe that their ideas and comments are valued and that they are not taken for granted, they become active members of the decision-making team. Library staff need to know that their role in providing service is important, their ideas are important, and they are valued participants in decision making. The role of the director and department heads becomes one not of telling staff what to do but of listening, discussing, and coming to a mutual understanding of the best way to serve. And this is done with an understanding and acceptance of the mission of the library to provide exceptional service.

Within the library, as within any organization, a way of making decisions or of deciding whether a decision is necessary results in a kind of internal practice. Although continuity in carrying out library policies and practices is necessary, there is also a local culture of how the library makes decisions. In some libraries, there is a very conservative approach to making decisions, where the major guide to new decisions is current and past practice. The assumption is that if something worked last year and is still working, it is probably the right thing to do. Some libraries value consistency over creativity and see new programs or new practices as dangerous. They often say that "if it ain't broke, don't fix it." The problem here is that a situation may not be so out of kilter that it is seen as being broke, but it may be on the way down. Those who look at each library program and activity as areas that can always be improved or might need to be replaced by something better are keeping a close eye on day-to-day operations and ensuring that they are working properly. Another element of the decision-making environment is whether or not the director and others with authority fear that they will lose some of their power if decisions are made in a participatory manner. For the conservative manager, the fear of loss of power and authority and the fear of the new exerts considerable pressure on the decision-making process and the way in which staff respond to the decisions that are made. In sum, "the quality of an organizational decision is largely a consequence of the quality of organizational intelligence and the quality of the decision making process."[4]

The Decision-Making Process

Peter Drucker outlined the following process for decision making.[5] First classify the type of decision to be made. Is it generic, unique, or a new kind of problem? Most decisions deal with issues that recur on a regular basis and are therefore generic. When one analyzes regularly recurring problems in an area, they may lead to an awareness of an underlying problem that needs to be fixed. For example, constant problems with a copy machine (e.g., out of toner, out of paper, often in need of repair) may highlight the fact that the staff member responsible for its operation lacks proper training, has too much to do, and cannot spend sufficient time tending to it, or perhaps the staff member should be replaced. With this information a decision can be made about the poorly performing copy machine. A unique problem may be new to this library, but has occurred elsewhere. While combining e-reference with more traditional reference service may be a new direction for one library, other libraries may have already tried it and will have insights into how to make good decisions about how to proceed. The unique problem that has not occurred before may be a sign that something new is happening. It is important to observe the unique situation to see how it develops and what one can learn from it. Although one cannot develop a policy or procedure for a truly unique situation, a rule, a policy, or a principle may be stated that will take care of similar situations.

The second step is to define the problem. All issues involved in the problem are to be identified. What do we know about the problem? Is it new and different from other problems? Once we have defined the problem and know what we are dealing with, we then set boundary conditions for the decision. What do we wish to accomplish in making a decision? What conditions must we satisfy? We then make a decision based on what is right rather than what would be acceptable. Making decisions based on what will produce a solution rather than what will produce the best solution is called *satisficing*; satisficing or "good enough" rarely works very well. It rarely moves the library forward. All it does is reinforce the status quo. After the decision is made, then one identifies the steps to be taken to implement the solution, who will actually take the steps, and how success will be measured. In making the decision and identifying the steps, those responsible need to have requisite information, resources, and the ability to carry out the decision. The final step in decision making is to evaluate its success. Were sufficient resources available? Did the individual have appropriate skills and support to succeed? And most important, did the decision support the library's mission and values?

Decision-Making Models

There are numerous decision-making models, but most decision making falls into five categories or some combination of these categories. The first of these models is the Rational Model, which is goal directed and problem driven.[6] There are agreed upon behaviors, which may or may not be written down. The library may have developed a standard procedure for decision making, and it is assumed that if each library staff member follows the rules and behaviors, the library will function well. There may be roles covering each activity, rules covering how information is used, rules covering resource allocation, and rules for reporting. In this type of situation, individuals are expected to follow existing rules to the extent possible, even when circumstances change. Goals for the library are set by trustees, funding agencies, and administrators, and all decisions are expected to fall within these goals. They look at past performance as the best guide for future activities. This attempt to control the environment by controlling who makes decisions results in a library that is not responsive to the needs of those who rely on it to meet their information needs and is not responsive to the changing skills and abilities of staff. Looking at past performance to decide how to function in the future is a little like driving a car over a route that has had several curves relocated as though nothing has changed. There is often more danger in sticking with the old way of doing things too long than in changing to the new too soon. Though the rational model may be intended to reduce uncertainty, it neglects the fact that we live in a changing world.

The Process Model looks at stages, activities, and dynamics of possible behavior. Researchers looked at a wide range of types of decisions made in government and for-profit organizations and found that there was an underlying decision-making structure. Because of a buildup of events in an area, it would become evident that a problem existed and that a decision was needed. The person closest to the situation would collect data, both internal and external. Using this information, plus actions taken previously in the organization, alternative solutions to the problem would be posed. After evaluating the alternatives in terms of the ways in which they related to the library's goals and were politically acceptable, and looking at the possible consequences of each alternative, a decision is made.

The above activities take advantage of existing regular activities within the library, and decision makers are aware of the relation of the problem to other library activities. Existing data-gathering activities in the library are utilized, as is the expertise and knowledge of the situation by staff. Resources available to address the situation are known, as are any time limits for a decision. How long it takes to reach a decision depends on the urgency of the situation, the time needed to collect relevant information, and the ability of staff involved to reach a decision.

The Political Model focuses on those who have authority to make decisions. The authority comes from the position to which they are appointed, and they are limited by that position. They are as powerful as the individual who appointed them, and their decisions reflect the priorities of that individual. Though this model rarely applies to library decision making, there are instances in which the library director has been fired by a mayor or city manager and an individual of his or her choice has been given the position. This may occur when the library director disagrees with the mayor or city manager about a policy or service and is replaced by a more pliable individual.

When the library has poorly defined goals and staff does not have a clear idea of the direction to be taken, decision making is difficult because there is no agreed upon direction for action. If the individual in charge is unsure of the direction to be taken or has not informed staff of how to proceed, the situation is even more difficult. Some directors have difficulty deciding how to approach a problem and may not be consistent in what is expected of staff. In this Anarchic Model, decisions are usually reactive in that they are made after a problem has occurred. There may or may not be any data gathering. The decision may or may not be in accord with other decisions made. If such an individual has decision-making authority in the library, that individual should be dealt with swiftly before too much damage is done.

When issues and information are thrown together in no particular order and decisions are the result of chance interaction among the following—choice, opportunities, problems, potential solutions, and participants[7]—we have the Garbage Can Model. "Like the garbage in a trash can, the decision depends on the mix currently available. There are *collections of choices* looking for problems, issues and feelings looking for decision situations in which they might be aired, solutions looking for issues to which they might be the answer, and decision makers looking for work."[8] When people say that they are just muddling through, they are most likely using this model of decision making. With the sophistication of data gathering and a good organizational structure in the library, there is no excuse for just muddling through.

How to Make Good Decisions

Some managers become comfortable with the status quo and "form habits about the acquisition and passing on of information, and in general establish values and norms that influence how the organization copes with choice and uncertainty."[9] Information critical to an issue may not fit into the routine structure, and its absence may result in major decision-making errors. The space shuttle *Challenger* is cited as a situation in which routine data collection and routine ways of decision making resulted in disaster, because the process was trusted more than the conflicting data. When one focuses on bureaucratic and political accountability in the library, it can have a way of downplaying reality. Choo says that "the analysis of the Challenger accident reveals failures and lapses in sense making, knowledge creating, decision making, and information management.[10] When one filters information through a dominant way of thinking that may or may not be valid, and focuses on process rather than the facts, information flow is blocked and good decisions rarely result.

Making a decision is a way to exert control over uncertainty. We are unsure of a situation, and if we make a decision, there is the assumption that we have solved the problem. This may or may not be true. In seeking information for decision making, we tend to rely on the following trial and error sources:

- Has the event occurred before? Is it representative of a category of events? Has someone experienced the event previously? Are we generalizing from a small number of events?

- We can recall familiar and recent events; for example, decisions by library patrons to attend a film series may be based on satisfaction with an earlier similar series. An outstanding event, such as the showing of a film inappropriate to the audience, may bias the attitude toward all films selected for the series despite evidence that the poor selection was a one-time event. How does one move forward?

- We can estimate the value of a decision by setting a baseline and then adjusting it. One approach to budgeting is to look at the current year's funding and then adjust it upward a bit to account for inflation and other elements. The decision makers do not question the appropriateness of the baseline of last year's funding, and rather than making a good decision based on earlier information, they may be making the situation worse.

The best way to make decisions is to

- look for situations that require decisions,

- seek information to assist in identifying a course of action,

- select a particular course of action, and

- review past actions as a way of evaluating new decisions.

Decision making is complex. It is impossible to gain all information, analyze it, and make a decision based on it. There is too much information, and it would take too much time to analyze. Organizations, including libraries, design and implement rules and routines to simplify the process. They therefore promote uniformity in the library, as decisions are based on a set of rules and procedures. The resulting conformity can restrict information, limit creativity, and result in poor decisions. Standard decision-making activities focus on what the organization has learned from experience. Tradition wins over innovation. Although we need structures to help us deal with the complexities of decision making, those structures may limit, constrict, and mislead us. We need to find the balance between an orderly way of making decisions and inviting innovative ideas that will move us forward.

And what happens when decisions are not good and lead us in unwanted directions? When we make a decision, the assumption is that we will make the best decision based on available evidence, but

- What if we lack critical information essential to a good decision?

- What if there is no clear cut, right decision?

- What if none of the possible decisions appear to be good decisions?

- What if personal bias, yours or that of someone else, gets in the way?

- What if there are competing groups supporting competing decisions?

- What about unanticipated and/or unintended consequences?

What does the manager do?

One solution is to seek advice. Gino suggests that in seeking advice, advice seekers tend to overvalue advice when the problem addressed is difficult and undervalue it when the problem appears to be easy.[11] They also tend to overvalue advice they pay for, assuming perhaps that free advice is useless. Nearly all managers seek advice from someone—colleagues, superiors, experts in the field. Gino also suggests that the advice seeker check to see if there is a bias in how the advice is given and/or received. His final advice is to "beware of being too willing to listen to others who are no better informed than you are." We need to trust those who make decisions, to trust that they have listened to others, have received and analyzed necessary information, and are unbiased in their decisions.

SUMMARY

Though we have a wide array of databases and other data-gathering systems to provide us with information to help us make decisions, it is the analysis of the information by individuals who are familiar with the workplace, who know the goals of the library and the needs of those who use it, that determines which information is most useful in a situation. We need good information-gathering techniques to provide us with requisite information, and we need experienced, creative librarians who understand what the information means and use that information to make decisions that lead us toward achieving the mission and goals of the library.

NOTES

1. Chris Argyris, "Interpersonal Barriers to Decision Making," in *Harvard Business Review on Decision Making* (Boston: Harvard Business School Publishing, 2001), 1–19.

2. Kenneth Cloke, *The End of Management and the Rise of Organizational Democracy* (New York: Jossey-Bass, 2002), 11.

3. Eric Bonabeau, "Don't Trust Your Gut," *Harvard Business Review* 81 (May 2003): 116–23.

4. George P. Huber, "A Theory of the Effects of Advanced Information Technologies on Organizational Design, Intelligence, and Decision Making," *Academy of Management Review* 15 (1990):63.

5. Peter Drucker, "The Effective Decision," in *Harvard Business Review on Decision Making* (Boston: Harvard Business School Publishing. 2001), 2–17.

6. James G. March and H. A. Simon, *Organizations* (New York: John Wiley, 1958), 162–63.

7. Kerry Grosser, "Human Networks in Organizational Information Processing," *Annual Review of Information Science and Technology* (Medford, NJ: Learned Information, 1991), 383–84.

8. Michael D. Cohen, James G. March, and Johan P. Olsen, " A Garbage Can Model of Organizational Choice," *Administrative Science Quarterly* 17 (January 1972): 1.

9. Chun Wei Choo, *The Knowing Organization: How Organizations Use Information, Construct Meaning, Create Knowledge, and Make Decisions* (New York: Oxford Press, 1992), 155.

10. Ibid., 163.

11. Francesca Gino, "Let Me Give You Some Advice," *Harvard Business Review* 84 (March 2006): 24.

ADDITIONAL READINGS

Kaufman, Arnold. *The Science of Decision Making: An Introduction to Praxeology.* New York: McGraw Hill, 1968.

Chapter 9

Library Organization

INTRODUCTION

The library organization is a small social system that is part of the larger social system in which we live. It is built upon and reflects the culture, attitudes, and behaviors of the larger system and serves as the structure that brings together people and resources to achieve goals. It is a tool for managing the actions of individuals and the structure for formal communication. Each library reflects its community and the values of those who are responsible for its operation. Each library also has both a formal and an informal organization.

Peter Drucker's view of organizational structure is that it follows strategy: what is the purpose of the organization, what should the results be, what are the components, and how should they be arranged?[1] He stressed that management is people, and it is their actions that energize the organization and management needs to look at today's technological and information rich world and determine how one manages ambiguity. In their book *In Search of Excellence*, Peters and Waterman stated that the organizational chart is not the organization but the point at which one begins to change.[2] It is often difficult to develop a truly different organizational structure, because the existing one may be very comfortable, and staff may not want to change.

Peters and Waterman stress that the purpose of an organization is to develop a way to serve the customer. There must be a passion for quality and reliability and the individual is more important than the organizational structure devised to do so. They identified seven variables that constitute an organization; structure, strategy, management style, systems, shared values, skills presently available or desired, and people.[3] They also found that the four basic human needs are essential to the success of an organization:

1. Need for meaning. Is what we are doing valuable? The profession of librarianship is built on meaning: the value of bringing individuals and information together for the benefit of the individual and society.

2. Need for some control. Each individual in the organization should have a measure of control of the work he or she does.

3. Need for positive reinforcement. Each individual needs to know if his or her efforts are appreciated, and if not, what should be done to correct them.

4. The degree to which actions and behavior shape attitude, and not vice versa.[4]

They stress that an organization needs to adapt to changing conditions and be agile in dealing with unexpected issues. When possible, decisions should be made quickly and by those closest to the situation. We need an organization that can move, change, and keep current with, and perhaps even ahead of, the issue.

TYPES OF ORGANIZATION

Organizations both shape and are shaped by the culture of which they are a part. Most individuals work for an organization, which provides them with the opportunity to earn a living. As a condition of their employment, they conform to the social norms of the workplace. And through the types of services it provides, the organization has an effect on the community it serves. Organizations in turn are shaped by their purpose, mission, goals, and objectives.

Over time, as attitudes toward the workforce have changed, organizations have also changed to accommodate the needs and interests of a better-educated and more independent workforce. Most organizations continue both to be highly centralized and highly structured even when the workforce is distributed over a wide geographic area. Though information technology and communications technology have made it easier for an organization to be dispersed over a large area when necessary, the structure is still highly centralized. Because of legal requirements, public opinion, federal regulations, and social action, organizations have also become more socially responsible to their staff and those they serve.

The underlying purpose of the organization is to provide a way in which individuals can be brought together to work toward common goals and objectives. The type of organizational structure that emerges depends on the mission and goals of the library. When determining what organizational structure is to be developed, one needs to keep in mind that the purpose is to organize individuals into a structure that will get the work done and will accomplish the mission, goals, and objectives of the library. In the fast-moving world in which we live, we need an organizational structure that is flexible and can respond to changing needs. Organizations evolve over time. In the beginning, they often use other organizations as models and then change to meet new circumstances. One would like to think that these changes are made thoughtfully, but more often than not, they are made in response to crises, changing demographics, technological changes, or other external circumstances.

The Formal Organization

The formal organization is clearly defined and can be presented on an organizational chart that indicates positions and the ways in which those positions are related to one another. Each position on the chart has a description that indicates the responsibilities of that position. The chart also indicates the level of positions in a hierarchical form in which each position level reports to the level above it. Communication flows downward in the chart through directives from those in higher levels to those in lower levels, and it flows upward with reports on the extent to which directives have been followed and their results. As the organization grows, the chart becomes more complex. New positions are added, and new reporting relationships may be indicated. This definition of the formal organization represents what some would consider the ideal situation. In reality, it is difficult to fit all position descriptions and all reporting lines into a chart and thus provide an accurate view of the organization. We live in a world in which change is continuous and there is the need to respond to new and changing needs. The formal organizational chart may still serve as a skeleton on which to structure the library's activities. If it becomes rigid and unable to change with changing needs, it becomes a strait jacket that interferes with the purpose of the organization.

The Informal Organization

Every library also has an informal organization, sometimes several informal organizations. The informal organization consists of "the unofficial and unauthorized relationships that inevitably occur between individuals and groups within the formal organization."[5] These relationships are informal and are not subject to control by the organization. They may be based on friendship or common interest. The informal organization meets social needs and the need for belonging that are not met by the formal organization. It may provide a means for staff members to become socialized to the expectations of the formal organization or in some cases, it may have its own norms of behavior, which may or may not be in agreement with those of the formal organization. For example, the formal organization may be strongly supportive of a diverse workforce, while those in the informal organization may prefer to deal with individuals with whom they relate immediately. Rather than welcoming a person who may represent a different gender, culture, or age group, the informal organization may place social barriers in that person's way.

The informal organization can function as a useful liaison between supervisor and staff. Its members may discuss instructions from the supervisor and agree on ways to carry out a task. It may serve as a means of informing the formal organization of staff concerns about issues such as workload or staff morale. In earlier decades, prior to the online world in which information is widely available, the informal organization built its own network, called the grapevine. Information moved rapidly along the grapevine to all parts of the library. Staff members were kept current on what was happening elsewhere in the organization, and the alert supervisor who tapped into the grapevine was able to know what issues were of concern to staff. The grapevine was not respected by many supervisors, who regarded it as a means of distributing inaccurate information; however, research has shown that it has a high accuracy rate. Today, information moves up, down, and across the organization much more easily than in the past, but the grapevine continues to provide an important means of assessing the attitudes and concerns of staff. When the informal organization and the formal organization share objectives, the organization is strengthened, but if those objectives are in conflict, the organization is weakened and will not function well. It is the responsibility of the supervisor to understand the role of the informal organization and to work with its leaders so that they work together to serve the community. Though managers can interact with the informal organization, they cannot control it.

The Bureaucratic Organization

In the early 20th century, Max Weber and others championed the bureaucratic organization as the ideal. This hierarchical structure was built on well-defined rules and roles, and authority came from the top of the organization and flowed downward. This hierarchy of offices existed with each office controlled by the one above and controlling the one below. Each position has its competencies and responsibilities. Written rules and records of past decisions provide direction for subsequent decisions. The person holding a position owes that position loyalty, is responsible for the use of the organization's resources, and is expected to carry out the duties of the position. Work life and personal life are separate, but it is expected that work life takes precedence, and for this loyalty one receives a salary based on rank. A final aspect of bureaucracy is that the individual holding a position does so at the pleasure of those in higher ranks. Obedience by the individual is to the office and not to the person holding the office. This model was refined over many years and is found in both for-profit and not-for-profit organizations. Though this model may work for situations that do not change, it is too rigid to adapt to new situations. In a bureaucracy, there is always a rule or precedent that can be brought out to support the status quo. Bureaucracy is impersonal, and the organization is more important than the individual. One can remove a person from a slot and easily place someone with similar credentials into that slot.

Other problems with bureaucracy are that, although it promotes stability, at the same time it is the enemy of change. It becomes rule bound to the extent that it is very difficult to address new situations. The organizational structure itself becomes more important than the purpose for which it was formed or the people involved. There are also many examples of promoting individuals based not on ability but on the basis of cultural or political views and a willingness to conform to the organization and its status quo. One critic said that the charge of incompetence of a bureaucratic organization may actually be the result of following a different set of objectives.[6] When, for example, a customer wants to get information on a particular product or service and cannot do so, bureaucracy is blamed. Perhaps the bureaucracy doesn't want to release that information, and the unavailability of the information is seen by the bureaucracy as success. It is easy for an individual or group to co-opt a bureaucratic organization to serve a personal agenda. Rules become very important, and it is assumed that if you make a rule, the problem is solved. A result of too many rules is that they inhibit responsible decision making.

During the period of our history in which the workforce was considered just another part of the machinery, having a highly structured organization was seen as the way to control the workers. This attitude toward workers gradually changed as the workforce became better educated and it became evident that there wasn't one best way to organize individuals. Why not develop an organization that respected the individual's abilities and interests? What is accomplished by forcing an individual into an organizational slot that deprives that individual of the ability to think creatively and make decisions in a changing world? Such an organization would still have goals, objectives, and the need to manage resources. This conflict between democratic ideals and authoritarian structure continues. When an organizational structure doesn't function well, some blame the individuals rather than looking to see if the structure is appropriate for the task.

The Virtual Organization

With the use of information and communications technology, we can develop a virtual organization, one that is not bound by time or space. Members of the library staff can work from home, another library, somewhere else in the country, or even abroad and still be connected to their colleagues as if they were present in person. As librarians look at the activities that occur in the library, it is possible to identify those that can be performed from another location. For example, online reference services can be performed from any location where there is a reference specialist and a computer. Reviewing materials as part of the selection process can be done in an online mode by a team composed of representatives from different branches. The team could also include subject specialists from anywhere in the world. Continuing education programs are increasingly offered online, and because students from anywhere can enroll in courses, one can offer a wide range of topics, even in courses that would have insufficient enrollment if they were offered from one location.

Library staff can look at their activities and determine which can be performed from a distance. Staff members who live at a distance from the library, who may have caregiving responsibilities, or who have short- or long-term disabilities may benefit from being able to work from home for part or all of the week. When possible, staff members need to interact with their peers in face-to-face meetings. Some libraries will expect staff members to work one or two days a week in the library so that they are socially connected to the library and feel that they are part of its social structure. There is an almost limitless opportunity to mix the virtual, online, work world with the world of nine to five, and this opportunity opens doors to library staff who might otherwise not participate.

One can also have virtual patrons, those who e-mail the library with reference questions, ask for books or other materials to be sent to them that they can renew online, and take advantage of the library Web site to plan activities. Though we may think that the virtual library is a very open environment, in fact it is highly structured and needs to be managed carefully. With appropriate thoughtful organization and management, the virtual organization becomes the virtual library that everyone can enjoy. And as the technology grows and improves, so will the opportunities.

The Learning Organization

All organizations have a life cycle. They are initiated, they grow and mature, and if not tended carefully, they will decline. Library staff members are responsible for maintaining a healthy library organization and for ensuring that it moves ahead. This doesn't happen without a plan and a process, which define the learning organization. Garvin says that the learning organization is "one skilled at creating, acquiring, and transferring knowledge and at modifying its behavior to reflect new knowledge and insights."[7] Learning organizations are problem-solving organizations. They look at issues and analyze information to make good decisions. They do not rely on opinion or political expediency, nor do they try to make the problem conform to what may seem to be a good solution. They try out new approaches to manage the library or to provide service and adopt those that are of greater benefit than the existing procedure.

Because these approaches are carried out on a regular basis within the library, they are small and incremental and keep the library learning and changing. When one has the goal of looking for new and better ways of doing things, these small steps are part of a direction and a plan. Without a direction and a plan, change may be seen as a constant churning and movement without a purpose, a situation that results in staff discomfort and unwillingness to change.

Learning organizations benefit from past experience; the experience of similar libraries; and the suggestions and ideas of staff, management, trustees, vendors, and those who use the library. New jobs may be developed that replace old jobs that no longer meet new needs. Librarians who are active in their professional associations learn new approaches and identify best practices. All of these sources provide a steady stream of new approaches that ensure the library is moving ahead as an organization and has not become mired in the issues and concerns of the past. Again, as with the virtual organization, the learning library, while open to new ideas and innovation, is well organized and well managed so that it can take advantage of new approaches.

TYPES OF FORMAL ORGANIZATIONS

As has been discussed, formal organizations have a structure that is clearly defined and can be described by organizational charts, position descriptions, and the flow of communication. The formal organization can be organized in a number of ways: by function, by geographic location, and in libraries by subject matter and/or format. Each of these is a response to the question, "What is the best way to get the job done?" Following this question, one asks how best to utilize personnel and resources to get the job done.

Organization by Function

The major functional areas of the library are public services, technical services, and administration (see figure 9.1). For each function there are specific tasks, and for these tasks, individuals with specialized education and skills are necessary. Within each major area, there are specialized activities. For example, within public services one finds units including reference services, children's services, outreach services, circulation services, and other services requiring direct interaction with those served by the library. The technical services area includes acquisition, cataloging, and collection maintenance. In some libraries, information technology activities are part of technical services; in others, they are part of a separate unit. Administrative services include financial services, personnel services, maintenance and building services, and any other activities necessary to provide the environment in which public and technical services can function easily.

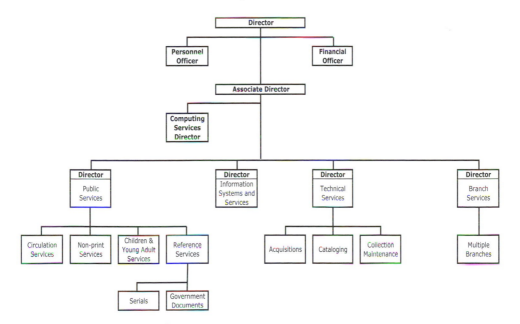

Figure 9.1. Organization by Function

The head of each functional unit and the head of the subunits serve as the library's experts in that area. These heads advise the director on those issues about which they are knowledgeable. They are up to date on the ways in which the services they provide are best conducted. They know what the latest advances in their area are and are active in their professional activities. They know whom they serve and the changes in their service area. For example, the children's specialist knows how children learn, at what age certain programs are appropriate, how to present those programs, and how to evaluate the results. The children's specialist interacts with other children's librarians in both school and public libraries to learn new ways of presenting programs and to coordinate program activities with schools so that children's school activities can be reinforced in the public library. Being active in professional societies provides another very important way to keep up to date on how children learn and how best to support that learning. The children's specialist also knows the demographics of the community served: age range of children, ethnic groups, socioeconomic groups, and any other ways to define the children in the service area. Trends in demographics are continuously sampled to be sure that library programs continue to meet existing needs.

Reference specialists, depending on the size of the library, can be divided by the format of the materials they use, such as print, nonprint, and online searching. They may be expert in one, more than one, or all formats of materials. As specialists in their particular area, they contribute important information to the planning and executing of library activities. Though they may not be knowledgeable about other parts of the library, their combined expertise is an important resource.

Organization by Geographic Location

When a library serves a large area, it may divide its services geographically, with a central library serving the entire service area and branch libraries serving specific population areas. (See figure 9.2.) Although the libraries are geographically distributed, they are bound together by common policies, common objectives, and a common organizational structure. The director and administrative staff of the central library, including the financial officer, personnel officer, and development officer, serve the entire library and ensure that the library functions in the same way regardless of location. The central library holds the largest collection and provides both public and technical services to the area, and branch libraries are often responsible for the same range of public services as the main library but do so for a smaller population. In most instances, the main library is responsible for centralized acquisition, cataloging, and processing of materials because it is more efficient and cost effective to provide these services from a central location

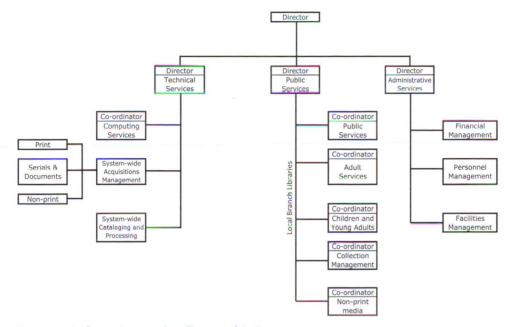

Figure 9.2. Organization by Geographic Location

In a library organized by geographic location, the central library usually has on its staff coordinators of major services such as coordinator of children's services, coordinator of reference services, coordinator of collection management, etc. The coordinator works with branch library staff to ensure that each branch library has access to the best ways to provide a service and that each branch has equal access to the library's resources in a particular area. Branch libraries often tailor their services to the demographic needs and interests of that smaller population. For example, if the branch library serves a largely Hispanic population, the collection may reflect local reading and viewing interests. A Spanish-speaking librarian may be available to work with families who are becoming familiar with the language and culture of their new country. Print and nonprint materials can be selected to meet the needs and interests of the population. The director of the branch library is usually responsible for the administration of the branch and for the public service programs and activities of the branch. Because the head of the branch library is a generalist and must deal with all aspects of service to a community on the front line of interaction with the community, this is an excellent training ground for tomorrow's library administrators.

With the availability of online catalogs and reference services, the branch library can offer many of the services available at the central library and do so in a more convenient location. The resources and services of the main library are available to everyone in the service area, and because branch librarians are attuned to the special interests of their community, the level of service is high.

Organization by Subject/Format

In large public libraries one may find the library organized by subject or by format (see figure 9.3). This type of library organization may have a sci/tech department, a fine arts department, a government documents department, a nonprint media department, and a local history department. Each department is headed by a department head, and reference services are provided for the particular subject area within the department. In some instances, circulation services may also be provided within the unit, but it is more likely that a centralized circulation department will be used. As with the library organized by geographic location, administration, policies, financial and personnel activities, and acquisition and processing services are centralized to ensure efficiency and uniformity. Information technology services are also managed centrally.

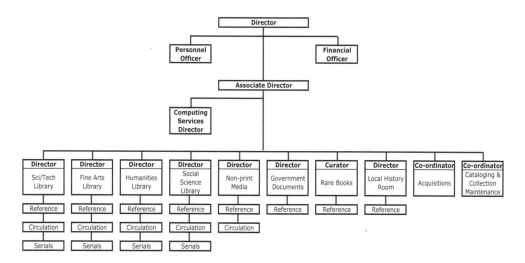

Figure 9.3. Organization by Subject

COORDINATION OF ACTIVITIES

Regardless of the overall organizational structure of the library, its purpose is to provide a way in which staff can work together toward the common objective of providing information to their community. The organization as a whole follows the same policies, rules, and regulations. Centralized guidance and authority are communicated throughout the library. Each member of the library community needs to feel a sense of belonging to a well-managed organization whose purpose they support. Each member of the community needs to know that he or she has an important role in achieving the objectives of the library.

Within the larger structure, each library unit has individuals with different areas of expertise and different priorities. It is the responsibility of the department head or the branch head to coordinate the activities of the unit with those of the library. This is the purpose of department head meetings, in which the library's plans and priorities are discussed and the contribution of each department is determined. Within each unit, the department/branch head makes sure that there is communication so that each staff member knows what his or her responsibilities are, how they are to be carried out, and how he or she will be evaluated. There must also be excellent communication among units so that they are working in concert with each other.

A question that always arises when one discusses organization is that of span of control: How many individuals should report to the same supervisor? Some say four to eight individuals is the right number; others provide another number. Championing a specific number has been replaced by a different approach, in which a variety of factors are considered. If the task being done is routine and staff members are well trained, one can supervise a fairly large number of individuals. An example of this would be circulation staff in a large public library. If the task being done requires a high skill level and there is the need for regular consultation with the supervisor, a narrower span of control is appropriate. Each library has its own culture and attitudes toward the delegation of work, and this may influence the span of control. The wise supervisor knows how to manage and how to provide the appropriate level of supervision and trust.

Centralization—Decentralization

We often think of centralization and decentralization of an organization in terms of geography, but in reality we are talking about decision making. Where are decisions made? How much of the decision making comes from the top, and how much is made at other levels of the library? In some libraries, the director and supervisors are known for their willingness to involve staff in discussion of issues and are comfortable with sharing decision making. In other libraries, those in charge are very reluctant to share decision making and insist that all decisions are to be made from the top. Policies and procedures have been developed by and for the organization to guide and control many daily activities. The objectives of the library also serve as guides to daily activities. A problem arises when policies and procedures are not reviewed regularly and the attitude "we've always done it this way" exists.

Ernest Dale, an expert in organizational design and management, lists four criteria for looking at the level of centralization—decentralization in an organization:[8] the greater the number of routine decisions made lower down in the organization, the greater the degree of centralization; the more important those decisions made lower down in the organization are, the greater the decentralization; the greater the number of functions affected by decisions made at lower levels, and the less checking of those decisions, the more decentralized the organization. In most decentralized organizations, routine decisions are not checked at all. Supervisors expect that their staff will make the correct decisions, and in those cases where there is concern about what those decisions may be, staff will consult their supervisor Trust in the ability of staff to be responsible decision makers is essential to a smoothly running organization.

When the organizational structure is rigid and slow moving, decisions take a long time to be made. In our current climate of continuous change, it is no longer possible to have an organization that relies on centralized decision making. What is needed is an environment in which decentralized decision making is supported by policies and practices that are reviewed regularly and in which decision making is pushed as far down in the organization as possible. This type of organization requires staff who are well trained, who nderstand their work, and are confident in their decision-making responsibilities.

Committees and Teams

Committees and teams are ways of organizing staff members and representatives of other stakeholder groups into units responsible for accomplishing specific tasks. In the library, there will be several types of committees depending on the needs of the library at a particular time. Standing committees are committees with specific responsibilities and specific membership. They meet regularly and advise the director on issues. Standing committees usually include a personnel committee, finance committee, planning committee, and development committee. Membership on a standing committee is often written into an individual's position description. For example, the financial officer is a member of, and usually chairs, the finance committee. Each standing committee includes staff members, a representative of the director, and often members of the board of trustees. Some standing committees have decision-making power, whereas others are advisory to the director and through the director to the board of trustees.

Ad hoc committees or task forces are appointed to serve for a specified period of time and are charged with a specific task. Once the task has been completed, the committee or task force is disbanded. Search committees, committees to recommend new software, and committees to respond to a community request for a program are examples of ad hoc committees. They are appointed by the director and staff and represent those in the library and community whose perspective and expertise are important components of the recommendation they will make. All committees and task forces keep records of their activities, which then become part of the library's records, so if someone should question their decisions or recommendations, a record is available. Committee membership provides an excellent opportunity for staff to meet and work with others in the library and the community.

Cross-functional teams and activities are also an excellent way of maintaining communication among different units. These teams may be charged to perform a task and in this way are similar to ad hoc committees, or they may be appointed for a longer term and be charged with dealing with concerns that affect more than one department. For example, the personnel officer may put together a cross-functional team to discuss the best way to provide in-service training for the library. Cross-functional teams are used to break down barriers between departments, provide the opportunity for staff to work together on common issues, and see that there are many approaches to the same issue and that each approach contributes to the solution.

Another way to improve communication between and among departments is to offer individual staff members the opportunity to work for an extended period of time in another department. A reference librarian may find that working in acquisitions provides a better understanding of the processes necessary to provide materials used in the reference department. A technical services librarian will find a new appreciation of how technical services processes help or hinder providing information to the public. A branch librarian may find that working at the main library answers many questions about how main library staff see branch activities and how the two do or do not work together. Not only does working in another department provide a greater understanding of how different tasks in different departments contribute to the mission of the library, it also provides useful cross training to staff members. The library always benefits when staff members come to understand and value the activities of others. And this is an excellent way to test interactions between and among units and make improvements when necessary.

INFORMATION TECHNOLOGY AND THE ORGANIZATION

Although the basic structure of the organization and the organizational chart remain essentially the same, information technology has had and continues to have a profound effect on the organization. It has changed the way we communicate, the ways in which we work, and even where we work. The combination of living and working in a global economy, and the presence of an increasingly well-educated and tech savvy workforce results in an ever-changing environment. While someone working in a bureaucratic environment tends to become more and more specialized in an ever-decreasing area of expertise, today's workers must continuously learn new skills, adapt old ones, and look for new ways of working and new kinds of services to provide. "Instead of a role anchored by the organization and codified by a job description, the new forms are offering a role defined by the task of the moment and the location of the worker."[9] Those who accept change and have become accustomed to continuous technological innovation find this an exciting environment; those who are less willing to learn new ways of doing things find this very stressful. Within any organization, any library setting, the manager will find some who welcome change, some who are threatened by it, and others who do their best to adapt.

A strong, adaptable organization is a learning organization that looks for new ways to move ahead. Depending on the willingness of staff members to learn and change their way of doing things, change may come slowly or more rapidly. The manager needs to be aware of how ready for change staff members are and plan carefully so that stress can be minimized. Staff need to know before a change is put into place. They need to be part of the change process and informed about the steps to be taken and what is expected of them. Even then, some staff members will not accept change, and one must keep in mind that a library is a social organization with interactive parts, so when we change one part of the organization, unanticipated change may occur elsewhere. Brown and Duiguid state that the organization is a social system with a collective knowledge that supports those who work there, and when technology disrupts the workplace, one must reach a new balance.[10] How can those working off-site interact with those working full time in the library? How can one supervise the work of a reference librarian who is conducting searches from home? Because a library is a social system, and staff members rely on collective knowledge to interact, how does someone working remotely tap into that collective knowledge? How does the staff member working from home or from a distant branch library connect with others in the library? New connections must be built so that people working on the same or similar tasks who are geographically separated may feel that they are a part of the social environment. Some supervisors have difficulty working with staff members who are not physically present and are not comfortable interacting with them electronically. Although it is possible to interact electronically only, there is a need to build in face-to-face interaction when possible. Staff members may work at home or at a distant location part of the week and attend staff meetings, social events, and other activities during which they can interact with others.

When one brings information technology into the library, it is not an add on, nor is it something that can be done in one part of the library or on one process. Early library automation was directed toward the ability to speed up traditional number crunching, data storage, and access. It soon became evident that information technology could be used for more things than just to replicate existing tasks. It also became evident that when one speeds up activities in one part of the library, there are implications for work flow elsewhere. To be successful in adapting technology to library processes,an overview of the organization is needed: what are its objectives, what current activities further those objectives, and can technology be used to support the activities? In this review, it is often found that some activities are no longer needed or can be combined with other activities. New processes may need to be developed that take advantage of the technology. The result of the review is a reshaping of library activities that takes advantage of the technologies available.

Not only do those in the workplace need to take advantage of new technologies to grow and develop, they need to take advantage of new ways of working. New skills are needed as "the new technologies also force adoption of more sophisticated mechanisms in the hierarchy of coordination, e.g., task forces, teams, project coordinators, and entire integrating of departments."[11] Traditional organizations divide activities into specific units. In libraries, we find public services, technical services, and administrative services, and each area is responsible for specific activities. The integration of information technology into the workplace has made it desirable to look at the library as a whole, and rather than dividing its activities into specific units, there is an emphasis on working in teams that focus on a particular program or activity. These teams may be made up of any combination of public, technical, or administrative services personnel who are appropriate to the task. A task-oriented library focuses on its role in the community and what it needs to do to meet expectations.

In a technology-rich library, we not only build teams representing all areas of the library, we may also scatter members of a department throughout the library and even have department members working in another location or from home. We no longer need to have all members of a department in the same place. When we no longer rely on word of mouth communication or the hard copy memo, we free individuals to work anywhere. And we also free up those individuals who formerly held staff meetings and wrote memos. Now, with one e-mail, the supervisor can communicate immediately with all members of the department or team and immediately receive feedback. Face-to-face communication continues to be very important because it connects individuals socially and builds a sense of belonging, but much of the routine communication can be done in other ways. If we follow the analogy of the organization as a body and the organizational structure as the skeleton, communication is the spinal cord and the nervous system. It connects all individuals and teams so that there is an ability to move in the same direction.

Redesigning an organization to take advantage of technology is not an easy task. Using rapid communication, the ability to store large amounts of data and analyze it for decision making and to streamline business processes such as ordering materials and managing travel accounts requires effort. The more mature the library, the more difficult the task is, as individuals have become accustomed to working in a particular way and to interacting with others both formally and informally in specific ways. As the public library is part of larger government structures, its administration needs to conform to the organizational structure of the larger entity. It is much easier to build new ways of organizing and working in a new library because ways of interacting are still settling in, and individuals are open to new ways of doing things.

Every day we learn of new opportunities offered by technology to create, restructure, and manage the library. No area of the library, from the director's office to the maintenance office, is unaffected by what we can now do better, faster, and often cheaper. We can organize our internal information into databases that provides us with a greater ability to determine the actual costs of our activities, identify any trends, and project in both the short and long term what our anticipated expenses will be. Access to external databases provides information on demographics of the community served and trends that will impact service options. These and other ways to collect and analyze information about the library in real time are important tools in managing the library and its resources in the best possible way.

Managers who involve staff in discussing new technologies and present them as a solution to existing problems provide a way for staff to become familiar with new ways of organizing and completing their tasks. They also give each staff member the opportunity to see how his or her job can fit into the technologically redefined operation and how a different way of doing things will benefit that person. This opens the door to discussion of new opportunities and how to implement them. Staff also need access to any necessary training in the use of new technologies and transition time to put them into practice, the process of building a new culture, the e-culture. "Fast open access to information and the ability to communicate directly with nearly everyone everywhere sets e-culture apart from traditional environments."[12] In this culture, it is no longer possible to hide information and to use the withholding of information as power.

E-mail has become a communication tool that we now consider indispensable for both internal and external communication. Even in situations where team members or department members are dispersed geographically or have different hours, everyone gets the same information at the same time. Communication flows in all directions: from the supervisor to team and department members, from them to the supervisor, and horizontally among team and department members. They can communicate in each of these directions to share progress and discuss problems and possible solutions. In some ways, this allows the merging of the formal and informal organization as policies and directives are discussed with both the supervisor and among staff. An additional benefit of enriched communication is that the teams and departments build community and a sense of belonging to their group. This is an example of how changing the information flow changes the organization.

Within the library and depending on its size, each of the numerous departments has its own teams, each with its internal communication. There is communication among these groups; with centralized services such as personnel, budgeting, or maintenance; and with groups external to the library. Units in one library may wish to keep in touch with their peers in other libraries or interact with subject specialists elsewhere. Their teams will reorganize continuously depending on the requirements of the tasks for which they are responsible. What does not change is the commitment to the goals and objectives of the library and the expectation that tasks will be completed on time and the work will be of high quality.

The tech-savvy organization has less direct control than the bureaucratic organization, where hierarchy and close control is important. The tech-savvy organization has a greater degree of individual accountability, which fits the expectations of today's workforce. It should not be assumed that information technology will save money or even simplify the organizational structure because of the cost of hardware and software and staff training; however, the organization itself has a greater opportunity to reform and reshape its structure.

Discussion of information technology and its effect on the organization changes daily as new technologies allow for new organizational structures and new communication links. We are just beginning to realize just how pervasive the changes are and the impact they have not only on the library as an organization but also on the library as a service provider. As library staff and the community become increasingly computer literate and computer dependent, changes will accelerate. As awareness and understanding of how an informed organization can and does work increase, there will doubtless be less and less patience with the slow-moving, highly structured organization. What does not change is the way in which individuals deal with new ideas and new ways of working. Some welcome the opportunity to learn new skills and apply them to their daily activities, while others prefer to do things as they have always done them. It is the supervisor's responsibility to help those who are hesitant to change and to encourage those who are already changing.

SUMMARY

Until recently, the library's structure has been hierarchical, with authority and communication moving from the director downward through departments and units to individuals. Recent innovations in information technology and communication have made it possible to develop a more flexible organization in which communication and ideas move in several directions. Organizations that are built around the talents and interests of staff and that take advantage of today's technology have the promise of being stronger and more productive organizations. "Information and communication technologies have the ability either to strengthen the existing bureaucratic structure or to serve as the web on which new structures can be built."[13]

NOTES

1. Peter Drucker, *Management; Tasks, Responsibilities, and Practices* (New York: Harper & Row, 1973).

2. Tom Peters and Robert H. Waterman, *In Search of Excellence* (New York: Harper, 1982), 3.

3. Ibid., 10–11.

4. Ibid., 102.

5. Herbert A. Hicks and C. Ray Gullet, *Organizational Theory and Behavior* (New York: McGraw Hill, 1975), 108.

6. Charles Perrow, *Complex Organizations: A Critical Essay,* 2nd ed. (Glenview, IL: Scott Foresman, 1979), 4.

7. David A. Garvin, "Building a Learning Organization," *Harvard Business Review* 71, no. 7 (July–August, 1993): 78–91.

8. Ernest Dale, *Planning and Developing the Company Organizational Structure,* Research Report 20 (New York: American Management Association, 1952), 105.

9. Bart Victor and Carroll Stevens, "The Dark Side of the New Organizational Forms, An Editorial Essay," *Organizational Science* 5, no. 4 (November 1994): 480.

10. John Seeley Brown and Paul Duguid, *The Social Life of Information* (Cambridge, MA: Harvard Business School Press, 2000).

11. Harvey Kolodny, Michel Liu, Bengt Stymme, and Helene Denis, "New Technology and the Emerging Organizational Paradigm," *Human Relations* 49, no. 12 (December 1996): 13.

12. Rosabeth Moss Kanter, *Evolve! Succeeding in the Digital Culture of Tomorrow* (Boston: Harvard Business School Press, 2001), 72.

13. Ann Prentice, *Managing in the Information Age* (Lanham, MD: Scarecrow Press, 2005), 101.

Chapter ➤ 10

The Impact of Technology on the Public Library

INTRODUCTION

Though technology has not changed the purpose of the public library—to bring people and information together—it has changed nearly every way we do so. It has changed the ways in which we can acquire, store, and access information. It has changed many of the ways in which we connect information to the individual and the community. It has impacted the administrative structure of the library staff, and has even changed the way in which libraries are built and furnished. Any projection of the impact of technology on library service is outdated almost as soon as it is published.

This is also true of efforts to assess that impact. For example, no one ever thought that the impact of the Internet on the library and on society at large would be as great as it has been. The initial impact was greatly underestimated, and we have only recently begun to understand that we are in the midst of an information revolution of massive proportions. This revolution is obvious, but how to plan while it is underway is not easy.

Planning in the midst of rapid change is difficult because one must keep the purpose of the library in view, move in the right direction, be aware of the changes taking place, adapt staff and services to incorporate changes, and at the same time stay within budget. One researcher likened the process to navigating a boat through rapids. It is essential to keep sight of landmarks along the shore to know the direction in which one is going, while at the same time keeping the boat upright and moving safely through dangerous water in the direction one wants to go rather than just being swept along.

Librarians need to reevaluate all aspects of the library's mission, goals, and objectives so that they can respond to the information expectations of the 21st century. We need to find and build our competitive edge not just through technological enrichment, but also by envisioning new services. This begins with reviewing the role of the library and clarifying its niche in an information technology rich world so that it continues to be a vibrant partner in serving the community and does not become obsolete. A major role is providing access to information.

The ways in which people access information continue to change, and it is important to reevaluate existing services and adapt them when needed to meet current and changing needs. Library users can access library services from any place at nearly any time, and their expectations of librarians have become more complex. Information seekers range from the self-sufficient user who seeks suggestions in navigating the many information sources available to the novice or reluctant user who wants someone to find the information for him or her. Rather than following a single model of helping individuals find information, librarians develop multiple models of navigating the masses of information to find needed information as easily as possible, and they evaluate the information once it has been found. Though the basic task is the same, increased access to information makes serving the individual's needs more complex. One way to increase access to information is through the information technology (IT) world.

PLANNING FOR SERVICES IN AN IT WORLD

How does one define the technology-enhanced library of tomorrow? How are librarians in public libraries adopting and adapting to new technology? The best road to the future is to bring together the knowledge and networking power of external experts, staff, and other stakeholders to develop an understanding of today's needs and resources, and to plot out the changes that will keep library services relevant in the future. This includes a willingness to practice forward thinking and take informed risks. It also includes knowing who today's users are and how that user base will change over the next few years. Not only will the demographics change, so will the technology and the needs and interests of users. We need to identify new areas of activity and new users so that we can provide appropriate services, and we need to be sure that the technology we select and use supports our objectives. We will be wise to take advantage of informal networks and use them to build momentum, excitement, and commitment to change; by combining their energy with good management and technological skills, we may be able to envision tomorrow.

We may envision new kinds of library shapes and services, each of which may be a facet of the new library:

1. We may develop a transparent library in which we enhance and expand communications at every level. All decisions—administrative, operational, or from a program or service development perspective—are available to staff and stakeholders. The benefit of continuous communication is that everyone can be

part of the environment of continuous change. The transparent library supports open conversations among all interested groups using blogs, wikis, electronic surveys, and other yet to be developed communication forms.

2. We may enhance the library's role as a learning commons that provides a learning space in which technology is incorporated into learning activities. This informal space provides an opportunity for social learning and informal collaboration among individuals and groups. This space is inviting, with real people with whom one can discuss issues and an opportunity to contemplate. As our use of technology increases, face-to-face human communication becomes less and less a part of our information activity. The library as learning commons helps to restore that most important component of living and learning, the human component.

3. New Internet-based communities are emerging that are centered around a specific activity or interest. We may wish to take advantage of Web 2.0 social networking services and develop an interactive library environment on social networking sites, including MySpace and Facebook, as a means of communicating with present and potential library users about services that are available. Highly individualized communication with individual users or groups of users is possible. Librarians might also wish to develop a presence on Second Life as a means of connecting with users.

4. We will want to develop a library Web site that is the virtual face of the library. The ideal Web site makes a good first impression on those who use it by being informative, always up to date, and easy to use. The information provided on the Web site is often the first introduction to the library and its services. One can access the library catalog, access specialized library databases, learn about the library, and learn about special programs. We use the Web site to market library services, evaluate them, and provide the opportunity for stakeholders to comment on them. For many individuals, the Web site is the first connection with the library.

Traditional library service divisions between technical and public services have blurred, and those areas often overlap. Units of the library organization itself often overlap in ways not previously possible. We can now distribute services electronically among branches and departments and can connect with other libraries and other types of libraries to share services, for example sharing access to library catalogs. We have multiple databases and multiple search engines to help us locate information. The primary library community we serve has expanded to include communities with which the library interacts or has an interest in interacting. How do we harness, or can we harness, this enormous amount of information and personalize our searching to the needs and interests of the individual user?

We face technical challenges, challenges to staff who need to be in continual learning mode, organizational challenges, and the challenges of managing services in an era of limited resources and unlimited change. Technical challenges are probably the easiest to deal with, as nearly all information agencies face many of the same problems, and libraries can share experiences and expertise. We are redesigning library catalogs to accommodate open access journals, blogs, and other new information formats. Although it is useful to use search engines developed by others, these search engines typically focus on the most easily available information and do not deal with information that is specialized or of local interest. What plans are in place to include in a library's information bank those materials that are unique to its service area? This is a technical, reference, and administrative question, as one needs a plan to identify and include these materials in a searchable format, expertise in making them available, and a financial and staffing plan to do the work. We need to maintain a balance between trying out each promising technological change and selecting those that will work best for the library and its clientele.

STAFFING

The organization is changed by the use of technology. We have decentralized workplaces, virtual workplaces, and overlapping work activities. Management is moving toward more integrated systems which require collaborative effort to complete tasks. The library manager is the communication hub for those in each of these workplaces and serves as the coordinator of the several teams. Work may be organized around the need to maintain a particular information system, with a team assigned to that task. The team may be a virtual team or a partially virtual work team, in which some members of the team are on-site while others are at distant sites.

The key to maintaining relevance in this fast-moving digital world is for staff to grow their expertise in working with new tools and in finding new and improved ways to work with information seekers. Library managers may need to develop new positions and position descriptions, such as the e-reference librarian, who is a highly skilled electronic resources searcher. They may also need to revise the organizational chart if new positions cross traditional boundaries of technical and public services. To prevent one's skills from becoming outdated, each staff member will have to keep ahead of the curve by always being in learning mode. Professional development in the form of formal courses, workshops, and training programs that introduce staff to new products and services are required components of each position. There can be no staff members who are reluctant to learn new skills, and this applies to every staff member, not just those with professional degrees. When one adds continuous staff development to the workload, adjustments may need to be made in position descriptions to ensure that staff members do not become overloaded.

New staff members usually bring with them a level of technical skill that serves as a good foundation for continuing in the learning mode.

Though existing staff may have varying levels of technological expertise, they understand how the organization works and the dynamic of the community served. Existing staff can work with new staff to educate them about the library's communities, and new staff can work with existing staff to introduce them to new technological skills and how to interact with new online communities. New technology such as iPhones, iTouch, or Kindle may be made available to staff so that they can experiment and become comfortable with new tools. They may decide which tools will be useful in working with the public or in carrying out tasks within the library. A mutually supportive environment in which learning and developing new skills strengthen the entire staff will ensure that library services are continuously growing and adapting and at the same time maintaining the focus on the user. This environment of continuous change and mutual support helps all staff cultivate their talents and learn from doing new things.

REFERENCE SERVICES

Librarians work with users to help them understand how to use and evaluate databases. The expertise and interest of the user varies, and the librarian will deal with individuals in different ways depending on the wishes of the user and that individual's expertise. Some individuals wish to have an online interaction; others appreciate having the opportunity to interact face to face. The librarian may spend as much time working with an individual showing him or her how to use a database or suggesting other databases or other sources of information as is spent in actually locating information. Many library users are self-taught and do not necessarily have the skills to use a particular database to the extent necessary to locate desired information. The reference librarian as expert searcher can assist in identifying appropriate databases, knowing which overlap, spotting errors, and sorting out what is reliable information and what may not be reliable. The librarian is therefore both information guide and information locator.

The reference librarian continues to serve as a guide to all types of information resources and is the expert who locates information not necessarily available on databases. This includes providing access to local history archives and capturing current information of local and regional interest. The reference librarian also prepares finding aids, catalogs, and subject guides that help users locate information. Today's librarian is comfortable in conducting reference interviews in a virtual situation without visual cues. Librarians have worked with chat reference and have used text messaging to provide quick answers to questions. There is a concern that virtual reference, particularly the ready reference "ask a librarian" type of service, could become so popular that it will exceed staff time available to provide it. If staff cannot provide an expected service, this reflects poorly on the library. Availability of resources and use of resources to provide service go hand in hand. Decisions about maintaining traditional services and newer services are often difficult when funds are limited and the library must choose among very desirable services.

Technical Services

In 1967 the Ohio College Library Center (OCLC) introduced its machine readable bibliographic database. This grew and became the basis for a computerized regional center that became part of a national network. In 1977 the Ohio College Library Center became the Online Computer Library Center (OCLC) and served as the basis for the national online catalog network we now have. Bibliographic databases paved the way for online public access catalogs.

OPACs were developed in the early 1980s. These online integrated catalogs were easy to revise and provided a better way to search for information than was possible with the traditional card catalog. These activities made possible access to library holdings from nearly any location. Because library catalogs are used so much more widely today than in the past, subject headings that organize information in specific ways and were initially intended to be used by catalogers and experienced searchers may make it difficult for other users to locate information. To make searching catalogs easier, there has been some movement to develop user tags. These tags would add subjects that reflect a particular community's terms and provide a useful interface. Other efforts to develop a more user-centered approach to an interface are under discussion, such as Functional Requirements for Bibliographic Records (FRBR), which would provide links through related items that make more sense to users than traditional subject headings. Technical services librarians have the continuing task of creating tools that can search across databases to allow for one-stop searching, to make the task of seeking information more efficient.

Google is in the process of developing online access to millions of in-copyright books and other written materials that are in the collections of libraries that participate in Google Book Search, a project intended to make millions of books searchable on the Web. Copyright owners will be compensated for allowing online access to their work. As with so many other technical advances, there is an assumption by some that libraries will become obsolete because everything one would want to know will be available online. But searching Google does not ensure that one will have found what one needs to know. Resources being available online does not remove the need for print resources or software that is not Web based. Even though books may have been digitized, the hard copy continues to be a valuable reference tool for those who lack access to the digital version or who prefer to work with the hard copy, and the hard copy provides a backup source should software change or digital copies be illegible. Further, it is much more difficult to change the hard copy written record than it is to adjust the electronic virtual record. This argues that there is a necessary role for the printed hard copy far into the future.

Of particular concern to all public libraries is their ability to provide Internet and computing services to their communities. In 2008 the Information Institute at Florida State University published a report funded by the American Library Association and the Bill and Melinda Gates Foundation. The report, which follows from earlier annual studies on the topic,[1] reviewed the current status of public libraries and the Internet (2007–2008). This report that looked at the issues and challenges libraries face "as providers of no-charge public access Internet and computing services." The findings indicate that "although public libraries provide substantial public access services and resources across a range of areas, their ability to do so successfully is not limitless and has reached a saturation point in key areas of their ability to maintain, enhance, and grow public access technology services."[2] The report describes the current status of Internet and computing services, indicates challenges that remain, and concludes that

> they are increasingly unable to meet patron demands for services due to inadequate technology infrastructure, costs associated with operating and maintaining that infrastructure, and bandwidth quality/availability issues. . . . If the trends described [in this survey] continue while Internet and Web-based service demands expand, public libraries may find themselves reducing network services and having reduced overall quality of bandwidth and technology infrastructure.[3]

This is a continuing study, with reports expected to be made available on a regular basis.

A report prepared by ALA's Office of Information Technology Policy, *Fiber to the Library: How Public Libraries Can Benefit from Using Fiber Optics for Their Broadband Internet Connections* (2009), suggests that the bandwidth issues indicated may have a fiber-based solution.[4] The authors walk the reader through the various issues and steps involved in moving to such a solution. They conclude by saying that if fiber doesn't work for you, try satellite.

Administration

A world in which technology infuses all aspects of the library organization provides new opportunities to build a new kind of organization with new roles. This opportunity may excite some staff members, while others will find an environment of continuous change threatening. Staff communicates with each another, vendors, the public, and other stakeholders in ways that have changed radically, with fewer face-to-face interactions and more online communication. Rather than meet "at the water cooler," staff members may communicate via a blog. The daily face-to-face interaction that is so important to staff teamwork and morale has been replaced to a large degree by more impersonal means of communication, which means that the manager must find different ways in which to build community in the workplace.

The organization will doubtless be flatter than the traditional library organization. Staff members will often work across organizational boundaries. Position descriptions will be much more fluid than in the traditional organization, with new tasks replacing old ones and reporting structures changing as tasks change. Teams will be responsible for areas of work, and within the team there will be staff with the expertise to do the work. This structure allows for more direct interaction among staff than the hierarchical organization it is replacing. For those who have been comfortable with "knowing their place in the organization," it is often stressful to change to an environment in which they are part of a team rather than the director of a part of the library's operations.

Teamwork does not allow for slackers or individuals who are not contributing to the organization. New kinds of staff may be needed: those who are comfortable with the technology and can manage the information technology aspects of the library business. Perhaps these IT hires will work for the library, or they may be part of a municipal or regional business center that manages the financial business of many units of local or regional government. Other library activities may also be contracted out, and the library manager will manage contracts as well as in-house activities. Much of the routine and labor-intensive work will not be done by people, although some tasks, such as shelving print materials, still require hands-on activity.

As librarians need to balance their digital resources and continue to maintain their print collections, decisions need to be made. What kind of library do you want yours to be: a learning commons, a place to do research with the support of librarians, a reading space? The decisions one makes about the type and role of the library in one's community has direct implications for the collection development budget. There are also direct implications for other elements of the budget: what kinds of furniture will support electronic access? Do we need staff with different skills? Do we need to hire new staff or retrain those we have? Because the square footage of a building is expensive to maintain, what size print collection can we afford? Should we have a popular reading collection, some reference books? Or should we invest in e-books? What about the size of the DVD collection? Each of these questions is a collection development question, a space collection, an architectural question, and a financial question.

ARCHITECTURE

A library that incorporates substantial technological access to information is a different kind of space than the traditional library. Do we need more shelf space for books, or do we need more tech space such as carrels and group work tables? How should the building be wired or rewired to accommodate an increasing level of communications traffic? Do we have outlets for laptops, wi-fi access? Should we take into consideration the desire for "green" buildings and erect a building for the future? How can our spaces be well designed so that they accommodate technology and are at the same time friendly and inviting? We still look at the library as place, and do not want to lose that important aspect of service and community identification. The library is a symbol of what the community stands for.

We should also consider the library's Web site to be the library's virtual building. It too should be thoughtfully designed so that it provides information in a way that is easy to access and the space is welcoming. The virtual and actual buildings should complement one another.

SUMMARY

Staying afloat in the rapids of technological change requires that we develop a means of keeping current with the many developments in IT and information access. Librarians may wish to develop an environmental scan of relevant information sources. It would include a list of Web sites to check on a regular basis; identify reports that review new technologies, such as the *Library Technology Reports* published by ALA; scan books and reports that provide information on technological innovation; and identify individuals who can be contacted for information. One might also wish to include materials produced by some of the companies whose products are of interest to libraries. The popular press should be included in this scan, for example, technology and technology policy articles in the *New York Times*, which may be early announcers of new tech policy such as the expansion of broadband to rural areas by the federal government.

Librarians should also attend workshops and professional meetings to try out and discuss innovation, and work with vendors and other suppliers to gain access to new technologies and try them out to see if they will enhance the library's services. In developing a list of regularly reviewed sources on the topic, include sources outside the library/information world, such as the publications of EDUCAUSE, which focus on information and technology in colleges and universities. Many of the concerns they address are shared by public librarians. Finally, add a local newspaper to the mix so that technical interests of your community can be included. As with any good environmental scan, sources should be reviewed for relevance, and if a particular source no longer provides information on desired topics, it should be removed. If a new source is identified, it should be included.

Staff members could be assigned a number of sources to follow and then come together periodically to discuss their findings. If a staff member has a particular interest, for example, in a new search engine, readers could be asked to check their assigned sources to locate relevant information, and they could then meet to discuss their findings. This would give decision makers useful information. Using blogs and other in-house communications, the entire library staff could not only participate in locating information relevant to needs and interests, but could also share it with others.

With a plan for scanning the information environment, its changing policies, and its innovations, and with a plan for sharing information, librarians will be well equipped to navigate the rapids of technological change.

NOTES

1. *Libraries Connect Communities: Public Library Funding & Technology Access Study 2006–2007* (Chicago: American Library Association, 2007).

2. John Bertot and Charles McClure, *Public Libraries and the Internet: Study Results and Findings* (Tallahassee, FL: College of Information, 2008), 1.

3. Ibid., 6.

4. John Windhausen, Jr., and Marijke Visser, *Fiber to the Library: How Public*

Libraries Can Benefit from Using Fiber Optics for Their Broadband Internet Connections (Chicago: American Library Association, 2009).

ADDITIONAL READINGS

Clark, Larra, and Denise Davis. *Library Technology Report 45:1: The State of Funding for Library Technology in Today's Economy.* Chicago: American Library Association, 2009.

Kaufman, Herbert. *Time, Chance and Organizations: Natural Selection in a Perilous Economy.* 2nd ed. Chatham, NJ: Chatham House Publishers, 1991.

Molz, Redmond Kathleen, and Phyllis Dain. *Civic Space/Cyberspace: The American Public Library in the Information Age.* Cambridge, MA: MIT Press, 1999.

Turkle, Sherry. *Simulation and Its Discontents.* Cambridge, MA: MIT Press, 2009.

Chapter 11

Services and Programs

INTRODUCTION

Public library services and programs are divided into technical services—those that are "involved in acquiring, arranging, and controlling the library's stock in trade; the materials of the collection"[1]—and public services, those involved in using the library's collection and expertise to serve the public. Though technical services and many public services have a long history as part of the public library, the introduction of technical solutions to many of these activities has changed and continues to change the ways in which services and programs are performed. It is necessary to stay abreast of innovations so that librarians may incorporate into their management those that make library operations more efficient and cost effective.

Technical services support the operation of the library and the care and management of the collection. Public services are those in which the public is directly involved with activities in the library. Public services include service to individuals and to groups.

Service to individuals includes readers' advisory, reference, and other activities aimed at individual informational and recreational interests. It also involves the opportunity for individuals to be in an environment in which they can learn and reflect independently. Service to groups goes beyond individual interests to encompass the entire community. The many programs that evolve from community interests and resources, coupled with the resources of the public library, provide a rich environment for learning and community building.

TECHNICAL SERVICES

Technical services staff support the acquisition, organization, and maintenance of the collection. They are responsible for helping to choose and order materials for the library and for seeing that they are ready for users.

Collection Development

Collection development is a series of activities that ensure the library's collection meets the needs of the community. Is the collection current? Is it balanced to include different points of view? Do the materials added to the collection meet the requirements of the library's collection policy? Although at one time books and periodicals were the mainstay of library collections, today's library includes a wide array of formats in which information is available: databases, DVDs, and many others. Collection building is directed by collection development policies adopted by the library's board of trustees and supported by documents produced by professional associations. Librarians responsible for collection development represent the several subject interests and age levels served by the library. For materials selection, they rely on respected reviewing organizations, the recommendations of noted specialists, and personal expertise. They also take note of popular fiction and nonfiction of interest to the community.

Purchasing librarians interact with the publishing and information distribution organizations in many ways. They buy materials directly from publishers and/or from jobbers, who take the orders and fill them from several publishers. They subscribe to periodicals and databases. They contract with database vendors for service. Often a group of public librarians will join together to negotiate contracts with database vendors. In larger libraries, the business office is responsible for managing these activities within the budget allocated to each type of material. If the library is part of a consortium or library system, these activities are often managed at that higher level. Purchasing of some information resources, databases in particular, can be highly competitive, and negotiation to get the fairest prices is part of the responsibility of the library's purchasing agent.

Cataloging and Catalog Maintenance

At one time cataloging of materials was the responsibility of individual libraries, and librarians pored over the Dewey Decimal Classification System to assign the proper number, and the Library of Congress List or Sears List of Subject Headings to assign the appropriate subject headings. But individual librarians no longer do their own original cataloging, except in certain circumstances when the library has unique materials such as local history titles. The librarian does not have to order printed catalog cards from the Library of Congress for each book to be added to the collection, or to wait until both cards and book are in the library before making the title available.

One of the earliest contributions of information technology to libraries was the development of automated cataloging and classification systems. From the beginning of the 20th century, the Library of Congress performed original cataloging, produced printed cards, and made them available to libraries. Then, at the end of World War II (1945), Vannevar Bush described a new machine he had developed called the Memex, which introduced the concept of an integrated library system based on a single, machine readable bibliographic master file of the library's holdings.[2] From this concept, the integrated library system and bibliographic utilities developed rapidly. By 1967 the Ohio College Library Center was established, with the goal "to maintain and operate a computerized regional library center that would serve all the academic libraries of Ohio and become part of any national network that might be established."[3] From this beginning OCLC (now the Online Computer Library Center) has grown to become a cataloging center for all types of materials for all types of libraries. It continues to conduct research, refine its role in providing cataloging and related services to libraries, and devise new ways of providing access to materials.

Today's public library catalog is online and is available in the library or from the library's Web site and can be searched by anyone who wishes to locate an item. No longer do librarians need to do original cataloging, file catalog cards for new books (and sometimes a nonfiction book would have a dozen or more subject cards to file), or remove cards for books that were lost or discarded. Catalogers no longer need to go through the card catalog every time a new edition of the Dewey Decimal Classification arrives to make changes in all relevant catalog cards affected by decisions printed in the new edition. The hundreds of catalog card drawers one could find in a large public library, academic, or state library have been replaced by a terminal.

The cataloging department has all but disappeared from public libraries. The central library of a system may have a cataloger who does original cataloging for the system and who deals with requests from reference librarians who have difficulty finding an item. For example, a researcher in children's literature was looking for *St. Nicholas Magazine*, which she knew the library had but was unable to find an entry for in the catalog. With a bit of detective work on the part of the cataloger, it was found under Saint Nicholas Magazine.

Not only have catalogers become a rarity, many typists, filers, and other clerical staff are no longer needed. Some individuals who enjoyed poring over the cards in the catalog may suffer from nostalgia, because while doing so, they learned new facts about an author or book. In older libraries, one could still find handwritten cards. Until the typewriter was standard equipment in libraries, librarians were taught library hand, a script guaranteed to be readable, and catalogers were expected to use it when writing catalog cards. When one looks at the curriculum of early library education programs, a course called "Library Hand" often appears. We have made great strides in this area in past decades, and those who experienced the early days of cataloging and the tedious work involved can truly appreciate the OPAC.

Processing of Materials

A number of tasks are associated with preparing materials for use, including placing call numbers on the book or other format, indicating the library that owns the material, placing bar codes or other electronic device on the book, etc. These activities are also much less onerous than they once were, partly because of advances in technology and materials. In many libraries, these activities are completed before the material reaches the library, either as part of the purchasing process or at a central library so that branch libraries need not be involved. The librarian no longer finds certain activities such as collation (before a book was rebound, someone was required to ensure that all the pages were still in the book and in the right order). In today's world, it is cheaper to buy a new book than it is to pay someone to do this type of task.

Circulation

Circulation services include the registering of borrowers and enforcing library policies regarding issues such as length of loan, overdue materials, and interlibrary loan. The circulation department is also responsible for checking materials in and out of the library, shelving materials returned to the library, managing copy services, and maintaining circulation statistics. It also maintains an inventory of the collection, reads shelves to ensure that materials are in the appropriate place, removes worn or outdated materials, and otherwise keeps the collection in good working order.

Here too, technology has allowed libraries to streamline the process. No longer do we use the date stamp at the end of the pencil to stamp the date due slip in the back of the book. We have progressed through several generations of processes for charging out books and materials, from manual systems to a variety of electronic systems. Bar coding of materials is widely used, and since the early 1990s when it was first suggested to libraries, Radio Frequency Identification (RFID) has been replacing bar codes in libraries.

RFID technology "is the use of an object applied or incorporated into a product, animal, or person for the purpose of identification and tracking, using radio waves." Most RFID tags "contain . . . an integrated circuit for storing and processing information . . . and an antenna for receiving and transmitting the signal."[4] RFID tags may replace or supplement existing bar codes, so a book, CD, or DVD may have both tags attached. The RFID tag usually includes the book title and any other identifying information that is desired. In addition to supporting the circulation system, the information on the tag can be used for inventory. It can serve as a security device and thus replace the security strip. Library cards may also be fitted with RFID tags. RFID for libraries caught on worldwide, and more and more libraries of all types have begun using it. In the United States the first large public library to adopt the system was the Seattle Public Library;[5] other public libraries have adopted the system since then.

RFID has several library applications that are helpful, particularly to circulation staff. One does not need to open a book cover or DVD case to scan an item, because tags can be read through the item. Borrowers can check out their own materials without needing assistance and can scan a number of books at the same time rather than scanning them individually. When returning materials, they are checked in using the same technology and can be sorted by call number so that they will be ready for reshelving immediately.

One can also conduct inventories of the collection without removing books or other materials from the shelf by taking a portable reader to the stacks and passing it over the shelves. It only takes seconds to inventory a shelf.

Where RFID has been installed, it has been received enthusiastically by the public because it is so easy to use. It also reduces the need for a large circulation staff. This is an excellent example of the library adopting a technology used in business and industry to streamline its services to the public, cut overall costs, and at the same time improve service.

Information Technology

The library's information technology staff is responsible for maintaining the various IT systems in the library. This includes upgrades, maintenance, and any other activities necessary to being certain that all are in working order. IT staff members provide backup to librarians or other staff who teach patrons how to use computers. They are part of the team that manages the library's Web site. In these and many other ways, the IT staff supports technical, public, and administrative services.

If the library is a department of county or city government, the IT department of the larger governmental unit often is responsible for library IT, and in addition to the above tasks, makes certain that library IT conforms to the structure of the larger unit. If the library is a branch of a larger library, though each branch should have its own IT staff member, the library and its branches conform to one set of technical requirements. Upgrades, adoption of new software, addition of new modules, and other changes are discussed by all the IT personnel in the system and with library staff before changes are made. It is helpful if the individual responsible for the library's information technology is a librarian, but if not, there should be excellent communication between the IT personnel and library staff so that they understand each other's needs and expectations.

PUBLIC SERVICES

The first public library service was to lend books, and for many years this was the only service. The early role of librarians was to select, purchase, and lend books or to organize books given to the library, be responsible for the collection, and make certain that lending rules were enforced. Although it was important to select appropriate titles, library duties did not require an individual to have any particular training. As the library assumed a more active role in the community, it became evident that specific skills in book selection and the ability to find specific information for users was increasingly important. In the late 19th century, as more and more public libraries were built, often with the assistance of philanthropists including Carnegie, Astor, and Lennox, among others, and as Melvil Dewey's library education efforts produced librarians who had training to manage collections and work with library users, library services and programs expanded beyond the circulation of materials to include reference services, readers' advisory services, services to children and special groups, and numerous additional programs and services.

Services to Adults

Services to adults grew as library collections increased and as more and more individuals looked to the library for self-education. After years of discussion and research, in 1957 ALA established the Adult Services Division and formalized adult services by identifying the following activities:

indirect guidance: reading lists, displays, etc

advisory services: informed and planned reading

services to groups and organizations: exhibits, reading lists, booktalks

library sponsored programs: films, radio, TV, discussion groups

community advisory services[6]

The Adult Services Division continued to grow, and in 1966 it merged with the Reference Services Division to become the Reference and User Services Division of ALA. With *The Planning Process for Public Libraries,*[7] adult services in the public library became accepted as an important component of its role in the community. The activities listed in 1957 were revised and expanded to include the following roles:

community activities center

community information center

formal education support center

independent learning center

popular materials library

reference library

research center

Community Activities and Information Center

As a community activities center, the library signaled that it recognized its responsibility to serve as a focus for community activities and information, that it has a role not just in being part of a community but in building community. As a community information center, it provides information on local governmental services, social services, and other services useful to members of the community. The public library is also often the repository of local history archives, so that it provides information not only on today's community but also on its history.

Formal Education Support and Independent Learning Center

As a formal education support center and an independent learning center, the library makes information about existing continuing and independent learning programs and resources available. In collaboration with the National Institute for Literacy, whose goal "is to ensure that all Americans with literacy needs have access to services that can help them gain the skills necessary for success in the workplace, family, and community in the 21st century,"[8] numerous public libraries support literacy programs. These programs include adult basic literacy, pre-GED, GED, and English as a Second Language (ESL). Such programs are important to the individual who didn't finish high school and to the immigrant who needs to learn English. More broadly, they are important to the economy because they are key elements in the continuing education and re-education of our workforce.

Information literacy is critical to everyone.[9] The increasing amount of information available on the Internet, and often nowhere else, makes it necessary for each person to have basic computer skills. For many, their only access to training and the Internet is the public library, and public libraries have accepted this challenge by making computer terminals and training in the needed skills widely available. Nearly 100 percent of public libraries provide these services. These skills are also important to the economy because information literacy is essential for many employment opportunities, not just finding jobs but also having skills needed to do the job.

Readers' Advisory Services (Popular Materials Library)

People enjoy reading, and it continues to be a favorite pastime for many. For readers, the public library provides not only information but also enjoyment. Fiction is food for our imagination and an opportunity for each reader to enter new worlds and have experiences not possible in everyday life. It may remind us that others have suffered and survived and thus provide a kind of solace. Nonfiction takes us into the lives of others and to other places, as well as providing a new recipe or clues on how to repair a car or buy a camera. It is an essential component of the library and the library user's self-education.

Readers' advisory services have been documented in libraries for more than a hundred years and practiced informally from the earliest days of reading. This "patron centered library service for adult leisure readers"[10] requires a knowledgeable librarian who reads widely, knows the library's collection, and is skilled in relating to the individual reader. In an earlier period (1920s and 1930s), librarians saw themselves as educators and would recommend "what was good for the reader" rather than what the reader might want. The resurgence of readers' advisory services in the late 20th century focused less on elevating the masses and more on the personal interests of the individual. The current philosophy is that "librarians already allocate resources—both time and money—to developing and maintaining their popular reading collection; such expenditures justify a similar commitment of staff to make the collections as accessible as possible to readers."[11] Readers' advisory librarians provide annotated lists, genre collections, book displays, bookmarks, and other means of sharing information about the collection that may lead readers to a good "new read." Though leisure reading may not be as intense a learning experience as a textbook, it provides opportunity for learning in a more relaxed fashion.

As 90 percent of library users come to the library to check out books and videos for leisure reading and viewing, it is important that they be aware of the range of choices available to them. The public library is the only agency that provides free access to printed books, electronic books, and audio books.

Reference and Research Center

The public library as reference and research center is one of its most important roles. Through its print and online resources, the library provides information on nearly any topic. Use of library reference resources has changed in a number of ways as more and more resources are available online and more and more individuals search the Web for answers to their questions. The library patron may ask a question directly of the librarian or use the library Web site to ask a question online. Some databases are also available on the library Web site, but the cost to the library of making them widely available tends to limit the number. A wide range of databases, however, is available at the library.

The typical information seeker who is computer literate will Google a question and if not satisfied with the answer, will then e-mail or directly ask the librarian. An example of this is the individual seeking medical information who finds that most of the sites easily available via Google are commercial sites or may be unreliable. The librarian suggests sites that are neither and that will provide the desired information. Though many individuals like to search for their information themselves, the librarian is available to suggest alternate strategies if the initial strategy does not work.

Examples of Adult Services Programming

Programs have been developed for adults by the public librarian, often in collaboration with other agencies in the community. The specific programs offered evolve from the community served: the geographic area, the residents, specific interests, and special needs. Rather than developing programs and hoping that someone will come, today's adult services librarian looks to the community for input. This is an additional example of the librarian looking to the community to determine community interests rather than deciding unilaterally what the community needs.

From demographic studies and by being an active member of the community, the librarian knows which ethnic groups live in the community and may also know about their concerns. Finding a job, learning English, and meeting other people in the community are important motivators for newcomers. Parents are always concerned about their children and will attend programs that will be helpful to them. Immigrant families wish to assimilate into the culture and need information to survive in the new environment. Programs developed by the librarians should be translated into the language that a particular group speaks and reads, and it is important to know where to advertise these programs so that those for whom the program is intended will know about it. A well-traveled public library director recently said that any program with an ethnic theme should revolve around food, as food is the universal language of welcome and sharing and will bring people together faster than anything else.

Public libraries have become a resource for the job seeker. Counselors are often available to help individuals find job postings, write their resumes, and submit applications. With software that provides interactive critiquing, the job seeker can craft a resume interactively until it is just right. Some libraries also give workshops in interviewing skills and others help the job seeker connect with job opportunities.

Public libraries are also a resource for individuals wishing to start a small business. Seminars are sponsored, and information on steps to take in starting up a business, sources of start-up finding, how to apply for a patent, etc., is available. Some public libraries maintain a business reference center whose librarian is a business reference specialist and will work with small businesses to locate information relevant to their needs.

The most popular database in many communities is Ancestry Plus. Programs in the library that help individuals trace their ancestry involve a different group in the community. For people whose families have lived in the area for generations, local history and folk life resources showing the contributions their families have made to the community are rewarding. These programs may also inspire those families to contribute memorabilia they have held or family stories that have been handed down.

Older community residents and new immigrants have valuable experiences they may wish to share with others. They join writing workshops to recount incidents in their lives from another time or country. In this way, their unique experiences can become part of the community's history. A writing program could focus on food, and the result would be a cookbook of favorite recipes from other times and places. Not only do these programs offer an opportunity to retrieve important experiences, they also provide an opportunity for community and sharing.

Programs that focus on community issues—the building of a cement plant in the community, a controversial new real estate development, or other activity that impacts many individuals—are part of the library's programs. Book fairs, book clubs, and many more events that create community are also part of the librarian's interaction with the community.

Many public librarians provide opportunities for individuals unable to come to the library to participate in library programs. Those living in senior housing, assisted living, and similar locations may have books, DVDs, and other materials delivered to them. If they have a computer, they can participate in activities listed on the Web site, such as viewing programs presented earlier in the library, searching the library catalog for a title, asking a reference question, and reading blogs on topics of interest. Those with physical disabilities have access to the Web site, and there are often additional programs directed toward their needs and interests. The opportunity to develop library programs is limited only by the imagination of the community and the library staff.

Youth Services

Programming for teens also evolves from the teen interests and concerns in the community, and as with adult programming, the librarian needs to know the community by reviewing the demographics of the teen population, which is a subset of the overall collection of demographic information. It is important to talk with teens to hear from them what kinds of programs and activities they wish to pursue. Library programs often serve as a catalyst for community activities of interest to teens. Treating teenagers as a client group is a fairly new concept; until the 1920s and 1930s most teens were part of the workforce. Not until after the Fair Labor Standards Act (1938) established working conditions, including the age when full-time work was legal, was there a sufficient number of teenagers in the community to take advantage of library services. Young people would come to the public library to get vocational and training materials and receive assistance in using them. Teenagers who had time to read were given classical literature "intended to improve their 'taste' motivated by [adult] fear that lesser texts would be harmful to a child's intellectual development."[12] Teenagers could work in sweatshops, and for many adults that was acceptable, but if they read a popular novel, they were in danger of getting unhealthy ideas.

Librarians began to look at why teens might not be readers and found that this insistence on reading books of "value" rather than what interested them was the problem. Another problem was that many teenagers had limited reading ability and found required reading difficult to comprehend. Librarians then began to encourage teen readers to read more adventurous, or romantic, reading as a way to expand young people's horizons and experience.[13] Library service to this group began to become more collaborative rather than directive.

Library services for youth became an important component of library service in the years after World War II. More books for teens were written. "Best Books for Young Adults" appeared in 1952. Awards for the best books and an award for the "librarian who made unusual contributions to the stimulation and guidance of reading by children and young people" were established.[14] The growth in the number of books and magazines aimed at teens was not only because teenagers as a group were suddenly important but also because they had been recognized as a new market with money to spend. During these years numerous authors of quality fiction for this age group emerged. They wrote about important issues and did so honestly.

Readers' Advisory Services for Teens

Librarians understand the importance of recreational reading. It increases the vocabulary, contributes to a higher level of critical thinking, and improves scholastic performance. Reading is an escape from today's problems into a world where one can learn about other people and other cultures, and in doing so may learn more about oneself. It is important to read what is of personal interest and appealing at a particular time. Someone else cannot tell a teen what to read, but they can make suggestions about what might be of interest. The readers' advisor for teens is a good listener, does not judge, and is very comfortable with the genre. Literature of interest to young adults differs from other genres in that most characters are teens, the protagonist is close to the experience rather than reflecting other times, and the issues and conflicts are relevant to a teen's life.[15]

Programs for Teens

Since the later decades of the 20th century, the number and variety of programs and services to teens have increased and continue to increase. Librarians work with schools to develop projects that make use of local history and other collections. One public library invited a history class to come use local history archives to learn through reading primary source materials, including diaries and letters, about how members of their community served on the battlefield during the Civil War. Not only did students use primary materials, they also learned about some of their ancestors and were able to make family connections to the past. This same library has archives from the Revolutionary War, and students were able to read accounts and visit battlefields. They used maps from the 18th century to identify where battles were fought or forts built. By using modern maps, they could see the changes that have occurred in the intervening years.

A teen concern that is often difficult to address is pregnancy. One librarian put together a program for pregnant teens and using library materials and guests, worked with the teens by providing information on health issues, what it means to become a mother, and the importance of staying in school. When the baby arrived they learned about parenting. One of the most important aspects of the program was that the teens had a place to go, someone to talk to, and a community of other moms in waiting who could serve as a support group during a difficult time.

Teens have established theater groups in the library to write, stage, act in, and produce their own plays. One group charged admission for their play, asking for a donation of food for the local food bank. Not only did they learn and have fun in doing so, they also contributed to the welfare of the community.

The Internet has had a strong impact on teens who have grown up using it for communication and information. They use online resources for their homework, to pursue personal interests, and to just have fun. A new twist on a long-standing library service is the use of games for learning as well as fun. Computer-based gaming is a very popular activity for teens. Librarians support gaming in numerous ways, from providing space to providing the software. Some libraries have a game day and other kinds of competitive activities. By collaborating with teens, learning about their interests, and suggesting ways in which these interests can be addressed, the library may provide a vibrant and always exciting environment in which teens feel they belong, can interact with other teens in a place not home and not school, and can at the same time learn valuable life skills. Today's teens are tomorrow's parents and taxpayers who will support the library in the future.

Programs for Children

For more than a hundred years, children have been important to the public library. Since the 1890s, public libraries have had children's rooms, children's librarians, and collections of children's materials. For children's services the first half of the 20th century was a time of consolidation, standardization, and broadening horizons. Children's librarians provide individual readers' guidance, book selection, and materials to enhance readings. They also provide storytelling programs to every age.

Demographics changed after World War II, and many families moved to the suburbs to raise their children. The families who moved tended to be white, while those who stayed were families of color. Many of the children's librarians stayed in the cities and continued to serve the children who remained. The New York Public Library had many well-known children's librarians, a number of whom were librarians of color. These talented women reached out to all the children of the city. Augusta Baker was one of many children's librarians of color who was influential both as a guide to children through her programs and nationally recognized storytelling abilities and as one who saw no limits to what a children's librarian can do. A new generation of children's librarians, building on the work of those who preceded them, worked with suburban children to create community in new areas. Their programming took into consideration the new demographics and perhaps different needs of the community.

For many years the Enoch Pratt Free Library in Baltimore, Maryland, has been among the leaders in providing children's services to a diverse community. In 1967 Lowell Martin, one of the best-known consultants working with public libraries, said, "The notable success in the public library has been children's services. High caliber children's librarians who selected 'not on the standards of popularity, but of quality' and in the public mind, it is thought of as of the most natural and significant activities of the public library."[16]

A program developed by The Pratt some 40 years later continues the tradition of quality and is an excellent example of the best in children's programming. The objective of the program was to find a way to interest immigrant parents of young children in early childhood reading readiness. An existing reading readiness program, "Mother Goose on the Loose," was translated into Spanish and became "Buena Casa Buena Braca" ("Warm Home Warm Hearth"). Children's librarians worked with a community organization that focuses on immigrant needs to refine the program. The organization (Maryland Committee for Children) has a specific focus on children and the quality of early childhood education. Its database of interested women with young children was used to contact parents to invite them to attend the program with their children.

"Buena Casa Buena Braca," like "Mother Goose on the Loose," used language, music, art, play, and positive reinforcement to help children learn important skills of social and emotional development.[17] Tips for parents on how to help their children continue to learn these skills were provided as well. After the program, while the children were eating and playing, caregivers had the opportunity to ask questions and discuss their children. Over the course of the program friendships were formed and at Thanksgiving they asked to have a celebration at the library. A potluck dinner was arranged, and each person brought a particular dish.

"The public library is widely touted as a place where democracy is strengthened by giving people equal access to technology through free computer use and training. We believe that the library also shows its strengths through personal relationships and program planning . . . and people become empowered through a positive relationship with an American institution."[18] So said the librarians responsible for this program that covered so many elements of what a public library is: learning, sharing, and community building through the use of the library's information and staff resources.

SUMMARY

Public library services provide the information and the people who work to build community through programs that respond to its concerns, needs, and interests. Public library programs evolve from the geographic, ethnic, cultural, economic, and other interests of the community. In a highly mobile society, it is important to have a place where everyone is welcome, where one can find information to help with everyday questions; learn about the world; meet people; discuss issues of common interest; and have a place to read, dream, and just be. And it is freely available.

The public library can be a magical place, opening new worlds by bringing performers to the library who may show us new aspects of music, dance, and acting and new ways of thinking. It stimulates cultural growth and an awareness and appreciation of one's community. It is truly the heart of a democratic society.

NOTES

1. Carleton Rochell, *Wheeler and Goldhor's Practical Administration of Public Libraries* (New York: Harper & Row, 1981), 335.

2. Vannevar Bush, "As We May Think," *Atlantic Monthly* 176 (July 1945): 101–8.

3. Alice Gertzog and Edwin Beckerman, *Administration of the Public Library* (Lanham, MD: Scarecrow Press, 1994), 146.

4. Jay Singh et al., "The State of RFID Applications in Libraries," *Information Technology and Libraries* 1 (March 2006): 24–32.

5. Ibid.

6. Kathleen de la Peña McCook, *Introduction to Public Librarianship* (New York: Neal Schuman, 2004), 185.

7. Charles R. McClure et al., *Planning and Role Setting for Public Libraries: A Manual of Options and Procedures* (Chicago: American Library Association, 1987).

8. McCook, *Introduction to Public Librarianship,* 196.

9. Association of College and Research Libraries, *Information Literacy Toolkit,* www.ala.org/ala/mgrps/divs/acrl/issues/infolit/index.cfm (accessed August 10, 2010).

10. Joyce G. Saricks, *Readers' Advisory Service in the Public Library,* 3rd ed. (Chicago: American Library Association, 2005), 1.

11. Ibid., 12.

12. Heather Booth, *Serving Teens Through Readers' Advisory* (Chicago: American Library Association, 2007), 2.

13. Margaret Hutchison, "Fifty Years of Young Adult Reading, 1921–1971," in *Young Adult Literature in the Seventies: A Selection of Readings,* 40–42 (Metuchen, NJ: Scarecrow Press, 1978).

14. Booth, *Serving Teens Through Readers' Advisory,* 3.

15. Ibid., 32; Linda Alexander and Barbara Immroth, "Youth Services," in *Introduction to Public Librarianship,* by McCook, 211–39 (New York: Neal Schuman, 2004).

17. Betsy Diamant-Cohen and Anne Calderone, "Buena Casa, Buena Brasa," *American Libraries* 40, no. 12 (December 2009): 41–43.

18. Lowell Martin, *Baltimore Reaches Out: Library Service to the Disadvantaged* (Baltimore, MD: Enoch Pratt Free Library, 1967), 17–18.

ADDITIONAL READINGS

Anderson, Rick. *Buying and Contracting for Resources and Services: A How-to-Do-It Manual for Librarians.* New York: Neal Schuman, 2004.

Durrance, Joan C., and Karen E. Pettigrew. *On Line Community Information: Creating a Nexus at Your Library.* Chicago: American Library Association, 2002.

Nelson, Sandra. *The New Planning for Results: A Streamlined Approach.* Chicago: American Library Association, 2001.

Pierce, Jennifer. "What's Old Is New Again; It's About Time Library Gaming Made a Comeback." *American Libraries* 40, nos. 6&7 (June/July 2009): 83.

Risen, Clay. "PacRat: The Fight to Preserve Old Video Games from Bit Rot, Obsolescence, and Cultural Oblivion." *The Atlantic* 305, no. 2 (March 2010): 30.

Smallwood, Carol, ed. *Librarians as Community Partners.* Chicago: American Library Association, 2010.

Walter, Virginia A. "The Children We Serve." *American Libraries* 40, no. 10 (October 2009): 42–55.

Regularly check the Web sites of the following ALA divisions:

Children's Services
Library Resources and Technical Services
Reference and User Services
Young Adult Library Services

Chapter 12

Staffing

INTRODUCTION

During the latter half of the 20th century, extensive changes in library staffing patterns were gradually implemented. Although technology was the driving force, other forces, including developing a research-based approach to library issues, the increasing professionalism of library staff, and the continuous pressure of limited funds to manage libraries, also played a role.

The *Public Library Inquiry*, based on social science research methods, conducted in the late 1940s and into the 1950s, was the first major research-based study of public libraries and served as an important benchmark for public library research. Among the several volumes published was one by Dr. Alice Bryan, dealing with public library personnel.[1] It was both a product of its time and an indication that public library personnel and their activities were on the brink of major changes. Within a decade of its publication, a research-based doctoral program had been established at Columbia University, with Dr. Bryan as a member of the faculty. Within the next 10 years, a number of schools of library science became schools of library and information science and had added doctoral programs to their curriculum.

Title II-B of the Higher Education Act (1965) was a response to the perceived need for professional librarians to manage the libraries that were being built under the Library Services Act (1956) and the Library Services and Construction Act (1961) and to fill positions in the many public libraries that were expanding into the suburbs and/or positions available in existing libraries. Title II-B provided funding for the education of librarians at the doctoral level, who were expected to populate faculty positions at the growing number of what were then called library schools. The legislation went far beyond this purpose and in doing so changed the way librarians were educated.

The first outcome was that work at the doctoral level required that students conduct research, thus beginning to build a body of research in a field known more for anecdotal writing or biographical accounts by and about famous librarians than for research.

Master's students were introduced to research as a way to solve problems. They were taught that two or three anecdotes about a problem were not sufficient evidence to make a decision. Research in many aspects of public librarianship continues to feed the curriculum and to educate librarians to have the tools necessary for decision making in a fast-changing world.

A second outcome was that research-oriented faculty began to replace practitioners as instructors. Many research-oriented faculty members were also experienced practitioners who brought the best of theory and practice to the classroom. Over the past decades, programs educating librarians and other information professionals have focused more and more on hiring faculty with a PhD or equivalent. One often finds that full-time faculty have the research base from which to teach and may have experience as a practitioner, To bring more reality into the classroom, adjunct faculty who are often practitioners are hired to bring their on-the-job experience to the classroom.

The result of this increasingly research-based curriculum has not only been an increasingly professionalized faculty in academic programs for tomorrow's librarians, it has also resulted in an increasingly professionalized librarian workforce. Graduates who are accustomed to making decisions based on research and evidence rather than anecdotes are expected to make better decisions and provide higher quality service, and they expect to participate to a greater degree in the library's decision making.

Concurrently with the increased professionalism of instruction, libraries were undergoing major changes because the computing, communication, and information revolution was beginning to change the ways libraries were managed and the ways they provided service. New phrases like "library automation," "online catalogs," and "information databases" were being introduced into the workplace and the curriculum. The new graduates were often expected to figure out how to turn these phrases into action. Although there were numerous forward-thinking librarians who had a glimpse of the future and acted upon it—including Fred Kilgour, developer of OCLC,[2] and Hugh Atkinson, an academic librarian known for his early understanding and adoption of library automation,[3]—most librarians needed to figure out how to adopt and adapt to this revolution in how things were done.

A third factor in what was to become a new way of working in public libraries was the increasing professionalism of other specialists operating at the local government level, those who were involved in aspects of public administration. For example, during the same period that librarianship was becoming more professionalized, planning as a profession received federal support, research-based faculty were educated, students received a research-based degree, and they were expected to provide a higher level of service than before. As was true of librarians, accountability for their decisions and for the level of service they provided began to be tied to the amount of funding they received from local tax sources.

If a public library is a good thing, public librarians should demonstrate that the library contributes to the community and is worthy of support. They should also demonstrate that it is a worthy steward of public funds. With the increasing squeeze on municipal budgets resulting in cuts in the library budget, librarians must demonstrate that they can do more with less and less.

The ability to manage the library well and to retrain staff members so that they learned other ways of providing service through the use of technology has been instrumental in helping public librarians cope with declining budgets. With the automation of business practices including financial records, libraries save time and money. At one time, ordering of books and other informational materials and supplies was a time-consuming manual operation.

Now this is a much faster and smoother operation, which may also be centralized in a library system and/or may be part of the municipal budget office. Librarians no longer do their own cataloging, except for the occasional title produced locally. They are part of online public access catalog systems; catalog card filing and other catalog maintenance activities are done electronically.

Circulation systems in some libraries have moved and in others are moving closer and closer to user self-check, and inventory can be done electronically so that fewer and fewer clerical support staff people are needed. The public library has been able to reduce staff costs while at the same time providing additional services to the community. Most of the reduction in staff costs has been in technical services rather than services in direct support of community programs and services.

At some point, as budgets continue to be reduced, public services suffer. The case needs to be made to and by the public and the public librarian that the role of the library—to inform, educate, and serve as a cornerstone of the community—is critical to that community. No other organization can do all these things as economically or as well as the library.

STAFFING PATTERNS

Staffing should be thought of as an integrated system for moving into, through, and eventually out of an organization.[4] It includes all methods of matching skills available with tasks to be performed, through hiring, placement, promotion, transfer, job restructuring, and training. The theory of staffing is based on individual differences in abilities and interest.[5]

Staffing patterns depend on the type of organizational structure. Public libraries are usually organized by function. They may also be organized by geographical location and then by function, or some areas may be organized by subject matter or format. A library with branches will have a staffing pattern different from a single location library. In a library with several branches, a variety of services may be conducted in the central library and the products shared with the branches, such as purchasing and processing of materials.

The organizational structure adapts to different conditions as the library grows. The organizational chart is the skeleton on which positions and activities are placed, and the chart shows relationships between and among the various activities in the library. New tasks are added, and those no longer needed are removed. Although the organizational chart shows a hierarchical structure, there are in fact many cross-functional activities at different levels in the chart. Teams are often set up to work on cross-functional activities or short-term projects.

A good way to observe how the library's organization and staffing patterns change over time is to review the library's organizational charts from previous years. Change is usually incremental, and only rarely will radical changes be seen. "Some say that an organization chart should reflect the strength of current employees and should be adapted to provide them maximum ability to grow their talents while others say that individuals must conform to the role(s) indicated by the organization chart. . . . In reality the relation between individual skills and what is posted on the chart depends on circumstances and the expectations of the director."[6] Roles and tasks of librarians and staff continue to change as more and more tasks formerly considered professional are shifted to support staff and the librarian assumes a higher level of professional activity in areas including long-range planning, development, and strategy setting.

Although smaller libraries tend to be less formal in assigning tasks, it is still important that they have an organizational structure with tasks assigned. Even though with a professional staff of fewer than five librarians, it is not possible to specialize in a specific area, it is still possible to assign primary responsibility for a specific area to one individual, such as children's and young adult services. In this type of situation, the director manages the library and also assumes responsibility for one or more other areas. Everyone is cross-trained and can do several things.

Developing Staffing Patterns

The Public Library Association (PLA) recommends a results model as the mechanism to develop staffing patterns. In this model, these are the aspects of staffing to be considered:

1. Identifying activities and when they will be performed.

2. Identifying abilities needed to accomplish activities.

3. Determining the number of staff in relation to patron use and staff workload.

4. Understanding how staff currently uses time.

5. Determining how to find staff to accomplish the library's priorities.[7]

The appropriate number and types of staff for library operations are determined by the population served. This is both in regard to total population and the demographics of the population. Some states have set standards for staffing on this basis. A problem with standards is that although they are intended to set base levels for staffing, they are often used locally as a target to aim at, and once the library has met the basic standard, some assume that no further growth is necessary.

Because of differences in community needs, the PLA moved from issuing standards for public libraries to developing a planning process for them[8] that provides guidelines for community-based planning and evaluation. "Staffing justification then comes from a local determination of programs and services needed."[9] This move from standards to planning is one of the major advances in public librarianship and has had a major impact on the ways in which public libraries are managed. Again, research, data collection, and decision making based on evidence rather than anecdote have become the basis for decision making. With this approach, librarians can plan for services and measure the success of the services planned. In an economy in which quantitative data demonstrating that community resources are used wisely is essential, the planning and evaluation model is an important component.

Discussion in the field has covered the appropriate ratio of professional staff to support staff within the library. The ratio of one to three was bandied about for some time, but there is no firm figure on which there is general agreement. Considering the speed with which existing tasks change and new tasks are added to the library, it is more important to have the right person for the right job than to worry about ratios.

CATEGORIES OF STAFFING

Library employees at all levels are the library's most important resource. They know the library's information resources and how to use them, they manage the resources, and they use them to provide a wide range of information resources to the community. Two-thirds or more of the library budget is allocated to personnel. It is therefore important to hire the best staff for the library and utilize their skills wisely within the library's staffing patterns. It is also important to work with staff to make sure they understand their jobs, do them well, and have the opportunity to grow through staff development and continuing education.

Professional Staff

Library staff members are typically divided into professional staff and support staff. A professional has special background and education "on the basis of which library needs are identified, problems are analyzed, goals are set and original and creative solutions are formulated for them, integrating theory into practice, and planning, organizing, communicating, and administering successful programs of service to users of the library's materials and services."[10] Initially, the special background and education referred to an individual holding an MLS and/or additional advanced degrees in library and information science. But with the proliferation of specializations in information technology, information design, fund-raising, business management, and other areas, the definition of professionals in libraries has expanded to include these degrees. Some librarians continue to insist that only the MLS-degreed library professional can be so called in a library, and all other holders of advanced degrees are support staff, but this distinction continues to blur over time.

Professional staff members are responsible for providing the expertise to direct library operations. They are responsible for the intellectual content of the library's collection and for its development and maintenance. They manage the ways in which technology impacts the library, provide specialized services to groups, and interact with the community. Those holding advanced degrees other than an information degree manage activities in their area of specialization, such as fund-raising, business, and public relations.

Support Staff

Support staff includes a wide range of positions, which are divided into technical and clerical. Technical staff may include personnel officers, business officers, or curators of special collections held by the library. Each of these positions usually requires education beyond the undergraduate degree. It also includes a large component of those responsible for maintaining the information technology systems in support of both public and technical systems.

Technical staff work throughout the library. They often manage the circulation department, copy services department, and other technical activities. They may be responsible for managing the library's Web site and blogs. In many public libraries, those with specific skills may be assigned responsibility for planning and managing programs. As the library profession becomes increasingly professionalized, more and more of the responsibilities and tasks once considered to be part of the professional's role are being delegated to technical staff. In some libraries, these technical staff members are often called library associates and typically have an undergraduate degree. They may manage a small branch, be responsible for carrying out outreach services, or conduct programs under the supervision of a professional librarian. This introduces many of them to library activities that then motivate them to seek a graduate degree.

Clerical staff members perform the routine tasks that are so necessary to the library's smooth operation, including staffing circulation desks, keeping the Web site up to date, working in the business office, and performing the many secretarial functions so essential to the library, such as providing support to the director and managing correspondence. Their education may range from high school graduation to an associate's degree at a community college. In many libraries, clerical staff are often the first individuals the public meets: they are at the information desk to provide directions, check materials in or out, and answer the phone. In these roles, they represent the library. The courtesy and efficiency with which they do their work influences how the public sees the library, and from a public relations perspective, an outgoing, friendly, and efficient clerical staff is invaluable.

In academic libraries or other libraries that are part of a larger organization, the maintenance staff is managed by the larger organization, but public librarians often hire and manage this staff themselves. If the public library is a department of city government, there may be a centralized service. Many public librarians contract with a local cleaning and maintenance service that keeps the building and grounds in good condition. The public librarian may also hire other services for specific purposes.

Most public librarians hire part-time staff. Individuals in this category may not currently be interested in full-time employment, may have particular skills the library needs but not enough to fill a full-time position, or may work during particularly busy times and for specific projects. Part-time workers may be part of the professional, technical, or clerical staff. The position description, required qualifications, and performance evaluation criteria are the same as for full-time staff. The only difference is in the hours worked and the benefits available.

Other staff categories include pages, who are typically student workers who shelve materials and do other routine tasks as needed. Student workers with individual skills may also be asked to contribute to the library in other ways. They typically report to a technical or clerical staff member.

Volunteers

Volunteers are a valuable means of linking the library to the community, and many libraries welcome volunteers to participate in library activities because they often bring specific skills and expertise. They may be invited to participate in library programs by sharing their experiences or by teaching a skill. They may donate their time to work with a special collection of materials that matches their expertise. Librarians may recruit community residents with specific skills, for example language skills, not available on staff. They may contact the library to offer their expertise.

When working with volunteers, it is important that they understand their role and the expectations of the library. Volunteers are interviewed by library staff members, who discuss with them the contributions they can make to the library's activities. This discussion includes the number of hours the volunteer will contribute, a work schedule, and to whom the volunteer will report. A clear statement of expectations, mutually agreed upon, serves as an agreement between the volunteer and the public library and includes the tasks the volunteer will perform, the resources and support the library will provide, and what is to be accomplished. It is also useful to set a time limit on volunteering so that at the end of that period, the librarian and the volunteer may discuss whether they wish to continue the arrangement. Library staff members need to know that volunteers are donating their time to accomplish specific tasks and should not be expected to do more than they have agreed to do. Volunteers receive no payment for their time, and their roles are always supplemental.

PERFORMANCE EVALUATION

The library has classification schedules that identify each position and how it relates to all other positions in the library. Position descriptions specify the kinds of work expected of the person holding that position, the knowledge skills and abilities to perform the tasks, and the minimum qualifications for the job. For example, the position description for Librarian I would state that the person holding this position performs professional duties under direct or general supervision and carries out duties as assigned. The individual would have completed the MLS or other degree approved by the American Library Association. The person applies that education by performing specific duties assigned under the supervision of a higher grade librarian. Employees in this class are assigned increasingly challenging tasks as they gain experience. Examples of work for Librarian I would be listed and could include providing reference services, supervising a medium-sized branch library, or conducting programs. This information is part of each employee's personnel file and also serves as the basis for evaluation of performance.

Classification schedules and position descriptions provide a necessary structure to provide stability for library management. In an environment of continuous change in which the library staff member needs to be flexible, they also prevent the library from changing as rapidly as is often necessary. The most useful position descriptions therefore are those that outline the specific knowledge, skills, and abilities that are needed and provide the supervisor and the staff member flexibility to adapt to tasks as needed. In this environment, some position descriptions and associated tasks will expand, while others will decrease and may even be eliminated. Staff members will need to learn new skills. Workflow patterns may change. Each staff member has a personal interest in reviewing his or her job description to know how expectations have changed in response to changes in library reorganization, technology, and/or funding that require elimination of some positions or the combination of related activities into one position

Today's workplace is outwardly seen as more diverse and more casual than in the past. Individuals work in a more self-directed fashion, and as long as they meet expectations, they have flexibility in how they do them. Not every position lends itself to this flexibility; for example, those dealing directly with the public are expected to be available at a specific time and place. Those working on other tasks, for example, Web site management, have more flexibility in their work patterns as long as the task is completed in a competent and timely fashion. This outward flexibility, however, is firmly grounded in the position description and expectations.[11] Performance review is based on the position description and the extent to which the staff member fulfills the requirements of the job.

The Appraisal Process

Library staff members deserve a regular periodic performance evaluation so that they know if they are performing their jobs in an acceptable manner.

The competent supervisor does a lot of evaluation "by walking around" and being aware of how well the library functions on a daily basis, but formal discussions between the supervisor and staff member are important ways for them to discuss the position, its expectations, how well they are meeting those expectations, and what they can do to improve their performance.

Many library managers are not comfortable conducting appraisals, and they may try to avoid the activity or may not spend the time necessary to make thoughtful assessments of an individual's performance. Because the productivity of the organization depends on each individual doing his or her best work, and because individual growth is related to the specific needs and interests of the individual, assessment is one of the most important roles a supervisor fills. Levinson identified the following purposes for performance appraisal and review:

1. To measure and judge performance.

2. To relate individual performance to organizational goals.

3. To foster the increasing competence and growth of staff.

4. To stimulate the staff members' motivation.

5. To enhance communication between supervisor and staff member.

6. To serve as a basis for judgment about salary and promotion.

7. To serve as a way to maintain organizational control and integration.[12]

It also provides staff members the opportunity to clarify issues, discuss their concerns about the position, and develop a plan for staff development and continuing education that will further the staff member's value to the library. A formal evaluation, dated and signed by both the supervisor and the staff member, is then placed in the staff member's personnel file. This process provides a record of the staff member's performance and is an important resource should the supervisor need to write a letter of recommendation or have concerns about the staff member's continuing performance.

Staff Development and Continuing Education

"Staff, not machines, will meet user expectations."[13] New ways of delivering services to an ever-changing and expanding community require that staff keep their skills up to date. Two levels of activity contribute to fulfilling this need: staff development that is conducted internally by library administration and continuing education that occurs outside the library. Continuing education includes workshops, seminars, and other short-term learning opportunities sponsored by graduate schools of information, professional societies, and other groups outside the library. As mentioned previously, a goal of the performance appraisal process is to identify ways in which staff members can learn new skills that will help them in their present jobs as they evolve and help them prepare for the next step in their careers. The appraisal process will help identify job-focused learning, but staff members, as adult learners, must be involved in determining what they need to learn and in "planning, executing, and evaluating their training and development and in assessing their progress. Educational programs work best when they are tailored to the individual and move from what the staff member actually knows to what the staff member wants and needs to know."[14]

The supervisor may be a valuable source of information to the staff member interested in building a career in the library professions, as can the professional associations, which present career workshops. Graduate schools of library and information science are also excellent sources of information. For staff members reentering the workforce, performance review and support in identifying the steps necessary to be successful in the world of work give them a road map to follow.

Continuing education establishes an environment in which personal growth is encouraged. Opportunities may be identified and guidelines for support established. Released time to take courses or attend a seminar, and tuition reimbursement when possible, are a valuable contribution, and in some situations the successful completion of a program may lead to increased responsibility in one's current position or possible promotion.[15]

The Learning Organization

The definition of a learning organization is one that is continuously looking at its environment and activities and encouraging new ideas. Peter Senge, author of *The Fifth Discipline: The Art and Practice of the Learning Organization*,[16] defines the learning organization as one that is continually expanding its capacity to create its future. He also said that the ability to learn faster may be the only sustainable competitive advantage. To develop the individual and the entire organization, he sees the need for five technologies: systems thinking, in which one looks at the entire organization and not just one aspect; personal mastery, in which the individual clarifies the personal vision; mental models that identify the way in which we think the world works; the building of a shared vision for the future that will guide the organization; and development of the team as a basic learning unit. He adds that individual development, career development, and organizational movement toward the learning organization are all aspects of the same activity. The organization that learns, and individuals who learn to support the organization and at the same time support individual growth, have the tools that will help them face the future.

SUMMARY

Since the latter half of the 20th century, public libraries have been on the fast track to the 21st century. While staying true to their mission of bringing people and information together to foster an educated society, they have developed research-based methods of management, adopted automation and information technology so that they are in the forefront of the information revolution, and opened access to the information age to everyone in the community. The public library has become what Senge calls a learning organization, one that continues to learn, to do, and to find new ways to serve the community now and in the future. Learning, as one faces future challenges and opportunities, never stops.

NOTES

1. Alice Bryan, *The Public Librarian* (New York: Columbia University Press, 1952).

2. Frederick Kilgour, quoted in *Wikipedia*.

3. Hugh Atkinson, quoted in *Wikipedia*.

4. Margaret Myers, "Staffing Patterns," in *Personnel Administration in Libraries*, 2nd ed., ed. Sheila Creth and Frederick Duda, 40–63 (New York: Neal Schuman, 1989).

5. Dale Yoda and Herbert Heneman, "Staffing Policies and Strategies," in *ASPA Handbook of Personnel and Industrial Relations*, vol. 4, 2 (Washington, DC: Bureau of National Affairs, 1974).

6. Ann Prentice, *Managing in the Information Age* (Lanham, MD: Scarecrow Press, 2005), 265.

7. Kathleen de la Peña McCook, *Introduction to Public Librarianship* (New York: Neal Schuman, 2004), 155.

8. American Library Association, *Library and Information Studies and Human Resource Utilization: A Statement of Policy* (Chicago: American Library Association, 2002); and www.ala.org/ala/aboutala/offices/hrdr/educprofdev/lepu.pdf (accessed August 10, 2010).

9. Ibid.

10. Prentice, *Managing in the Information Age*, 282.

11. Ibid.

12. Harry Levinson, "Management by Whose Objectives," *Harvard Business Review* 81, no. 1 (January 2003): 107–16.

13. Sheila Creth, "Personnel Planning and Utilization," in *Personnel Administration in Libraries*, ed. Creth and Duda, 118–51 (New York: Neal Schuman, 1989).

14. Prentice, *Managing in the Information Age*, 301.

15. Creth, *Personnel Administration in Libraries*, 145–46.

16. Peter Senge, *The Fifth Discipline: The Art and Practice of the Learning Organization* (New York: Doubleday, 1990).

ADDITIONAL READINGS

American Library Association, Library Support Staff Certification Program. *Final Briefing Document.* Chicago: American Library Association, 2009. Available at www.ala.apa. org-lss.

Bernfeld, Betsy. "Developing a Team Management Structure in a Public Library." *Library Trends* 53, no. 1 (Summer 2004): 112–28.

Cortada, James W. *How Societies Embrace Information Technology: Lessons for Management and the Rest of Us.* Hoboken, NJ: Wiley, 2009.

Martin, Lowell. *Library Personnel Administration.* Metuchen, NJ: Scarecrow Press, 1994.

Mayo, Diane, and Jeanne Goodrich. *Staffing for Results: A Guide to Working Smarter.* Chicago, American Library Association, 2002.

Montgomery, Jack G., and Eleanor I Cook. *Conflict Management for Libraries: Strategies for a Positive, Productive Workplace.* Chicago: American Library Association, 2005.

Pollock, Miriam. "Cruel to be Kind." *American Libraries* 39, no. 9 (October 2008): 49–50.

Reed, Lori, and Paul Signorelli. "Are You Following Me?" *American Libraries* 39, no. 10 (November 2008): 42–44.

Chapter ▶ 13

Marketing and Public Relations

INTRODUCTION

Marketing and public relations are extensions of communication. Each presents the library to the community in different ways and for different purposes, and each is integral to the organization. *Public relations* is "the function by which organizations, including libraries and media centers, establish and maintain open, two way communication between the organization and its various publics."[1] It involves knowing your community in order to serve it better. It "helps management to keep informed on and responsive to public opinion, defines and emphasizes the responsibility of management to serve the public interest, . . . keep abreast of and effectively utilize change, serving as an early warning system to help anticipate trends."[2]

Marketing "is a dynamic function which identifies the needs of users, and the attendant activities by which the library meets these needs and communicates these activities to the public."[3] It is also defined as "the effective management by an organization of its exchange relations with its various markets and publics."[4] In marketing, one assumes that the purpose of the organization is to determine the needs and wants of the customer and to meet those needs. Whereas selling focuses on the seller and the products/ services being sold, marketing is customer focused and aims at providing greater customer satisfaction. The purpose of the organization is to serve as the structure to meet the customer's needs and wants. Social marketing, which is the marketing of ideas rather than products, is what the librarian often does.

Several related activities are found under the public relations/marketing umbrella. *Advertising*, paid communication whose function is to inform, persuade, and remind,[5] is the oldest form of telling others what an organization or business is about and has included those selling something posting a billboard in a public place or sending someone out to tell others about what they were selling. Most advertising is done by for-profit organizations, and its focus is on providing a product/service at a price. *Publicity* is news that is created by an organization and is reported in the media free of charge. For example, the public library may be hosting a well-known author and wish to inform the community of this newsworthy event.

Promotion provides information intended to change public attitudes. When the public librarian initiates a campaign to show that the library is much more than books and invites the public to visit and participate, that is promotion. *Propaganda* is a technique intended to change public opinion and may be used for good or ill. Informing the community about the benefits of healthy eating that is based on research and intended to improve life is a good. Lying to the community to persuade them to vote a certain way is not good. *Community relations* is the process of enhancing the image of the organization by being active in community affairs. Publicity and propaganda have often been seen as less than honorable uses of communication, but they too have a role in presenting an organization's products and services to the community. As long as one acts honorably and ethically in communicating with the public, each of these activities has its uses.

WHY PUBLIC LIBRARIANS NEED TO KNOW ABOUT PUBLIC RELATIONS AND MARKETING

Public librarians provide services that are essential to the community: information to help solve problems, get a job, or pursue education; films, books, and other resources to inform and entertain; access to computing, training in its use, and access to the Internet; and many more services for all ages. But unless members of the community are informed about their availability, they will not know to come to the library and use these services.

Communication is a two-way process involving the library and the entire community. The librarian needs to know about the community to provide programs and services that meet its needs, and the community needs to know that those programs and services are available.

Spreading the word about the public library is accomplished on many levels. Trustees and librarians need to connect to the community by joining local organizations and being active in them. They may offer to provide information on topics of interest to the organization, offer to speak to a group on a particular topic, and be willing to support the activities of the organization. Trustees, whether elected or appointed, should reflect a range of community interests.

Do librarians and trustees maintain working relationships with elected officials, not only at budget time but year-round, so that local government is aware of library programs and what they contribute to the community? Do librarians work with local government officials and community groups to collaborate on programs? Are local government officials kept informed of ways in which the library can increase service to new neighborhoods with new branches or serve an underserved group, given added resources? Are local officials convinced that the library's stewardship of tax dollars shows that it is a good community investment?

Library staff at all levels are important participants in the process. Every time someone comes to the library, how that person is greeted, the way in which his or her requests are handled, the courtesy with which that person is treated says something important about the library. Are library staff members never too busy to be of service? This is important whether it is an in-person visit, a phone call, or a virtual visit. Are books and other materials shelved in a timely manner, or are filled book carts in evidence in many areas? The look of the building is important. Is it well organized, clean, safe, inviting, and well lit? Is it easy to navigate, and are signs appropriately placed?

Are the grounds or adjoining businesses an appropriate setting for the library, and is the parking lot well lit? All of these factors tell the visitor if the library is well managed and if it places a high priority on customer service. All of these activities are part of the library's informal marketing and public relations program and are essential to its survival and success.

A Bit of History

In 1876, the founding date of both the American Library Association and *Library Journal*, an article stating that "good personal relations between librarian and reader were essential" was published in the latter.[6] Articles dealing with one or another aspect of public relations have appeared in the library press regularly since that then.

John Cotton Dana, director of the Denver Public Library and later the Newark, New Jersey, Public Library and president of ALA in 1896, "exhorted the membership to 'see that your library is interesting to the people of the community, the people who own it, the people who maintain it'."[7] This is the same man who was the first to encourage the use of publicity to increase use and support of public libraries, and for whom the John Cotton Dana Award is named. The John Cotton Dana Library Public Relations Award, the most prestigious award of the American Library Association, is given annually to honor outstanding library public relations activities.

Writing in 1935, Gilbert Ward stated that "in the long run, a public library usually depends for its prosperity and usefulness on what the public thinks of it. What the public thinks of it depends in turn not only on the character of the books and the services, but also on what the librarian does to make its books and services known."[8] Public relations for the library had two goals: to promote use and to obtain support. He added that "publicity should seek to emphasize the worthwhile, the useful, the wholesome and the timely book, and to ignore the title of doubtful quality."[9] His examples of articles about the library and ways in which to design newsletters and similar public relations items appear dated some 75 years later because society has moved on. But his stated goals, to promote use and obtain support, remain important basic goals.

Ward wrote at a time when newspapers were the primary medium for providing information on libraries and their activities. The mimeograph machine was used to prepare announcements and booklists. Radio had just become available as a way to inform the community about the library. Television was decades in the future, and the Internet, with its multitude of opportunities to inform others about the public library, may have been a science fiction possibility but hardly imagined as reality.

Although public relations and marketing have been around in some form for a long time, it wasn't until the 1970s that the not-for-profit sector adopted these means of identifying customers and their interests. Philip Kotler's[10] work in the 1970s provided a foundation for much of the publications about how to manage public relations and marketing in the not-for-profit sector.

Following on his work, library professionals including Cosette Kies[11] and Darlene Weingand[12] provided useful guides for librarians on how to go about developing, managing, and evaluating public relations and marketing programs. Guides and handbooks on these topics continue to be published on a regular basis.

Public relations is seen as an antidote to lack of awareness about the public library and its contributions to the community and to each individual. It is a means of breaking down stereotypes about the library: that it is not an up-to-date information resource but is full of outdated information resources, that it is for women who like to read romance novels, that it is a nice place for children, and that "librarian" is just a fancy name for clerk. The goal of public relations is to replace these faulty images with the truth: that the public library is not only an up-to-date information resource, its staff will help patrons learn basic computing skills and access the Internet and assist them in searching for information they need. It has programs and services for all ages that help to inform and educate. It is a community service that provides information on all aspects of an issue, has no requirements for participating in activities other than that being a member of the community whose taxes support the library, and is free.

The Public Relations Plan

In getting this message to the community, it is essential that the public librarian have a process and a plan. That process is made up of five activities, each of which is an important element of the activity:

1. Identify the organization's relevant publics.

2. Measure images and attitudes of the relevant publics toward the organization.

3. Establish image and attitude goals for the key publics.

4. Develop cost-effective public relations strategies.

5. Implement actions and results.[13]

Once these steps have been taken and the necessary information has been collected about the demographics of the community served and their attitudes toward the library, the next step is to develop a library plan for action, which includes the elements discussed below, many of which are present in the library's long-range and strategic plans. Think of the public relations/ marketing plan as a companion plan to the others, while focusing on making the community aware of the library and its contribution to the community. The goals and objectives of all plans are held in common.

As in any planning process, the first step is to review the library's mission and its goals and objectives. Do the goals and objectives mesh with the current demographics of the community, and do they respond to current interests and needs? Do the programs and services provided meet current needs? Has the community aged and therefore needs to pay more attention to seniors than children? Have new groups moved into the community who need different services? Is the librarian reaching out to the community on the Web? Does the library have sufficient Internet access for the increasing number of individuals whose only Internet access is the public library?

To what extent and in what ways does the librarian currently inform the public about the library's services, and how well is the job being done? Are there gaps in informing the various groups about services available? Have surveys been used to determine levels of community satisfaction with library activities and the ways in which they are informed of those activities? Has there been an analysis of mass media coverage? Does information about the library and its services appear regularly in the local newspapers and other outlets? Does the information focus on library resources and activities? Is the coverage positive? What are public attitudes toward budget cuts for library services?

The next step is to review current ways of informing the community and identify those activities that work well in reaching the intended audience with appropriate information in a timely fashion, and identify those activities that do not meet this standard. What steps need to be taken to ensure that all publics are informed of information they need? In this step, one should identify each program and each potential audience and set objectives for each.

A budget and timeline are then developed to support new public relations ventures and to revise existing ventures that have not met expectations. If the library does not have an individual or unit responsible for public relations, someone should be assigned to manage the program to evaluate its success and revise it as needed. Success is measured by the extent to which the community responds to the library in a positive way. This may be determined by attendance at specific programs that have been announced in the media; by votes for or against a bond issue to enlarge the library, build a branch, or build a new library; or by citizen responses to threats of budget cuts.

Staff members need to be part of the input into goal and objective setting; program planning; and the ways in which the community is made aware of programs, activities, and library issues. They are directly involved with those who use the library and hear comments and suggestions by patrons that have the potential to improve programs, the ways in which activities are managed, and the overall public relations program.

Marketing

Marketing is a management process that encompasses analysis, planning, implementation, and control to identify both product or service and the public's willingness or desire to receive that product/service in exchange for something of value.[14] Marketing is not selling, which focuses on the seller and the product/service being sold.

Marketing is customer focused and measures both customer needs and satisfaction. The marketing approach must be an organizationwide attitude that focuses on customer satisfaction and what needs to be done to enhance that satisfaction.

Philip Kotler[15] stresses the fact that marketing is an exchange process The organization offers or exchanges something of value for something else of value. "If the organization's purpose is to serve social needs, then marketing can be seen as a social process."[16] In marketing, one selects those target populations most likely to bring results. Marketing is aimed at "achieving organizational objectives . . . [and] relies on designing the organization's offerings in terms of the target market's needs, not the seller's personal ideas."[17] It is user oriented, not seller oriented. Libraries do more than select target markets and serve them. As a publicly supported organization, the library is committed to serving the entire community. What marketing can do for library planners is provide a methodology for describing the total community and for selecting groups within the community to which it can direct specific programs while at the same time providing a quality level of service for all. The methodology provides the data to justify those decisions.

The Marketing Audit

It is difficult "to be all things to all people" when budgets are cut, and difficult decisions must be made about where to focus resources. Collecting data through the use of a marketing audit is one way library planners can make informed decisions. A *marketing audit* differs from needs assessment and community analysis in the following ways.

The *needs assessment* is based on customer-expressed needs, and data are often collected using surveys and interviews. *Community analysis* focuses on the entire community, not just the user. It takes a "snapshot" of a point in time through collection and analysis of demographic data and projected growth patterns. Data collected at a point in time will change, and that is taken into consideration when planning. The marketing audit collects data on present and potential customer needs and interests and demographic data on the community. It also conducts an environmental scan to identify trends and analyzes the internal environment of the organization, thus providing the most comprehensive set of data for planning of the three.[18]

It is also necessary to determine how the library is perceived. Is the public library seen as an organization that has the reputation of being able to deliver desired services? Does it have adequate resources, equipment, and staff expertise to deliver those services? Does it provide a pleasant environment in which to take advantage of services? Kotler cautions that a potential customer may respond to his or her perceptions of the library rather than to reality. He defines image as "a set of beliefs about an object"[19] that vary from person to person and differ in clarity and complexity. Someone who has not visited the public library for some time may be unaware that today's Internet-connected library is much different from the library of a decade or two ago. This perception may interfere with current reality, and the potential user may not think of the public library as the first place to go to learn about and to use Internet resources.

Interviews and focus groups are often used to determine what the image of the library is within certain groups. Marketers want to know if image is determined by how individuals perceive the organization and whether that perception is due to personal bias or lack of information. Services highly regarded by some may be seen as out of date, too costly, or of no interest to others. It is essential to pay close attention to the ways in which services are perceived and to ensure that the perception of them is positive.

Market Segmentation

A market segment is part of the overall market and may be defined by geographic area, type of market, or a number of other factors, including income, lifestyle, personal interests, level of education, and loyalty to the organization providing the service or product. Is the individual open to trying new services or products? Once a specific market segment has been identified based on geographic area, age group, educational level, or other variables, services tailored to specific needs and interests are developed. One may often provide for the needs and interests of a targeted market more efficiently than for a larger market in which the interests of a smaller group may be lost.

It is important to ask, "What specific market niche does your product or service fill? What niche do you want to fill? If a library wants to be seen as the first stop for those who do not have computers at home to go to for instruction and access to the Internet, how will it design the service so that achieve that objective? What does that library do that is special and not done elsewhere? What is the competition? How does it evaluate the service in order to ensure continuous improvement?"

Public library staff and trustees in the past have seen themselves as providing special services for which there is no competition and have believed that there is no need to be concerned about identifying a niche. In our highly competitive social, political, economic, and technological world, we no longer have the luxury of ignoring our competition, and we need to identify it.

Internet cafes, coffeehouses, and even McDonalds advertise wi fi and are among the places one can go to get online if one has a laptop and knows how to use it. School library media centers provide Internet access but usually not on weekends. For those seeking job information, unemployment offices are available during certain hours. What does the library do that makes its services more attractive? Is it availability of workstations, hours open, convenience of the location, someone who will assist the individual who is having difficulty using the technology? The public library can make a powerful case that it fills an important niche in the community and serves many individuals not otherwise served, and in doing so, it meets important educational and social needs.

The Marketing Plan

The library's marketing plan describes the target audience, identifies problems and opportunities, lists measurable objectives, produces a budget, and includes an evaluation plan.[20] The target audience has been identified through careful analysis of the data collected and the decision to focus on specific targets as priority areas. For the public library these targeted audiences receive special services above and beyond the services provided to all. What is the library's justification for developing programs specifically for a target market? Can it justify spending additional funds for the program? What are its expectations, and how does one know if the program is successful?

If studies have indicated that there is a large number of new arrivals in the community whose first language is not English and who are families with young children, this points to the need to provide preschool readiness programs directed toward this target market. A plan is developed identifying problems and opportunities. Is there any other community agency serving this need? Is it possible to cooperate with that agency? What resources and services are available? What new expenditures are needed? What are the long- and short-term objectives? Can the library achieve the objectives using available resources? Can those objectives be stated in measurable terms?

Sometimes a self-selected target group appears in the library, and it is the responsibility of the library to develop a means of providing services to them. The library, as a place for the unemployed to get access to online resources, help filling out job applications, and resources for writing resumes, is very busy during periods of high unemployment. As more and more employers ask and even require that job applications be submitted online, more and more individuals need assistance, and the library is open in the evening; has workstations, software, and online information; and has people who can provide guidance in their use.

HOW THE PUBLIC LIBRARIAN USES MARKETING INFORMATION

In the late 1970s the Baltimore County (MD) Public Library's mission statement stated that the "library will collect materials most users do read or use, provide them as soon after publication as possible, and have enough copies to meet demand promptly."[21] This bold statement contradicted a century or more of an attitude that librarians should buy what the reader should read or use rather than what the reader wanted. It was received by the library community with varying levels of acceptance. This is an example of using market research to identify what people want and then getting it for them.

Other examples of using marketing to enhance the library include borrowing ideas for display from local stores. Where should the latest materials be put so that they are seen immediately? How should the children's area be decorated so that it is bright and inviting? How can the library Web site be designed so that it is graphically pleasing, information rich, and easy to use? One way to answer the last question is to visit other Web sites, not just library sites but those of online businesses.

In addition to learning what people want and benefiting from the ways in which items are displayed and marketed, the value of marketing for nonprofit organizations is that the techniques for data gathering provide extensive information about the community and how it wants to be served. Data gathering also provides information on trends in the demographics of the service area. One may identify trends in the development of new information products and in how people use information. It is possible to look ahead and project what steps the library needs to take to stay in the forefront of information delivery to the community at large. This information is essential for long-range and strategic planning.

A second benefit of using market research in the library is that one can identify the library's market and target markets that need special attention. It provides the information to plan programs for specific groups in a timely manner. Is this service a new service? Does it replace a service that no longer has an audience? Is it a variation of an existing service? How does it fit with similar services?

Of particular importance is the ability to use marketing information to demonstrate to the community and its elected officials that the library fills a unique need and its decisions are well reasoned and fact based. Determining outcomes of specific activities is a difficult task. When each program has an evaluative component that collects data on a regular basis, it is possible to know how many individuals have taken advantage of that service. It is more difficult to quantify the contribution to the community of the service beyond anecdotal information.

One may ask what difference a preschool, pre-reading program for small children of immigrant parents has made to the community. If those children are ready for kindergarten and get a better start in their formal schooling, one can measure this and demonstrate whether the library program made a difference. A child who gets a positive start in school saves the community money and is more content.

One also may ask what difference the time spent with unemployed people helping them use job banks, fill out applications, and prepare resumes has made. This is easier to measure than a child's success in school, because one can determine how many of those people found jobs and how long it took them. This is another example of how the public library supports the community economically by helping individuals become more independent and productive.

These are the facts that are important when the community presents its rationale for library funding. Using market research, that rationale can be more targeted and provide the kinds of information government officials deal with. Just saying that the public library is a good thing and therefore should be funded is no longer enough. Good will only goes so far. Hard data plus good will are much better.

SUMMARY

Marketing and public relations play an important role in determining whom we serve and how we make the community aware of services available. The public library has moved to a central role in connecting individuals and information, and its programs and services extend to all areas of the community. With the library Web site serving as a virtual branch of the library, service is available 24/7. The 21st-century library needs to place itself front and center in the community, and it is through marketing and public relations that today's public library makes itself known to the community it serves.

NOTES

1. Cosette Kies, *Marketing and Public Relations for Libraries* (Lanham, MD: Scarecrow Press, 1987), 5.

2. Rex F. Harlowe, "Building a Public Relations Definition," *Public Relations Review* 2 (Winter 1976): 34–42.

3. Kies, *Marketing and Public Relations for Libraries*, 9.

4. Philip Kotler, *Marketing for Non-Profit Organizations* (Englewood Cliffs, NJ: Prentice-Hall, 1975), x.

5. Harry R. Cook, *Selecting Advertising Media: A Guide for Small Business* (Washington, DC: Small Business Administration, 1977), 1–3.

6. Kies, *Marketing and Public Relations for Libraries*, 18.

7. Ibid., 20.

8. Gilbert O. Ward, *Publicity in Public Libraries; Principles and Methods for Librarians, Library Assistants, Trustees, and Library Schools*, 2nd ed. (New York: H.W. Wilson, 1935), 1.

9. Ibid., 54.

10. Kotler, *Marketing for Non-Profit Organizations*.

11. Kies, *Marketing and Public Relations for Libraries*.

12. Darlene Weingand, *Marketing/Planning Library and Information Services*, 2nd ed. (Englewood, CO: Libraries Unlimited, 1999).

13. Kotler, *Marketing for Non-Profit Organizations*, 382.

14. Ann Prentice, *Managing in the Information Age* (Lanham, MD: Scarecrow Press, 2005), 171.

15. Kotler, *Marketing for Non-Profit Organizations*, 382.

16. Prentice, *Managing in the Information Age*, 172.

17. Kotler, *Marketing for Non-Profit Organizations*, 6.

18. Weingand, *Marketing/Planning for Library and Information Services*, 129–32.

19. Kotler, *Marketing for Non-Profit Organizations*, 129–32.

20. Robert H. Wilbur, ed., *The Complete Guide to Non-Profit Management,* 2nd ed. (New York: Wiley, 2000), 66.

21. Shannon Mattern, *The New Downtown Library* (Minneapolis: University of Minnesota Press, 2007), 5–6.

ADDITIONAL READINGS

Alman, Susan Webreck. *Crash Course in Marketing for Libraries.* Westport, CT: Libraries Unlimited, 2007.

Cronin, Blaise, ed. *The Marketing of Library and Information Services 2.* London: ASLIB, 1992.

Walters, Suzanne. *Library Marketing That Works.* New York: Neal-Schuman, 2006.

Chapter ▶ 14

Program Evaluation

INTRODUCTION

"Measurement is the collection of data representing the state of the library, its services and users. It provides objective data on efficiency and effectiveness to assist decision making."[1] Measurement compares what is with what ought to be. For many traditional librarians, the idea that one could measure something as special and unique as library service was unthinkable. This attitude became untenable during the 1960s for a number of reasons. After a time of increased funding for libraries during the 1950s, resources again became limited and librarians found themselves in competition with other publicly funded services including fire, police, and social services for the funds that were available.

Library managers and managers of other units of local government began to use measures of effectiveness and efficiency to justify their services. They began to see that measurement of services was a useful, if still somewhat distasteful, tool for justifying support. Also during this period, management at the town, city, and county level, including library management, became increasingly professionalized. And because of the growth in PhD programs in library and information science and the replacement of many practitioner faculty members with research faculty, the curriculum in LIS programs shifted to a more research-based program, in which students became more comfortable with the use of research methodology, which they then would transfer to their work environment.

Similar changes were also occurring in public administration and other fields that affected local government agencies. Applying strategies developed in business environments to the public library as well as to other government and not-for-profit agencies became standard practice. Faculty who combined

169

research competence with operational experience had the expertise to conduct research on ways in which one could plan programs and develop ways in which to evaluate them. This provided library managers with tools they could use to measure library performance. It became increasingly evident to library managers that they needed to evaluate the services they provided to show that a service met its intended goals and objectives, was well managed, and was cost effective. Because public library services are in competition with other services provided by its funding agency, the public library must be able to show that its services are relevant and efficient, and are being used prudently.

The movement toward an increasingly professional management of libraries has benefited from the leadership of the American Library Association (ALA) and the Public Library Association (PLA), a division of ALA. PLA's *A Planning Process for Public Libraries*[2] was the first of a number of guides for planning and evaluation published by ALA during the 1980s. These guides introduced many public librarians to the processes of planning for library service and measuring those services.

PLANNING AND MEASURING

Planning

The *Public Library Inquiry* (PLI), a series of studies of public libraries, their services, and their users, was conducted in the late 1940s and early 1950s by the Social Science Research Council and funded by the Carnegie Corporation. It laid much of the foundation for later study of public libraries. Because these studies were conducted by a social science agency rather than by library professionals, the findings contrasted dramatically with the view of the field that was published in the library press of the period. These research-based studies provided a solid base for future study and action. One of the best-known volumes in the PLI , Berelson's *The Library's Public*, focused on demand for services: "Who is the library's user, and what does he want?"[3]

The approach to library service from the perspective of the user has become a core element in planning and evaluation of services. Following the lead of the business sector, similar planning activities were taking place in other not-for-profit agencies as they moved to a more professional way of doing business.

The publication in 1980 of *A Planning Process for Public Libraries* was a major event in public library management.[4] The planning process begins with the collection of appropriate data, the purpose of which is to evaluate current library services as the first step in planning for future services. The authors stressed that "library management requires a system of data, or statistics to provide information for decision making, to meet the reporting requirements of local, state, and federal authorities, and to allow for comparison with other libraries."[5] This system is built up a coordinated system of data collection based on determining what is needed, how it will be used, how often the data will be collected, how often they will be reported, and who is responsible for these efforts. Once one knows the types of data to be collected, it is relatively easy to put into place a management information system that will allow for continuous collection of data online that can be accessed on demand. With such a system, data collection is always up to date, and one can print out reports in real time rather than having to wait for them. One can also print out reports at regular intervals.

Performance measures provide us with much of the information needed to review the extent to which the library's goals have been met. They also provide us with data that help us monitor library activities on a continuing basis. Library statistics alone are not performance measures, but they contribute to them. Library statistics—including number of books and other print and nonprint media, number of borrowers, program attendance, number of reference questions answered, and number of users of computer terminals— have been collected since libraries were established. The types of measures have varied depending on the library services provided. When looking at ways to measure service, library managers tended to collect statistics that were easy to collect and quantify. They often did not take the next step, which would be to ask, "What do I need to know that will help me plan for the best use of library resources to serve the public?" There appeared to be a disconnect between the collection of information and how it could be used to plan for and evaluate library programs.

Measuring

Performance measures emerged in the 1960s as a means of evaluating service, of responding to the often asked question, "Did users get what they wanted?" Two approaches emerged: those, including Ernest DeProspero, who aimed at developing simple and easy-to-use measures, and those who based their very complex measures on operations research methodology. Although the operations research methodology was used in innovative ways, those using it were not always aware of library operations, and their results were difficult to assimilate. There are no right or wrong measures; there are poorly designed measures and measures that are not consistently and carefully applied. Measures do not diagnose the causes of problems. They do show where problems that need further study may be located.

The purpose of measurement is to use objective data about library operations to determine how well the library has performed in achieving its goals and objectives so that one can make decisions about allocating and reallocating resources. Performance measures focus on output and effectiveness and "are an analytical tool which provides a manager with the means to evaluate the activities of his/her organization as to the results produced and the extent to which these results fulfill pre-designed objectives."[6]

Using performance measures, service can be evaluated to determine the following:

- **Effectiveness:** How well does a service satisfy the demand?

- **Cost Effectiveness:** How efficient are the library's internal operating systems?

- **Cost Benefit:** Is the value of the service worth more or less than the cost of providing it?

Output Measures for Public Libraries builds on *The Planning Process for Public Libraries*. Its focus is on how to collect data "representing the state of the library, its services and users."[7] Numerous data-collecting tools are presented, from which librarians may select those that answer specific questions about what they do and how well they do it. The criteria the authors use to guide in the selection of the appropriate measure are relevant to any selection of measures for evaluation and include the following:

- **Validity:** Does the tool measure what we want to know?

- **Reliability:** Are the results of the measurement consistent?

- **Comparability:** Can we compare the results of the measures over time and across like situations?

- **Usefulness:** Are the results of the measurement activity used for decision making?

- **Precision:** Many measures, particularly user surveys, have a margin of error. Is that margin of error such that the results are not useful?

- **Cost to gather:** Are the data collected worth the effort made to collect them?"[8]

The purpose of developing and collecting objective data on the library is to determine how good it is and how it can become even better. Using objective measures, it is possible to quantify performance in relation to objectives achieved and services delivered. It is possible to get feedback on performance and an evaluation of service. If, for example, we want to know if by changing the way in which books are checked out we have speeded up service, reduced complaints, and done so without adding staff, we can develop measures as part of the planning process to collect relevant data to determine whether the change has met expectations. The data collected support decision making and "as libraries become more and more complex, management needs objective, standardized data on which to make decisions."[9] Measures that describe the existing situation are compared to goals and objectives to determine the extent to which those goals and objectives were met. The process of goal setting and the measuring of those goals is cyclical.

The goal is set and a level of expected performance is indicated. Broad-based criteria are developed from which one can formulate measures. Specific operations and procedures are set out that are critical to achieving the goal. One applies measures to the operations, and data are collected and analyzed to determine the extent to which the goal was met and to see how closely actual activities match the goals. Using this information, goals are reviewed and revised as appropriate and the cycle begins again. Typical measures include user satisfaction, availability and use of materials, quality and use of facilities, and the quality and use of information services.[10] It is relatively easy to measure inputs (e.g., materials purchased) and outputs (e.g., materials circulated); it is much more difficult to measure outcomes(e.g., user satisfaction with the materials and the uses to which the materials were put). Input and output measures are objective and easy to support, but outcome measures are subjective and more than one interpretation may be made.

It is easy to skew data gathering and thus to receive an incomplete or inaccurate result. The data-gathering tool must be designed so that it collects data relevant to the program or service. Also, collecting just one measure for a program or service provides an incomplete and therefore inaccurate picture of the situation. For example, circulation statistics measure the number of materials checked out, and this is a useful number. It does not give a full picture of the use of the collection. Were the books checked out the only ones the user consulted or looked at while in the library? Were the books checked out those the user really wanted, or were they what was available at the time? Were the books from a particular area of the library, such as the children's collection, young adult collection, or adult collection? Was the user a child who wanted to have access to the other collections but was limited to the children's collection? Was the user an adult selecting materials from the children's and/ or young adult collection?

Analysis of use requires a set of related measures that reflect why certain titles were chosen. Another limitation on objective measures is that they reflect the use of existing services but do not necessarily address other roles of the library, such as its socioeconomic role in the community or its archival role, and how these roles affect service. One may also manipulate measures to provide a desired rather than an accurate picture. By measuring attendance at particularly well-attended programs in a series rather than by measuring attendance at all programs, one could say that the series was more popular than it actually was. It is important to be very careful how data are collected to ensure that they tell the full story and do so accurately.

In addition to measuring the success of library services, it is also useful to measure the effectiveness of library operations. By using questionnaires, interviews, and observation, one can learn how the library makes decisions and what the results of those decisions were. It is possible to learn how well different units in the library communicate and how well they support one another. It is also possible to measure the success of a particular management style, the level of enthusiasm of the staff, and their success in reaching out to the community. These and other measures of the way in which the library functions can be measured, the data analyzed, and adjustments made to improve the library's operation.

Since the 1970s many studies of library services and users have been done, and the result is a large number of interesting, independent studies. Because few of the libraries used the same methodology, asked many similar questions, or collected comparable data, few generalizations can be made. These studies also focused on output measures, such as what the library accomplished. They did not take the important step of tying output to input, such as the resources the library needed or had to be successful in providing service. Therefore they were not particularly useful for looking at what resources would be needed to achieve a certain level of service as measured by outputs. Another limitation of these studies was that they were often conducted in isolation: one service or unit in a library, one library in a system. Unless a program or a library is seen in the context of its library, its system, and its community, the review provides an incomplete picture. A library program relies on the library for its resources, its goals and objectives, and a level of direction. A library in a system of libraries relies on the direction of those who manage the library system, and their success is directly related to the overall expectations of the higher authority. Individual studies conducted out of the context of the library, the library system, and the community have a limited usefulness beyond that specific situation.

EVALUATION

Evaluation uses the measurement process to ask the question, "Are we doing things right?" Are the library's services provided efficiently? Have they met the stated goals and objectives as laid out in the planning process? This not only includes how well the service was performed by the library and the level of the service, but also can be used to relate user satisfaction to user expectations. *Effectiveness* carries evaluation a step further by asking, "Are we doing the right things?" Both of these terms relate to a data-gathering, data-analysis, and data-reporting process, and each includes qualitative and quantitative elements as well as value judgments. Each also assumes that evaluation is an important and permanent part of the planning process and that it will be carried out systematically and on a regular basis. There is also the assumption that evaluation contributes to an environment of continuous improvement.

It has been suggested that the library is a system and that there are tradeoffs in evaluating it.[11] Depending on the perspective one has in data gathering, different sets of measures can be used. If the emphasis is on physical input such as staff, equipment, or materials, one set of measures is used. If the emphasis is on the dynamics of the library, another set of measures is used, and if the focus is on user satisfaction, still another set is used. It is important to select measures carefully and to be sure that they measure what one wishes to measure. Measures to assess short-term activities may differ from those used to look at long-term activities. As measurement and evaluation became a standard part of the planning, operating, and evaluation cycle, more attention began to be paid to the quality of service as expressed by users. There is no consistent definition of what an effective library is, and criteria for assessment change based on circumstances. In determining what to measure and how to measure, one must be aware of the different perspectives each measure may take. Deciding which measures to use is as much a political as it is a managerial decision.

The Use of Consultants

Library managers may wish to hire a consultant to conduct a survey of library activities and programs and/or to recommend and implement specific means of measuring and evaluating the library's activities and programs. There are specific reasons why library managers, in consultation with trustees, opt to conduct a survey. They may wish to have an independent survey of the library conducted that can serve as a benchmark from which to develop new programs. They may be concerned about library operations and wish to have an outside review that can serve as a basis for reorganization. They may wish to have an evaluation of library services to use as part of a public relations effort to inform the community and the funding agency about what the library does and the resources it needs to do even more, and to provide a path to the future. In addition to providing an overview of the library's management and its activities, when a survey is conducted by an outside expert, the result is an objective view that may have major benefits for the library and the community.

The quality of the survey is directly dependent upon the skills and experience of the individual hired to conduct the study. Lowell Martin, the most widely recognized and respected surveyor of public libraries in the latter part of the 20th century, whose work not only resulted in major steps forward for the libraries surveyed but also set a standard and a path forward for all public libraries, described the proper roles for the surveyor:

> [The surveyor] may have specialized knowledge neither possessed nor expected to be possessed by the administering librarian or the local staff. Examples are the building expert, when a new structure is in prospect, or the cataloging expert when a change in a classification system is under consideration. Or the surveyor may be called in as a friend of the court to help make the case for a line of action the librarian wants or may already have proposed. The surveyor brings his prestige to the cause or his power of convincing, or both . . . but I question this type of survey when the so-called expert is used essentially as a rubber stamp. The survey and the surveyor seem to me to be most useful when they are called upon to analyze a genuinely complex situation, with disparate factors and hard alternatives ahead.[12]

An excellent example of Lowell Martin's work is his study of the Chicago Public Library, *Library Response to Urban Change*, published in 1969.[13] It follows from earlier studies of the library, takes a thorough look at the library at the time, and projects library development and growth for the next decades. Thoughtful, well organized, and well written, it continues to be a model for what the skilled consultant who knows libraries and who is well aware of their role in the community and society can produce.

Where does the library director find consultants who have the skills, experience, and vision to design, develop, and carry to completion a complex survey of the library? Former directors of public libraries who have retired and are willing to serve as consultants are often asked to do so. Faculty of LIS programs who have experience in the public library sector are another resource. Consulting firms often advertise that they have the skilled personnel to conduct surveys. If the staff they recommend have skills specific to the public library, or if a staff member is willing to work with a librarian, this will augment the research skills of the staff member. One does not want to hire a generic survey expert whose skills are in the process of surveying organizations and who does not understand the unique role of the public library. When looking for an individual to conduct a library survey, it is advisable to check with the state library agency, other librarians who have worked with consultants, and colleagues who are members of the Public Library Association.

When a library survey is conducted by a skilled expert who understands the role of libraries in society, understands management, and has a vision of what public library service can be in the future, the survey can serve as a blueprint for action, a benchmark on which to build, and a roadmap to the future.

Political Components of Measurement and Evaluation

Because program evaluation is a highly political and often politicized activity, the new administrator needs to answer the following questions early on:

- How are the programs for which I am responsible measured?

- What measures are used, and is there agreement on what they mean?

- Do they actually measure what they are supposed to measure?

- What am I supposed to do with these measures?

- What if I think, and can demonstrate, that the measures are faulty?

A problem with numbers, particularly when they purport to measure something that is difficult to measure, such as level of satisfaction or other subjective element, is that they are believed even when they should not be. This is a very political area, and one needs to tread softly while at the same time questioning the data that appear to be inaccurate. The data may be fine, but it is important to be able to verify that. Or the data may relate to a small area of inquiry and will not generalize to a larger group.

One of the places where power lies in the organization is in the process of measuring its performance. This is a key to levels of funding, earning prestige, and good public relations. Perhaps because data gathering in the service area has many subjective elements, and perhaps because librarians often leave the design of data-gathering tools and the data gathering itself to someone else within or outside the library who may or may not understand the services being measured, the data gathering may in some instances be suspect. For one reason or another the information may have been manipulated for political purposes. Trusting data at face value is dangerous. Those who have designed the data-gathering tools and have collected data should be willing to discuss how they did so. This step ensures that the data are clean and unbiased. It is important to understand how the programs for which you are responsible are reviewed, by whom, and for what purpose.

When a supervisor knows and is comfortable with the ways in which programs are reviewed, there is a level of control over how they are managed not otherwise possible. And this cycles around to goal setting, planning, and resource allocation. Often data gathering, measuring, and evaluating are neglected by the supervisor who sees doing things as more important than looking at what one is doing and why. This same awareness is important for any staff member and provides a measure of control over one's workplace and place in the organization. The clerk who knows how the work is evaluated, such as the number of items processed, error rates, etc., will work within those measures. And clerks are rightly concerned that changes in procedure could change the measures and therefore perhaps improve or harm their status. The new employee, either technical or professional, who learns if things are measured and if so, how he or she can develop some personal control over his or her work and workplace.

Program evaluation is part of all activities, and as the need to produce more and better with fewer and fewer resources continues to be the management mantra, evaluation will continue to be an increasingly important part of everyone's work life. It is important to a new staff member to learn if the workplace is measured and how it is measured. If it is not measured, what measures should be considered? These measures may be informal and for personal use if one is the supervisor. It is guaranteed that at some point supervisors will be asked to evaluate programs for which they are responsible, and it is important to be prepared. If the workplace has measures, learn what they are, how they are applied, what they measure, and what they omit. If there are questions about validity and usefulness, ask them. It is a wise approach to check out how programs for which one is responsible are measured and evaluated and also to check out how one's activities are evaluated.

STANDARDS

Most types of libraries, including public libraries have developed standards for performance within their professional organizations. Early standards were often very brief and focused on specific quantitative statements, such as the number of books per capita, size of staff, or per capita funding. Although these standards were intended to provide a baseline for support, they were often treated as a goal. Once a library reached the standard, funding agencies might decide that they had met the goal and further support was not needed. As library management became more professional and the library associations became stronger advocates for quality service, and particularly as the planning processes and performance measures became more generally a part of public library activities, the more generic standards gave way to a more individualized approach. Each public library is unique, and within the framework of the requirements of its governing and funding agency, it should be able to determine its own performance criteria and how it will evaluate performance.

Standards provide a benchmark for measuring the level of achievement. With agreed upon criteria, the library manager establishes outcomes, both quantitative and qualitative, and arrives at a clearly stated set of expectations for planning, funding, collecting, and maintenance of facilities and equipment.

Outcome measures are set for the expected use of collections, services, and resources. Using the standards as a benchmark, the library manager can then evaluate the library in terms of its success in meeting agreed upon levels of performance. When common standards are used among libraries, librarians will be able to look at their performance in relation to similar libraries to identify best practices and change their approaches to programs. When they find models in other libraries that appear to work better, they can transport these approaches to their own libraries.

SUMMARY

Program evaluation is an important component of the planning cycle because it provides information on how well programs are performing and which programs should be augmented, continued as they are, or considered for reduction or closing. The use of measures and standards to evaluate library activities provides continuous information to those planning for and executing library programs. The process responds to stakeholder concerns about what they receive from their support of the library. It also responds to those who may have concerns about how well the library is managed. Program review and evaluation meets the library director's responsibility to be accountable.

NOTES

1. Nancy Van House, Mary Jo Lynch, Charles R. McClure, Douglas L. Zweizig, and Eleanor Jo Rodger, *Output Measures for Public Libraries,* 2nd ed. (Chicago: American Library Association, 1987), 1.
2. Vernon E. Palmour, Marcia C Bellisari, and Nancy De Wath, *A Planning Process for Public Libraries* (Chicago: American Library Association, 1980).
3. Bernard Berelson, *The Library's Public: A Report of the Public Library Inquiry* (New York: Columbia University Press, 1949).
4. Palmour, Bellisari, and De Wath, *A Planning Process for Public Libraries*, 84.
5. Ibid.
6. Ibid.
7. Van House et al., *Output Measures for Public Libraries,* 1.
8. Ibid., 5.
9. Nancy Van House, Beth Weill, and Charles McClure, *Measuring Academic Library Performance: A Practical Approach* (Chicago: American Library Association, 1990), 3.
10. Ibid., 5.
11. Rosemary Ruhig DuMont, "A Conceptual Basis for Library Effectiveness," *College and Research Libraries* 41, no. 2 (March 1980): 103–11.
12. Lowell A. Martin, "Personnel in Library Surveys," in *Library Surveys,* ed. Maurice F. Tauber and Irlene Roemer Stephens, 124–25 (New York: Columbia University Press, 1967).
13. Lowell A. Martin, *Library Response to Urban Change* (Chicago: American Library Association, 1969).

ADDITIONAL READINGS

Brophy, Peter. *Measuring Library Performance: Principals and Techniques.* New York: Neal Schuman, 2006.

Choo, Chun Wei. *The Knowing Organization: How Organizations Use Information to Construct Meaning, Create Knowledge, and Make Decisions.* New York: Oxford University Press, 1998.

Dudden, Rosalind F. *Using Benchmarking, Needs Assessment, Performance Improvements, Outcomes Measures and Library Standards: A How-to-Do-It Manual.* New York: Neal Schuman, 2007.

Markless, Sharon, and David Streatfield. *Evaluating the Impact of Your Library: The Quest for Evidence.* New York: Neal Schuman, 2006.

Matthews, Joseph R. *Measuring for Results: The Dimensions of Public Library Effectiveness.* Westport, CT: Libraries Unlimited, 2003.

McClure, Charles, et al. *Planning and Role Setting for Public Libraries.* Chicago: American Library Association, 1987.

Van House, Nancy, and Thomas Childers. *The Public Library Effectiveness Study: The Complete Report.* Chicago: American Library Association, 1993.

Walter. Virginia. *Output Measures for Public Library Service to Children.* Chicago: American Library Association, 1992.

Chapter ▶ 15

Financial Planning

INTRODUCTION

Financial planning undergirds financial management. One must first plan for library services, prioritize those services, and then apply financial resources to that plan. The amount of money one allocates to services provides a means of prioritizing them. Each of these activities is conducted in a complex and ever-changing environment. External trends (political, economic, technical) affect planning and budgeting as much if not more than internal data showing how funds are currently allocated or what the use of specific library services has been.

The library administrator is sensitive to these forces and learns how to interact and anticipate trends that affect the library's environment and services. To do less would mark the administrator as a person lacking vision. The administrative structure within which the public library is located as well as local, state, and national policies and actions directly affect what the library can do, and as the demands and expectations of the user community change, programs and services to anticipate and meet these changes must be put into place. The library administrator, working with staff, anticipates the effect of these changes on the library and its services.

A further consideration is how professional standards may affect recommended levels of library service. Standards set by professional societies may run afoul of political and economic realities. Taking these factors into consideration, library administrators make decisions based on current and past practice as they relate to library objectives. Staff members often tend to focus more on internal activities and the success of their current programs and activities, and some may be unwilling to change their current activities to the extent necessary to meet political, economic, and technological realities. It is the responsibility of the director to bring together an awareness of external trends and internal activities to ensure that library activities are responsive to the external environment. The director is also responsible for making sure that external stakeholders know the bases upon which decisions for library planning and funding are made. This includes government officials, funding agencies, and the public.

Because public libraries depend largely on local government for their funding, local government officials must be kept informed of library plans and expenditures. When economic times are difficult, it is essential that the funding agency be aware of the highly important role the library plays in the community, that it is fiscally responsible, and that its services are particularly necessary to the community during difficult economic times. This is accomplished through regular interaction among library leaders, government officials, and members of the community.

BUDGETING

Budgeting is the allocation of scarce resources to meet specified objectives. The first step in the budgeting process is planning. The first step in planning is to collect data both in the external environment and within the library. Management has become increasingly professionalized in the nonprofit sector, and there is an expectation by local government that all agencies of local government will have prepared and kept up to date strategic and long-range plans to serve as guides for the services they provide. Nearly all organizations that rely on the tax dollar for support are expected to have a planning process in place. Though staffing within the library may change and levels of funding may vary, the fundamental purpose of the library, which is to provide the community with information and access to information, does not change. The planning process provides a path to the future for librarians to follow as they develop the budget to pursue stated goals.

Decisions on how to spend tax dollars for library service are influenced not only by resources available and the determination by local government officials of how much of those resources are to be allocated to library service, they are also influenced by factors that emerge from political, social, and cultural considerations. Information service as provided by the library is a public good in that it is an activity without political boundaries, has high social benefit, is carried out over a long period, and enhances our quality of life. Although its benefits are difficult to measure, it is generally agreed that the library is indeed a public good and worthy of public support. Other examples of a public good include the national highway system, museums, and education.

As a planning and decision-making device, the budget has a number of purposes. It is primarily a plan of action for the budget year based on the resources it can realistically hope to receive. The budget is directly linked to performance evaluation, and there is an implicit contract between the library and its funding authority that given a specific level of funding, the library will provide a specified level of service. As is true of any planning process, the budget is a way of highlighting how different programs in the library, and outside the library, are related and mutually dependent. Wildavsky describes the budget as a political act in that resources are requested from a funding body.[1] It is a plan of work in which activities are listed for the ensuing year, and costs of objectives stated.

The budget is a prediction of what staff wishes to accomplish. It can highlight or hide objectives depending on the personal interests of the planner and the perceived political climate. It is a means of control, as the level of funding per program will, to a large extent, determine the level of activity. The budget is a type of agreement between the organization and the funding body that outlines priority needs, sets objectives, and promises to meet those needs and objectives to the degree possible with funds allocated. Once the funding body accepts the budget, it is a precedent on which the library can build in succeeding years. Particularly in difficult economic times, it is essential that the library have a reputation for planning carefully and using public funds responsibly.

The planning process looks both to the long-term projections of three to five years and what actions need to be carried out early in the period to meet long-term goals and the next year's activities. Concurrently, a long-range budget with cost estimates for goals and objectives is developed in addition to the annual operating budget, which focuses on what needs to be accomplished in the next year to meet both long-term and short-term goals. Budgeting for multiyear special projects is usually part of the capital budgeting process and may have even longer time frames depending on the activity. A building project may have a budget that spans five or more years. Special activities and their budgets, though part of the planning/budgeting process, are separate from the annual budget, but each is focused on meeting long-term goals in a different way.

The Budgeting Process

Budgeting is not a one-time activity that occurs just before budget documents are due to be submitted. It is a year-round, ongoing process that requires continuous communication internally and externally so that one has the necessary information for decision making. The library budget committee, which is a standing committee, is chaired either by the budget officer or the library manager (if there is no budget officer). It represents both internal and external stakeholders, typically including library staff members, and may include members of the board of trustees, representatives of Friends of the Library, and others whose input is essential. The bulk of data gathering and budget building is usually the responsibility of two or three committee members, led by the budget officer, if one is on staff, or by the director. Other committee members serve as critics and reviewers who ensure that the document is an accurate representation of the library and its objectives.

Data gathering is conducted regularly through the use of management information systems (MIS) that maintain a record of income and expenditures, plus other internal data such as current staffing levels, the current value of equipment and buildings, book stock, and access to electronic information systems. From information on equipment and buildings, questions about how up to date they are and when replacement is necessary can be answered. Looking at current staffing, one can determine whether existing staff levels are sufficient to meet current needs, and if the staff's current responsibilities and expertise match program needs. Information gained from review of existing programs and recommendations for changes is analyzed to determine if the program should have increased support, steady support, or reduced support. Anticipated changes in the community can be derived from community analysis and other demographic data. When collected on a regular basis, community analysis data describe the current population served and can project changes in age, educational level, ethnic background, and economic levels so that library programs may be adjusted to meet the needs and interests of a changing clientele.

Environmental scanning provides a look into the future broader than that provided by community analysis and can highlight trends and issues that may impact library services. In addition to internal and external statistical data, one also needs to consider issues that are not quantifiable, such as the impact of possible legislation affecting access to the Internet by minors or the impact of an increase in the minimum wage have on the library's ability to increase support staff. What advances in technology will the library want to incorporate into its operations, and how will they affect current services? Responses to these questions will be a combination of statistical projections and subjective input.

The budget committee will look at the library's long-range plan to determine the progress made during the current year and make revisions with the needs and resources of the upcoming budget year in mind. Expenditures in support of each objective in the long range plan are determined on a regular basis throughout the year to ensure that anticipated and actual costs are in line. This also allows the budget officer to make adjustments to the budget when necessary throughout the year. At times during the year, a crisis may arise when resources may have to be pulled from one part of the budget to meet a need elsewhere. During difficult economic times, the funding agency may have to reduce the amount of funding promised to the library, and the library staff will need to make difficult decisions rapidly. Having a long-range plan with agreed upon goals and objectives that have been prioritized, as well as the accompanying budget, library leaders have the structure to deal with unanticipated cuts.

When cuts are necessary, decisions should be based on the data used for planning and budgeting, keeping in mind that core activities must be protected. Programs with a lower priority will receive reduced funding or be cut. It may be necessary to revise the long-term goals and objectives. The decisions made should be sensitive to the political environment and the needs of those using the library. They should be carried out in such a way as not to damage the long-term viability of the library and its most important programs. This is an excellent example of how the planning and budgeting process work together to provide information needed for good decision making.

Types of Budgets

Each library has two types of budgets: the *operating* budget, which is an annual budget that specifies how funds will be spent during the year, and the *capital* budget, which is multiyear and is used to support large-scale activities such as a building program and land purchase. The capital budget is separate from the operating budget, and its income can come from numerous sources: endowments, fund-raising campaigns, contributions, and similar nontax sources. In some instances, the capital budget is used as a vehicle for accounting for income that is not intended to be part of the operating budget. When special purpose grants have been awarded under a government program or by a foundation or other source, they are handled separately and are not part of either the operating budget or the capital budget.

The operating budget comes in several variations, three of which are most commonly discussed: the line item budget, the program budget, and the performance budget. Other budget formats, for one reason or another, are rarely if ever used, including the lump sum budget, the formula budget, and the zero-based budget. The most primitive type of budget is the lump sum budget.

From the Past

Funding agencies bypass long-range plans and budget proposals in making *lump sum* allocations. Funders may look at a prior year's allocation and add a small increase or, if funds are limited, may decrease the allocation. This type of approach shows a lack of interest in the library by the funding agency and tends to reinforce the status quo. Where lump sum budgeting for the library is provided, the librarian then takes the long-range plan and the objectives and allocates funds from that lump to prepare a proper internal budget.

Formula budgeting was developed primarily for the academic setting. Funds were allocated based on a complex formula that takes into account size of collection, anticipated growth by discipline, size of student body, number of faculty, and other factors. Then, projecting anticipated growth, a budget figure would be calculated. Fortunately, this system collapsed from its own complexity.

Another system little used today is zero-based budgeting (ZBB). A product of the 1960s and 1970s, ZBB was developed with federal government agencies in mind. The initial step in this process, after the long-range plan was completed and objectives for the following year were set, was to ask, if each program was essential to meeting stated goals and objectives. If so, a continuum of support for the program was developed, from absolute basic support to full support, and this was done program by program. Once a continuum had been developed for each, programs were prioritized and the level of funding per program was determined by its priority level. If budget cuts came during the year, one could cut programs based on the priority that had been set. Though ZBB was a helpful planning tool, the complexity of the process and the amount of time necessary to build a continuum for each program was too complex and time consuming for regular use.

Line Item Budgets

The traditional budget format is the line item or object of expenditure budget. In this format, each element of the budget—books, periodicals, staff, and equipment, among others—is listed and a dollar amount indicating anticipated cost over the next year is placed next to it. Typically those responsible for developing the budget would use the prior year's budget as a guide and increase each category depending on anticipated costs such as increases in salary, materials, and maintaining the building.

This type of budget is easy to construct because it is based on the expenditures of the prior year. It is also easy to cut, because the funding agency sees no relationship between, for example, cutting electronic information access and the service it supports. The line item budget is not a planning document, and it is difficult to determine the library's objectives for the year from looking at a list of components. It's a bit like describing a cake by listing the ingredients. The experienced baker may be able to visualize what the cake will be, but to the inexperienced, the list is just a list of things.

Program Budget

The program budget is an outgrowth of the movement toward a greater emphasis on planning for services. Beginning with the identification of the library's mission (Why are we here? What is our purpose?) and the formulation of goals and objectives to carry out the mission, the program budget is a concrete means of expressing what the library is, why it is important, and what its goals and objectives are. The program budget begins with a statement of goals and objectives with a listing of programs and functions necessary to meet those goals and objectives.

The library's programs, including circulation services, reference services, children's services, and each of the programs necessary to carrying out the library's goals, are listed and a detailed line item budget is prepared for each program. The same process is followed to determine costs for technical services, maintenance services, and administrative overhead (which includes public relations, staff training, and the salaries of top library managers. In a true program budget, a percentage of administrative and maintenance services as well as technical services (overhead costs) will be allocated to each program, and there will not be separate programs titled "technical services," "administration," or" maintenance." Some libraries do this, while others continue to have separate program areas for these services.

The initial development of a program budget takes time because it is necessary to determine staff costs, overhead costs, and information resource costs for each program. Once prepared, the program budget provides a clear picture of the costs of each library program. When funds are added to the budget, one can see where they will be placed, and when funds are cut, the staff, the funding authority, and the public can see what is being cut. More and more libraries are moving toward the program format because it provides a much better indicator of what their priorities are and what they cost. If local government requires a line item budget, and many still do, it is relatively easy to combine the line item budgets of the library's programs and produce one. Because the program budget is a much better indicator of what the library is and does, the librarian often prepares two budget presentations, one to meet the funding agency's requirement and one to describe what the library does.

The Planning (Performance) Program

The planning program budgeting system (PPBS), more commonly called the performance budget, adds an additional step to the program budget. That additional step provides a means of showing how each program contributes to the overall library goals and objectives. Using output measures, such as numbers of online searches, number of attendees at a program, or circulation figures, one can see what has been accomplished with the funds allocated to a program. Although it is relatively easy to calculate output measures showing tasks that have been completed, materials circulated, or programs attended, it is much more difficult to gather information to support library outcomes.

Determining how a library has enriched the lives of individuals by providing health information, helping the community understand issues of global warming, or raising awareness of demographic changes in the community is more difficult. As funding agencies move more and more toward requiring evidence of what the dollars they have allocated to the library and to other services do, performance measures become an ever more important tool for explaining the value of library service.

Budget Approval Cycle

The budget cycle has five components: preparation, submission, approval by the funding agency, execution, and audit. For each step there are formalized procedures, and models have been devised to carry them out. Budget preparation, as has been noted, is a year-round activity, beginning with the review of existing goals and objectives as stated in the long-range plan. Once revisions of the goals and objectives based on the level of progress to date have been made, and a general statement of anticipated costs has been developed, the next step is to prepare the budget.

The budget year may not coincide with the calendar year. The federal government's budget year begins October 1; state budget years begin July 1, April 1, or some other date. The library's budget year begins the same date as the budget year of the funding agency, which begins the same date as the state's budget year. Using the appropriate date as the beginning of the budget year, library planners develop a calendar to guide their budget activities during the year. Dates assigned to each activity should be in sync with internal activities and in compliance with external requirements and guidelines. Libraries that receive federal funds, such as those for a special project, will need to set a separate calendar that begins October 1 for those funds. Should funds come from another source, such as a foundation that has a different calendar, a separate calendar for reporting will be necessary.

Following from review of goals and objectives and an analysis of internal and external data, the budget director prepares estimate forms for each library department so that department heads can make their requests for support in a consistent manner. Once the departmental requests have been completed, they are consolidated into a single budget, which is the budget estimate for the following year. The next step is to hold departmental hearings so that department heads can discuss their budget estimates, justify costs, and present their cases for funding their departments and programs at a particular level. Part of the discussion is the consideration of entering into or renewing consortium agreements to negotiate better prices for goods and services than would be possible if individual libraries contracted with providers.

Based on these discussions, the budget is revised and sent to the library director, who reviews and if necessary revises it with the assistance of the budget director. The budget is then sent to the board of trustees, who review it and have the opportunity to make changes. And then it goes to the municipal, county, or other government agency of which the library is a part. The next step is usually a closed hearing, during which library representatives are given the opportunity to discuss their budget and the ways in which the library continues to provide benefits and services to the community. The brief budget presentation includes goals and objectives, the previous year's accomplishments, new programs proposed, programs to be deleted and why, and a brief statement of what is requested to provide even better service..

The library is but one of numerous departments making their case for funding, and officials appreciate a brief and to-the-point statement. An open hearing, in which the overall budget is discussed, provides citizens with the opportunity to support, object to, or otherwise comment on the budget. Hearings, both private and public, are partly informational, partly political, and to a lesser extent financial. How librarians present their cases and how they are received by officials and the public is particularly important. Although libraries are appreciated and seen as important to the community, when allocations are made, requests for libraries are typically considered after police, fire, health care, and other services have received allocations .A final review of the budget takes place, and it is approved based on anticipated revenues. This cycle, often called the "management control cycle," is a continuous process beginning with planning and budgeting, going on to operating and accounting, and ending with reporting and analysis and then back to planning.

Throughout the year, the library's budget officer regularly prepares reports indicating how funds are being spent, and at the end of the fiscal year a summary statement is prepared indicating both financial data and a statement of the extent to which goals and objectives have been met. On a regular basis, not necessarily annual, an outside auditor will review records to determine that appropriate accounting principles and practices have been followed. Regular audits ensure that the library conforms to accepted standards and is appropriately accounting for funds entrusted to it.

Prudent library administrators make a continuous and consistent effort to represent the library, its purpose, and its needs, and to highlight its accomplishments as they work year-round with local government agencies to maintain a good working relationship with those who make decisions about the library.

Planning and Budgeting in a Growth and No-Growth Environment

Depending on the state of the economy, planning and budgeting may take place in a growth environment, in which there is an expectation that resources will be available to develop the library and its programs. When the economy is strong, tax revenue allows the necessary resources to cover new acquisitions, programming, and perhaps even new staff and new facilities. At other times, the librarian is faced with a no-growth environment.

When the economy is not strong, fewer taxes are collected and fewer resources are available to support the community. Programs may be cut and even be eliminated. Library planners cannot wait until resources are cut to make decisions. They must identify core activities as part of the planning process so that when cuts occur, they will know what those core activities are and will make decisions to protect them. Library planners, as part of the planning process, should also identify programs that can be made smaller, be put on hold, or if necessary be eliminated, should a budget crunch occur. These decisions require that the library planners be aware of other libraries and information resources and services in the community and how they interact. If cuts are necessary, a coordinated effort that recognizes how and where librarians can collaborate to support one another is essential.

DATA ANALYSIS

As planning has increasingly become a team activity that involves more and more members of the library staff, there is an increased need for staff to be knowledgeable about data needed for decision making and the ways in which they can be used. Library data are available from library records and from the library's management information systems. These are raw data and must be analyzed to answer questions such as how much it costs to process a book, answer a reference question, or read a story to a child as part of a children's program. A number of techniques are available that take data and turn them into usable information. As one develops a budget for library activities, it is important to know how to establish cost.

Unit Costs

Cost is defined as a monetary measure of the amount of resources needed for a particular purpose. Unit cost is the amount of resources used to produce one unit for a particular purpose; that may include how many units can be produced and may also include how much time a staff member spends completing a task.

To calculate unit cost for unit production, one divides the total cost of producing a specified number of units by the number of units produced. The resulting figure tells us the average cost of production per unit:

$$\text{Unit Cost} = \frac{\text{Cost of Producing N Units}}{N}$$

Using the unit cost, for example, of processing a book in year one, and then calculating the unit cost for year two, one can see if the cost has increased during that time. One may also compare the unit cost of processing a book in one's own library to the unit cost in another library to see if one's costs are in line with those of similar institutions. One may also vary the ways in which a book is processed to see if there is a less costly way to do so.

Personnel as Unit Costs

In developing unit costs, it is very important to include all costs attached to the activity. Because information service is highly labor intensive, personnel costs are usually the largest component of unit costs. In calculating the salary component, it is necessary to factor in both wages and benefits. An individual is paid for approximately 40 hours of work. Because vacation time, sick days, and time during the day allocated to non-job-related activities come out of the 40-hour week, a more accurate figure is arrived at by calculating the actual hours worked in a week plus benefits. The actual productive hourly cost may be as much as a third higher than the hourly wage when these considerations are factored in. If the hourly wage of a children's specialist is $45.00 per hour, the resulting wage may be closer to $55.00 per hour. One then adds in the cost of training, supervision, meetings with vendors, staff meetings, and other tasks not directly related to working with children.

To obtain the above data, cost studies are conducted in which each staff member accounts for how he or she spends the work day. Being asked to report on activities for each 15-minute segment of time over a specified period, usually a week, is time consuming, and staff often resent having to do this. They may assume that they are suspected by their supervisor of not working hard enough and not doing their jobs. It is very important to discuss the purpose of the study and to assure them that there are benefits to them of the study. The time study may show that a staff member has been given too many tasks to complete within the time frame or may be completing tasks that could be assigned to someone at a lower pay grade. It may also show that the job description is out of date and may need adjustment.

Depreciation as Unit Cost

Depreciation is another important component of unit cost. All equipment, desks, workstations, and copiers, among other things, have a usable life span and at some time will need to be replaced. Although furniture has a relatively long life span, workstations and other electronic equipment have a brief usable span. For accounting purposes, a percentage of the replacement cost of the item should be part of the cost of performing the task for which it is used. Several depreciation models exist, the most common of which are straight line depreciation and declining balance depreciation. The simplest is straight line depreciation, which is calculated in the following fashion:

$$\text{Annual amount} = \frac{\text{purchase price minus salvage value of item when replaced}}{\text{number of years between time item purchased and when replaced}}$$

For example, a copy machine when new cost $2,400 and is scheduled to be replaced in three years. Assuming a salvage value of $300, annual depreciation will be $700. With straight line depreciation, one makes the assumption that the copier will decrease in value an equal amount each year, when in fact it may decline faster in the first year. Using declining balance depreciation is useful with items such as automobiles, which decline rapidly in the first year and then depreciation levels off. In neither case is inflation factored in, nor is the fact that with advances in technology, yesterday's copier may have cost more than a new model. Costs of replacing equipment or book stock usually will be higher than the original cost. Given these variables, depreciation figures are best seen as estimates.

Other Program Costs

Additional program costs include the cost of leased equipment and supplies, the building's replacement costs, rental and any off-site storage, and administrative costs. If the program under study uses any percentage of the equipment, the percentage of cost applied to the study will reflect the percentage of use. Subscription services and any parts of services under contract would be treated in the same fashion. Costs of supplies (e.g., pens, papers, disks) and the cost of storing them are added.

The building or part of the building occupied by the program is part of the cost. Per-square-foot costs of the building are usually calculated annually and are used for a number of purposes. They include replacement cost, assuming a 25-year-life span; insurance, maintenance, and heating and cooling. If the building is rented or leased, per-square-foot costs are based on annual rental and any costs not in the rental agreement. For the unit cost of an activity, multiply the square foot costs by the number of square feet used by the program. One of the reasons for off-site storage of little-used materials is that per-square-foot cost of housing a large collection may become a burden to the library.

Administrative overhead includes salaries of administrators, staff training, public relations, and other activities of benefit to the entire library. A percentage of the administrative overhead is assigned to each program depending on the size of the program and whether or not any special training or public relations support has been provided.

Fixed and Variable Costs

Another component of calculating unit costs is to identify fixed and variable costs. Fixed costs are those costs that do not change regardless of the amount of use of that service or item. For example, heating and cooling the library costs the same amount regardless of whether one or one hundred individuals are in the building. Variable costs change depending on the number of people using a service or the number of activities involved. If a trainer charges a flat fee to train staff in the use of a new database, it is a fixed cost; but if the trainer's charge is based on the number of individuals attending the session, that is a variable cost.

Cost Accounting

Cost accounting is the identification of the cost of providing a specific service. Although its focus is on financial data, the process of cost accounting is a management tool for the entire library. Its purpose is to link effectiveness to cost so that one can make comparisons between and among similar activities. This information allows the library manager to select the best approach. In the for-profit sector, studies to determine the actual cost of programs and services are a regular part of the budgeting and accounting process. This type of study was resisted for a long time by many in the nonprofit sector, who argued that one could not put a price on the interaction between client and service provider. It became increasingly necessary for those in the nonprofit sector to determine the cost of their services, and though the attitude toward cost accounting has often not changed, the reality is that studies must be undertaken and the results factored into the budget.

The process of conducting a cost analysis includes the identification of all current library activities, which are then grouped into major task categories. Broad functions are then identified. Tasks are assigned to appropriate functions. Organizational units for which costs are calculated are identified. Production units, in which volumes added is the measure, are defined. A study by Mitchell identified four units within the library:[2] the processing production unit, in which volumes added was the basic unit; the reference service production unit, in which the average time taken to respond to each traditional query was the measure; the bibliographic instruction production unit, for which the number of individuals instructed was the measure; and the circulation production unit, in which the cost per unit circulated was the measure. Although this study used an academic library, the units and the methodology work well for the public library. Methods to accomplish cost analysis change, but the basic units do not.

An additional benefit of cost analysis is that when one group's activities are listed under their tasks, it is quickly evident if the same or similar task is performed differently in different places. Tasks may change because of personal preference or changing needs. The initial description and expectation for the task may be too theoretical to translate into performance. Looking at work from the level of the task and how well the task description relates to reality is a basic building block for position descriptions and the possible need to revise them. One can also determine work flow patterns in the library by this type of analysis. Because approximately two-thirds of the budget of the library is personnel costs, any information that can be gained to utilize staff more efficiently is useful. If tasks can be redesigned to have fewer steps, be completed in less time, and use fewer resources, savings can be realized and the library will, at the same time, operate more efficiently.

Cost Benefit Analysis

The purpose of cost benefit analysis is "to determine the economic feasibility of developing alternatives to the current system. It insures that the user receives the best possible return for the investment."[3] Using cost benefit analysis, one can identify the cost of a program or activity and determine its benefit. One can look at different program options and determine the benefit of each alternative in relation to the cost. Although the cost figures are objective and can be supported by fact, the benefit aspect is subjective and cannot be assigned a direct dollar value. When a funding agency asks if "the cost of a children's program is worth the money," the librarian can provide dollar figures for cost but cannot quantify in the same way the learning that results or the pleasure experienced by the child. Despite this, cost benefit analysis does have an important role in making decisions about programs and activities.

Financial decisions have an impact on the way the library is seen by the public. If insufficient funds are available to maintain the building and grounds, the library may look unkempt. The way it looks will affect the way it is viewed by those who work there and those who use it. How rapidly the library moves ahead technologically and how current its collections are demonstrate to the public how forward looking and innovative the library staff is. Financial decisions not only affect how the public views the library, they also affect staff morale. The staff member who has worked long and hard to develop a new program or revamp an existing program to enhance its value will respond positively when additional funds or other resources are found to carry out the changes. When library staff recognize funding allocations as being wise decisions, they will be supportive. If they see allocations as being made to support pet projects or based on favoritism, they should and will object. Staff satisfaction or dissatisfaction impacts not only staff attitude toward the library and perhaps one another, it also impacts how they serve the public. Data that support funding decisions should be available to and shared with staff, and at times stakeholders, so that they understand the rationale for decisions. The extent to which staff perceive that funding decisions are made fairly and based on good business practice will affect the way in which they view the library administration. One of the measures of the library's value to the community is in the amount of funding it receives. Within the library, the value of a particular program is assessed by staff based on its level of support.

Information service results are largely intangible (quality of information, level of intellectual effort expended, uses of the information, and users' satisfaction with both the information and the service), and are therefore difficult to measure in dollar figures. But it is important that the library use dollar figures as one way to measure this and other services as an input to setting priorities. When one measures the cost of, for example, e.g. information services, children's services, or outreach services, they may appear to be much too costly for the benefit obtained. It is at this point that one looks at the social, educational, economic, or other benefits to society and determines that the program benefits are of sufficient value to continue the program. An example is health information programs, which are present in many public libraries. Their benefit to the health of the community, though not easily measurable in dollar figures, is positive, given the value to the individual user of the information gained. Another example is remedial education. Although the costs of remedial education are high, the cost of a person who cannot function in society because of the lack of an education is much higher.

Part of the discussion of cost benefit is to look at the private and social costs of an activity,[4] differentiated thus: a private cost is what a person or organization gives to receive a good or service; a social cost is what society must give up to permit the individual to receive a good or service. As an example, the cost of a DVD to the consumer may be equivalent to the cost of producing, transporting, and selling the DVD. Here the consumer pays the entire cost. Federal health care programs are subsidized by society, and the consumer pays only a part of the cost. Libraries are social costs in that they are subsidized by taxes and the user pays little or nothing for the service. This is an extension of the definition of the library as a public good: library service is paid for by society to enhance the social environment.

Benefits are measured by the willingness to pay. Although there is little information on what society or the individual is willing to give up so that library service will be available, one can gain a fair idea by looking at the funding priority level of the library at budget time. The community may place a high value on libraries, but when it is confronted with the need to decide who gets the money, the library may lose out to fire and police protection. When fees are charged for library services, use of the services typically drops sharply. In developing his cost model, Mason indicated that it is difficult to separate the value of the service that provides information from the value of the information itself.[5] He concluded that there is no way to measure the actual social benefits of either information or information services, although it is generally accepted that those benefits exist.

Public library service, like public education, is a collective good that, once available, is available to everyone in the local tax area. Everyone in the tax area pays for all locally supported services. Some groups, such as the middle income middle class, use the library more often that other groups. Other groups, by their choice, do not use the library at all. Some benefit more from one service than from another, but all have equal access to the services. What they do or do not use is their choice.

Cost Effectiveness

Whereas cost benefit is used to measure the benefit of a particular activity or product to an individual, an organization, or society and relate this benefit to the actual cost, cost effectiveness is used to measure the extent to which the objectives of the library are met. For example, if the head of reference is concerned about the number of reference questions asked and answered and the cost of each, the cost effective approach would be to increase the number of reference interactions and reduce the unit cost. The cost benefit approach would pay greater attention to the types of reference interaction to ensure that there was a high quality of satisfaction on the part of both the librarian and the user with the service performed. Then, if that quality could be maintained or enhanced at a lower cost, changes in the interaction would be implemented. Cost effectiveness is an objective statement that can be supported by data. When it is used in a situation in which individuals interact, it should be tempered with an awareness of the benefit of the activity.

Model Building

A model is defined as a simple version of a complex reality. Because libraries and library services are complex organizations, it is often helpful to build a model of the library services so that one can visualize the major components and how they fit together or do not fit together. When one designs a model, only the major components are identified, so it is relatively easy to see how they are organized. Major components of the library include circulation services, reference services, and children's services, among others. Once secondary components such as interlibrary loan or specialized research services are set aside, it is fairly easy to see how the major units are organized and interact. One can as a later step add in the secondary elements. Development of models is a way of educating staff about the interaction of different units. It is also a good way to see how a new interaction between/among units might play out. To an extent, the model is an analog for the library itself, which may make complex activities easier to understand. The model may be in the form of a narrative, a matrix, a flow chart, or another type of diagram. When software for model building is used, it is possible to manipulate the variables in the model and see what happens when one changes one or more variables.

Cost Behavior Analyses

One uses cost behavior analysis to project cost behavior to future activities. If library planners want to investigate the possibility of opening a branch in a currently unserved neighborhood, they will need to ask the following questions. What is the likely cost? What are the sources of funds to build and equip the branch? For how many years will the proposed branch meet community needs before it will need to be expanded? Planners will need to conduct a demographic study of the community and project client needs. Is it a young community with current and future needs for children and young adult services? Is it a retirement community with needs for services to a mature population? What are the community trends and likely changes?

In addition to profiling potential users, it will be necessary to project the cost of services to be provided. Software is available that allows planners to input current costs, current demographics, and a list of services and their costs that are projected to be needed on day one of the new branch. Using this information, it is possible to anticipate expected first-year costs. By using first-year anticipated costs and seeing how they may change due to inflation and other variables, one can project the costs of the branch in future years. Libraries tend to manage their activities based on past performance rather than on future projections.

> If libraries are to do the best job of managing information in the public interest, they must know the costs of strategies designed to pass on this information, they must be prepared to identify, measure, and control costs so that the results they want can be afforded, and the quantity and quality of information they believe is appropriate to their clientele is available given the financial resources available.[6]

FINANCIAL CONTROL

The final step in the financial planning cycle is financial control. Reporting library expenditures and accounting for how funds entrusted to the public library have been used serve a number of purposes: political, financial, and evaluative. Documents prepared to respond to reporting requirements are used to evaluate, modify, and refine the library's long-range plan as represented by the budget, which sets the stage for the next planning/budgeting cycle.

The Reporting System

Program budgeting and performance budgeting were designed to improve the way in which resources are allocated and managed. Each of these formats is backed by a long-range plan from which the annual budget derives. It lists programs and services, provides an estimate of those programs and services, and develops line item costs for each. Evaluation of programs and services is built into the system. Once the funding agency approves the budget and allocates funds, the library will set up its books for the next year. The financial management system is set up to keep track of expenditures and ensure that funds are being spent for the purposes indicated in the budget. It is also used to maintain control of expenditures and facilitate evaluation. Data from the management system may be used to modify the budget if expenditures in one area exceed budgeted amounts or if, because of economic problems, the amount budgeted for the library is cut. Data from the financial management system are printed out on a regular basis and shared with department heads, trustees, and others responsible for the fiscal health of the library. The format and content of the reports may vary depending on the audience, but in all instances must be accurate, clearly written, and easily understood.

Regardless of whether they deal with for-profit or nonprofit organizations, accounting systems have similar functions and are regulated by standards responsible for uniform accounting practices, such as the Financial Accounting Standards Board or the American Institute of Certified Public Accountants. The emphasis in application of the standards to nonprofits differs from that for the for-profit sector. A nonprofit is" an economic entity that provides without profit to the owners a services beneficial to society and that is financed by equity interests that cannot be sold or traded by individuals or profit seeking entities."[7] Public libraries fall into the category of organizations that are "involuntarily supported by government entities." Decisions made by those governing the public library are intended to meet the needs of the community, and the function of the reporting system is to keep the public informed about how resources are used and the results.

Although accounting principles have been published for reporting by several types of nonprofits and are fairly consistent, state statutes governing reporting are less so. Some states have no practices written into law or practices inconsistent with those approved by national accounting organizations. The federal government makes available audit guidelines to be used in reporting the use of federal funds. Because of this mix of reporting directives, a number of non-profits may have financial systems that do not follow approved standards. If concerned about whether or not reporting standards in the library are appropriate, it is useful to hire a certified public accountant who has experience with non-profits to review processes.

Users of the Reporting System

Those who review annual reports, regardless of the type of report, are interested in knowing how money was used and what was achieved. In designing or adopting accounting and reporting systems, it is important to make information easily and clearly available. It is possible to mask expenditures in a cleverly prepared annual report, but this activity benefits no one and when detected can ruin confidence in the organization.

Tax-supported organizations such as the public library are required to complete standardized reporting forms. These forms are filled out by every unit of local government that receives funding. The forms make it easier for the municipality or county to aggregate data, but they may include categories that do not apply to the library and may omit categories important to describing library activity. The forms may not have been updated for some time and may not reflect expenditure lines for technology or for services not available a decade ago. Several categories may be lumped under one heading, such as books, with no place to record expenditures for periodicals, DVDs, and other information formats. The income section may have a category for government grants but not for gifts. It is not possible to present an accurate picture of library expenditures when items are forced into slots that are not descriptive of the content. An answer is to complete the reports required by local government and then prepare a second report that accurately describes what was spent. This latter report may be used to inform both library staff and the community about library activities.

Regardless of the format of the report and the intended audience, each report contains similar information, beginning with an introductory section that describes the library and how it reports, continuing with a financial report that provides summaries of operating budgets for prior years so that one may compare current income and expenditures over an extended period, and including a statistical section covering income and expenditures from all sources, changes in levels of support, and the degree to which support meets any stated standards.

External groups who are policy makers, such as the city manager, mayor, or board of trustees, need general information on the overall health of the library. What was accomplished during the year with the library's allocation? What was deferred because of lack of funding? What important programs could be provided, if additional funds were available? These are knowledgeable individuals, and they anticipate receiving information in measurable terms. These stakeholders expect to receive brief reports that include information needed for decision making.

Library management needs the same information as well as detailed information on the cost of daily operations. Each department head, in addition to the overall report, needs specific information on how resources were used in that department and what the results were. The reporting activity is part of the evaluation process promoted by program and performance budgeting and serves as a building block for the next budget cycle. The director and administrative staff's report provides an overall picture of the library's operations, how funds were used, and what was achieved. This information is useful for overall planning and monitoring of services. Information that reflects the size of the collection, number of workstations, and current condition of the building is also used for insurance purposes.

Taxpayers, library patrons, and those who do business with libraries, such as jobbers and contractors, have a right to know how responsible the library is as a steward of public funds and what the community has received from the library in the previous year. One of the ways in which the library regularly demonstrates its ability and desire to serve the public is through its annual reports. These reports vary greatly in the way in which the information is displayed, often depending on the particular constituency receiving the report, but similar information is included, such as the number of people served, the kinds of service provided, the size and composition of the information resource, staff expertise available to the user, and information on special programs and their success. This type of report is both report and public relations document that answers the question, "What did we get for the funds expended to support library service?" Those receiving the report then decide if they got their money's worth.

An example of this is the use of value calculators, which are appearing on library Web sites. Various services provided by the public library are listed, next to which the library user indicates the number of times the individual or a family member uses that service. The retail value of the service is calculated, and a dollar figure representing the value of library service to the individual or family is calculated. An excellent example of the value calculator is that used by the Chelmsford Public Library in Chelmsford, MA (www.chelmsfordlibrary/org/library_info/calculator.html).

ACCOUNTING

Accounting is the technical aspect of recording quantitative data about income and expenditures of the library, a way of recording its assets and liabilities over time. It is "an information system for maintaining financial records of an organization and for communicating significant fiscal events both within and without the organization."[8] Definitions of accounting systems follow:

- *Financial accounting* is a kind of score keeping that tracks where the money comes from and where it goes. It is the basis for developing reports. The following terms, some of which have already been mentioned in this chapter, are regularly used by accountants.

- *Cost accounting* is the process of determining the cost of a product, service, or activity. It is used in a number of ways: for budgeting, comparison with standards, cost analysis, and general comparisons with actual and historical costs.

- *Historical cost* indicates the cost of an item or service at the time it was purchased for use. Historical cost is the figure one uses to record assets and expenditures.

- *Standard cost* is the identification of what the cost of a product or service should be. Standard cost may be determined through extensive study of the cost of a product or service or may be an informed estimate.

- *Unit cost* is the cost of providing a specific product or service. It is the most common way of expressing cost.

Accrual and Cash Accounting

Accrual accounting is a way to report both liabilities, including accounts payable and assets, as well as cash. Accrual accounting provides a more accurate picture of the library's assets and liabilities than does cash accounting, which reports cash only. In accrual accounting, once an item is ordered and a purchase order signed or a contract for service signed, an encumbrance is placed next to the appropriate line in the budget. Because the public library is tax supported, and tax-supported organizations are expected to pay for goods and services during the year in which they are encumbered, encumbrances are expected to be paid during the fiscal year.

Encumbrances against the budget are classified as liabilities. Long-term expenditure activities such as upgrading technology or building programs are typically recorded elsewhere. Short-term liability is recorded in the annual budget, and long-term liability appears in the capital budget.

Rules vary regulating the extent to which libraries and other-tax supported agencies may save (carry over) funds from one budget year to another to purchase expensive items one cannot buy within one year's budget. Because fiscal policy in many government units states that expenditures in a year must equal income, and tax rates are set with that policy in mind, it may be required that all funds be spent in that year. It has become evident that this policy hampers the ability to budget and pay for expensive items such as new software and hardware or new furniture, and the policy has been relaxed in a number of states. However, there is usually a percentage of the budget, often about 10 percent, beyond which one cannot carry over funds.

Depreciation Accounting

How does one take into account the general wear and tear on buildings, equipment, and other items that do not need to be replaced on a short-term basis? Depreciation accounting is the process used to do this. Because nonprofit agencies provide services rather than making a profit, some experts say that depreciation accounting, which is a way to charge the use of fixed assets against anticipated revenues, is not appropriate for them. Because nonprofits are seen as operating on a year-to-year basis, some say that depreciation accounting is pointless. Those who support depreciation accounting in nonprofits say that there must be a way in which to report the organization's assets accurately and to develop an orderly way of replacing equipment. If depreciation accounting is not part of formal reporting, library planners should maintain an informal record of depreciation and planned replacement.

Accounting and reporting are based on the principle of historic cost (cost at time of purchase) and do not reflect the effects of inflation on current value of assets or on purchasing power. One may approach the differences between historical cost and current cost in a number of ways: adjust historical dollar amounts to reflect changes in general price levels, adjust in relation to the current price of specific items, or record the current price of specific items and adjust for changes in the general price level.

Fund Accounting

Libraries receive funds from numerous sources in addition to tax revenues, which are their major source of funding. These include gifts and grants, income from investments, and income from book sales and other fundraising activities, all of which are voluntary contributions, and fines and fees, which are involuntary contributions. Grants from federal and state agencies are another source of funding. All funds have specific requirements governing their use. Some are to be used for specific purposes, whereas others are to be invested and the earnings used to support specific activities. Each source of income must be listed along with any limitations on use, for example, a gift to support a specific program. The library is legally and morally committed to spend funds according to the specified use. Each special fund has separate records of income and expenditure, and its identity is maintained at all times. If no limitations on use of the income exist, those funds go into the general operating budget. Funds received from federal and state agencies are handled according to the requirements of the grant.

The overall income statement for the library consists of two sections, one identifying funds that go into the general operating budget, such as tax revenue allocations, monies from library fund-raising activities, fees, and fines, and the second listing all special purpose funds and any income derived from them during the period covered by the income statement. If the library has a capital fund, it is maintained separately from the operating budget, and within the capital fund, any special funds and allocations are identified.

Accountability

The board of trustees, the public library director, and other library managers are accountable to local government and to other government agencies that provide funding for the library and are required to comply with all laws, regulations, and policies. Honesty in the use of funds and efficiency in how they are used to benefit the community are hallmarks of the successful library director and staff. Libraries are also measured by level of performance, and measures for performance are typically part of the long-range planning process. Three types of performance indicators are involved: operations, impact, and social. *Operations indicators* or *output measures* state in nonfinancial terms what was produced with the money spent. Here one uses number of reference questions answered, number of books and other materials processed and circulated, and number of programs and attendance. Program indicators address the extent to which the library has met a public need. As combinations of both operations indicators and measures of accomplishment, they have both quantifiable and qualitative elements. The availability of a job line and assistance in resume writing in the public library may have increased the ability of individuals to find jobs, which has improved their quality of life; this is an example of a measure of accomplishment. Social indicators are qualitative measures and deal with changes in society because of a library program.

In one community, a number of library programs were aimed at looking at the relationships among community groups as they had or had not changed because of the civil rights movement. Community members were invited to discuss their views, they interviewed those who had been involved in marches and other activities, and because of these and related programs, a dialog began to take shape and people began to talk with one another about how to change the community. This is the kind of social change a library can foster. And this is the best kind of accountability.

FUNDING SOURCES

The public library receives the majority of its budget from local government sources. The library chartered to serve a town or city receives its budget from the town or city. In many states, libraries serve the county, and in this instance, the county is the primary funding source. Because many public libraries, particularly those in the northeast, were established by their communities, there is a considerable diversity in how they are organized and the "community" they serve. Some libraries are a department of local government (e.g., Oak Ridge, TN), some are chartered to serve all or part of the community or a special district, and others have a more interesting history. For example, the Hyde Park (NY) Free Library was chartered to serve the Hyde Park Fire and Water District. Both rely on local government for the bulk of their funding. Additional sources of funding include state funding, funding from federal sources, and funding from private sources. In addition, some libraries receive fines and fees for service. Many public libraries and their Friend of Libraries also have fund-raising activities, including used book sales, arts and craft sales, and similar activities.

Funding from Local Government Sources

Public library funding is essentially a local responsibility. Although there has been discussion by some legislators and librarians about the possibility of state and federal agencies taking on a greater share of the funding, the public library is and will doubtless continue to be funded at the local level. It is therefore very important that the public library director know the local tax structure, those responsible for the local budgeting process, and the budget priorities of local government officials. In suburban areas where there is interdependence of services between areas and/or with a municipality, the library director needs a good understanding of the bigger picture. Support of the public library is a local decision related to the community's ability to pay, its attitude toward library service, and the role taken by community leaders and librarians in making the library central to the community.

Local taxing powers are granted by the state, and most local government units have the right to tax property. The rationale is that local property owners should be responsible for supporting the services of their community because they are the beneficiaries. Other taxes such as sales tax, income tax, and special assessments may be granted to localities by the state and may also be rescinded. Any limitations on taxing powers enacted by the state, such as exemptions for educational or religious organizations, have to be complied with at the local level. Over the past century or more, property taxes have been the major source of local government income. They have also been in constant decline while sales and income tax revenues have increased. Because of the inequity in availability of property taxes, there is a great diversity in the level of support and therefore the level of service provided by public libraries throughout the United States. In those areas in which more than one public library provides service within a county, local public libraries may band together to provide services and may ask for support from county government. This is one of the ways in which libraries work together to provide a better resource base.

Funding from State Sources

Not until 1956, with the enactment of the Library Services Act (LSA) by the federal government, was there much state involvement in public library funding. LSA funding stimulated state-level efforts to develop and plan for library service. Prior to this, some states would give small grants to libraries, usually to spur them to prepare required annual reports. Public libraries were low on the priority list of state agencies, and without federal stimulus, they would continue to be so. To obtain federal funds for libraries, states were required to have a state-level agency responsible for library development and a long-range plan for libraries. Regional agencies took shape within the states with various types of governance structure and services. For a number of states, the governance structure and the long-range plan have served as a means of allocating state as well as federal funds.

States may provide substantial direct support to local libraries or may develop systems of public libraries within a region and support the local library through the system with services paid for by the state. To receive state funding, local libraries must meet certain requirements, such as meeting minimum local funding requirements, being open a certain number of hours, having a required level of professional staff, being willing to share resources with other libraries, and filing annual reports.

State funding for local libraries is intended to meet state-level priorities, such as resource sharing. In many states, the resources of a local agency may not be used by people in a jurisdiction whose taxes did not purchase them. This means that materials purchased by a local library cannot be used outside the taxing area; but if state funding is involved, materials are not limited to one community. State resources make it possible to provide multijurisdictional activities and thus provide regional solutions to information access. In addition to funds specifically allocated for library services, state legislation in support of other activities may include library support. For example, each state has an arts council or similar agency that is responsible for developing programs in the arts. Part of the funding comes from the National Endowment for the Arts and the rest from state funds. Library programs may qualify for support for activities such as lecture series or other community programs. With few exceptions, library programs are often not well supported at the state level. Though they have few enemies, they have few vocal friends. Legislators do not place information services to the community very high on their priority lists. When extra money is available, libraries may receive some of it, but when funds are limited, libraries are among the last agencies to be considered.

Funding from Federal Sources

Funding from federal sources has been available since the mid-1950s, and though minimal (1 to 2 percent), it has had a major impact on planning and the development of innovative services. Beginning with the Library Services Act (1956) and continuing to the present with the Library Services and Technology Act, federal funding has been used to extend public library service to the many unserved areas of the country by instituting statewide planning, establishing cooperative networks, and encouraging resource sharing. Today, most of the federal funding for public libraries is distributed through the Institute of Museum and Library Services (IMLS) to each state, which then uses those funds to support programs of importance to libraries throughout that state.

The American Library Association (ALA), through its Washington Office, serves as the lobbying arm of ALA and keeps Congress informed of the importance of libraries and the need to fund them at an appropriate level. ALA provides up-to-date information on funding for library programs and programs that include education, the humanities, the arts, and many other important societal functions. Though funding for many programs that directly or indirectly support libraries was severely affected during the period 2000–2008, the Library Services and Technology Act has had increases in some of its programs.

The best way to stay informed about federally funded programs of concern to libraries is to access ALA's Web site on a regular basis and check its latest information on federal funding. You will find listed not only library programs but also programs in support of reading, the Library of Congress, the National Endowment for the Arts, and the National Endowment for the Humanities. This Web site is a MUST for anyone concerned about federal funding for libraries and interested in keeping up to date about current trends.

Funding from Private Sources

For the past century, more than 26,000 private foundations with a combined wealth of many billions of dollars have served as a source of funding for programs and activities directed toward the improvement of the quality of life. Much of that wealth is in a limited number of foundations, including the Gates Foundation, the Carnegie Foundation, the Rockefeller Foundation, and the Ford Foundation, and approximately two-thirds of the foundations have assets of less than $250,000. Each foundation has specific interests that it will fund. As foundation assets are largely intangible and depend on the stock market and the state of the economy, funds available at any one time will vary. Nevertheless, foundations carry out a wide range of activities and provide opportunities to conduct research, institute programs, and carry out other activities to enrich the community for which tax dollars are not available

Many foundations, particularly the smaller ones, focus on a region; others focus on a social issue such as AIDS research, educational improvement, or research dealing with global warming. In addition to being aware of the purpose of a foundation, its financial resources, and the state of the economy, those seeking funds should be aware of any patterns of giving. A number of national foundations have a pattern of giving that includes libraries. These include the Carnegie Foundation, the W.W. Kellogg Foundation, and the Gates Foundation. National foundations tend to support national issues such as access to information rather than supporting a particular library. Library managers and policy makers will find The Foundation Center Web site an invaluable online resource to learn about foundations, their interests, and their resources (www.foundationcenter.org/).

Businesses and industrial corporations often set up foundations within the communities in which they are located as a means of enhancing their image and supporting the community. These foundations tend not to have endowments and funds available vary from year to year, depending on their annual profit margin. Maintaining good relations with these entities is an important part of the role of library managers and fund-raisers.

Bond Issues

In certain situations, such as the need to build a new library, make additions to the existing structure, or invest heavily in technology, library trustees may wish to float a bond issue. When they ask the community to finance long-term projects, they are asking for a direct voter response about how valuable the library is to the community. To be successful, the library must have a track record of providing excellent service to the community and show that the community values the library as an important asset. Local officials are responsive to the local economic climate and how the library enhances it. They will not support an activity, particularly the borrowing of funds, unless there is a strong reason to do so.

Laying the groundwork for a bond issue is a long-term activity. It must begin early and be planned carefully by a group representing both the library and the community. The planning group should be broadly representative of the community, and the wider the range of groups represented and the ideas presented, the more directly responsive the approach will be to the community and its needs. A bond issue requires approval by local government, but the final decision is made by the voters. To get voters to support a bond issue through their votes requires a great deal of effort. When voters appreciate the importance of the bond issue to the community, they will get out and vote.

Other Sources

Other sources of income include fees for service and fines. Fees may be collected from individuals not residents of the community who wish to use library resources. Fees may also be charged for specific library services that go beyond basic services. There is much discussion about which services should be fee based and which should be free. Some planners and local government officials assert that charging for specialized services will place the cost of these services on the specific user rather than on all users and will generate another revenue stream. Although there is some merit to this argument, fees for service will not solve the problem of insufficient income.

Another source of income is fines for overdue materials and payment for lost or damaged materials. In most communities, libraries are allowed to keep the fines they collect, but in others, fines are part of the general revenue of the community. A final source of revenue is fund-raising through the many community activities that may support libraries: art shows, lectures, bake sales, and other ways in which the community shows its interest in the library and its programs.

SUMMARY

Financial management is a means of bringing planning and funding together. One plans for current and future programs and allocates funds so that programs are prioritized. It also includes being aware of sources of funding, being a responsible steward of funds, and reporting regularly to funding agencies and to the public, so that there is a general understanding of how library resources are allocated and spent, and what the community has gained from the expenditure of their tax monies.

NOTES

1. Aaron Wildavsky, *The New Politics of the Budgetary Process,* 2nd ed. (New York: Harper Collins, 1992).

2. Betty Jo Mitchell, Norman E. Tannis, and Jack J. Jaffe, *Cost Analysis of Library Functions: A Total System Approach* (Greenwich, CT: JAI Press, 1978).

3. B. T. Stein, *A Cost Benefit Technique for Research and Development Based Information* (Kent, UK: Wellcome Foundation, August, 1970), 7.

4. Robert M. Mason, "A Lower Bound Cost Benefit Model for Information Services," *Information Processing and Management* 14 (February 1978): 71–83.

5. Ibid.

6. Helen Drinan, "Financial Management of On-Line Services, A How-to-Guide," *ONLINE* 3 (October 1979): 14–21.

7. Emerson O. Henke, *Accounting for Nonprofit Organizations* (Belmont, CA: Wadsworth, 1977), 1.

8. United Way of America, *Accounting and Financial Reporting: A Guide for United Way and Not-for-Profit Human Resources Organizations* (Alexandria, VA: United Way of America, 1974), 3.

ADDITIONAL READINGS

Gerding, Stephanie Rawlins, and Pamela H. Mackellar. *Grants for Libraries: A How-to-do-It Manual and CD-ROM for Librarians.* New York: Neal Schuman, 2007.

Hasperslaugh, Phillipe, Tomo Noda, and Faras Boulos. "Managing for Value: It's Not Just About the Numbers." *Harvard Business Review* 79 (July–August 2001): 65–73.

Irvin, Hal, and Rosalind Meyers. "Can Your Auxiliary Services Compete?" *NACUBO Business Officer* 35 (May 2002): 29–31.

Matzer, John J., ed. *Practical Financial Management: New Techniques for Local Government.* Washington, DC: International Financial Managers' Association, 1984.

Prentice, Ann E. *Financial Planning for Libraries.* 2nd ed. Lanham, MD: Scarecrow Press, 1996.

Shim, Jae K., and Joel G. Siegel. *Financial Management for Nonprofits*. New York: McGraw-Hill, 1997, 358–62.

Smith, G. Stevenson. *Managerial Accounting for Libraries and Other Not-for-Profit Organizations*. 2nd ed. Chicago: American Library Association, 2002.

Swan, James. *Fundraising for Libraries: 25 Proven Ways to Get More Money for Your Library*. New York: Neal Schuman, 2002.

Turock, Betty J., and Andrea Pedolsky. *Creating a Financial Plan: A How-to-Do-It Manual for Librarians*. New York: Neal Schuman, 1992.

Chapter **16**

Into the Future

INTRODUCTION

"A library is a place to go for a reality check, a bracing dose of literature, or a true reflection of our history, whether it's a brick and mortar building constructed a century ago or a fanciful arrangement of computer codes. The librarian is the organizer, the animating spirit behind it, and the navigator. A librarians' job is to create order out of the confusion of the past, even as they enable us to blast into the future."[1]

During the latter half of the 20th century, the public library transformed itself from a relatively conservative community service into a proactive information organization that has become the community hub for accessing information in all its forms and formats and for introducing community residents to the Internet and how to use it, while continuing to fulfill its mission to bring people and information together so that every individual has the opportunity to become more informed about the world. Although at one time some thought that the public library had become an artifact of the past, the actions of forward-thinking librarians and information technology experts who envisioned the public library as the people's information center, not just in a print world but also in a virtual world, and supported by professional associations and philanthropic organizations, brought public libraries into the 21st century with new tools and new enthusiasm to fulfill their purpose.

To lead the community into the next decades, public librarians needed to understand the community they served and to be aware of its current and projected needs and interests. They needed a plan for moving forward and to become comfortable with what technology could do to support that plan and the activities it laid out.

209

Librarians also needed to believe in the possibilities before them and to reach for the future with enthusiasm. As they began to use new information technologies to manage information resources and serve increasingly diverse communities, being a librarian became one of the most exciting and forward-looking careers. Librarians know how to find and use information and now have a virtually unlimited set of tools they can use to accomplish that task in support of the community in which they live and those who inhabit it. As one library user said, "Forget about nostalgia for yesterday's public library. Librarians are now ahead of the curve."

Looking toward the future, there are numerous unanswered questions and questions yet to be asked. We are now fully immersed in the information age but are still learning how to use information to better our lives and society. Much of the world is still in the agricultural age, and the first world has yet to come to terms with how to use the tools of technology to make this a safer and more productive world for all. Librarians need to continue to identify and explore new possibilities to do what libraries have always done: bring people and information together for the benefit of society.

Technical issues are not the only issues librarians need to address. There is the issue of funding. Nearly 200 years ago, the first libraries to be publicly supported were the recipients of local tax dollars. That model, with some variations, continues to the present day. Since those early days, the public librarian has assumed a greater role in supporting community groups and individuals with their-self education and has provided additional services, such as those helping individuals find employment. The tools we now use are more varied and more expensive than they were in the mid-19th century. We need to take a careful look at the funding model for public libraries to see if it fits current needs. We have to keep abreast of the changes in the communities we serve: Who are they, what are their needs and interests, and what are our plans for serving them? Public libraries are on the fast track, and to stay there, it is necessary not only to use the best means of providing service at the least cost, but to do the homework and try out new things so that we continue to uphold that standard.

LIBRARY FUNDING

Public libraries are funded in large part by property taxes collected by local government. Typically, 70 percent of the library budget comes from this source. Other sources of income include state and federal support, often in the form of grants for specific purposes. Several philanthropic associations also include public libraries among the groups they support. Some funds are also available from programs sponsored by Friends of the Library, including the sale of used books and community events. In some communities the library is allowed to keep library fines; in others, fines go to the general fund.

Public libraries have always been among the most poorly funded public institutions. When the economy is prospering and there is enough money, libraries receive funding sufficient for their needs, but when the economy is slow, libraries typically are harder hit by budget cuts than other services supported primarily by local taxes. In the 1960s, which was a period of rapid growth and great social upheaval, followed by decades of slow growth, support for libraries and library service ranged from slow growth, to steady state, to decline.[2] It has been recognized that during periods in which the economy grows slowly and workers have difficulty finding employment, additional social and educational services are needed to support those out of work so that they can make the transition into an economy often different from the one they left. Despite the fact that public libraries assumed a large share of this responsibility, their budgets were reduced at a time of great social need.

A similar situation occurred during the 2008 economic downturn, when public libraries experienced flat or declining funding. Total public library operating expenditures tend to vary little from year to year and typically align with inflation rates (3–6 percent annually). During this period, the majority of any increases were in urban areas and suburban library systems, with little or no budget increase in budgets of libraries serving smaller communities.[3]

The Public Library Funding and Technology Access Study preliminary findings for 2009–2010 reported responses to questions about the stability of public library operating budgets from year to year. It was found that in most cases there was no increase in funding. If increases occurred, they barely kept pace with inflation.[4] In a 2009 survey of Chief Officers of State Library Agencies (COSLA) conducted by the American Library Association, a majority of state libraries reported decreases in local public libraries in the 5 to 10 percent range.[5] At the same time, 77 percent of state library agency budgets were cut, thus preventing state agencies from assisting local public libraries as much as they had in the past.

Again, decreased funding and its impact on staffing levels occurred at the same time that public library usage increased at a rapid rate. During difficult economic times, the public library provides important services to job seekers: listings of jobs, help in writing resumes, and other support. It also provides Internet access to community members, many of whom have no other access and must rely on the public library for access to and training in how to use the Internet. In addition to these rapidly expanding services, the library continues to support a variety of self-education activities, children's and young adult services, community support services, and the many other activities expected by the community.[6]

"Library funding is a result of political decisions made in an environment much broader than that of the library. Overall policy and fiscal policy are determined by citizens and their elected representatives. Voters and local, state, and federal government officials set the broad policy outlines for publicly funded institutions, including libraries."[7] It is the role of library advocacy groups to keep the community informed of the roles the public library plays and show how these activities improve the economic and educational climate.

In this environment of reduced resources and increased demand, each public service, including libraries, must reassess its programs and accompanying costs to see how far the resources can be stretched. Since the *Public Library Planning Process* became part of every public librarian's toolkit in 1980,[8] public librarians have used community data to develop long-range plans and set strategies that take into account limited support from the local tax base. Public librarians are in competition with all other locally supported services, including fire and police, and they need to make the case that the public library is also a basic service that supports the community.

Public librarians are concerned that the current funding structure for public libraries, primarily based on the local tax structure, is no longer adequate. The community expects the library to be their information resource and online access. It is either their only access or the backup access when their own search strategies are insufficient. This requires hardware; software; subscriptions to databases; and staff members with expertise in training new computer users, working with the public to help them navigate databases, designing and maintaining the library's Web site, and the many other tasks associated with quality library service.

Librarians have developed additional revenue streams, including private monies coming into the system, foundation support, and partnerships. A librarian in New England reported that though the town pays for the library building and staff, she is responsible for raising dollars for the collection, technology, and other materials. With a combination of grants, gifts, and endowments, she is able to purchase materials and support innovative programming for a rapidly changing community. Community groups have underwritten specific library programs in which they have a specific interest. For example, the Korean American community in one city donated funds for the purchase of materials in Korean. They recognized and appreciated that the library was spending money for Korean materials, but they wished to add to the amount so that Korean American residents would have access to additional resources.

Public librarians have shared information resources with other agencies in the community, for example, sharing medical information materials with a hospital library so that the patrons of each library would have added access at no additional cost. The list of collaborative efforts with the community is long and creative. In each of these activities, it is important that it is understood that the librarians do not support a particular point of view, that there are standards for additions to the collection and for programs that must be applied. Numerous philanthropic foundations support public libraries by underwriting research, supporting specific programs, or purchasing equipment.

The Bill and Melinda Gates Foundation has been instrumental in networking activities in public libraries and funding research. The W.K. Kellogg Foundation and other national and regional foundations also support libraries. The Institute of Museum and Library Services invites libraries to submit proposals for federal funding.

Though community efforts on behalf of the public library are important, one should not fund services as important as those provided by the public library on bake sales and donations. These are important added soft money resources, but the basic service must be funded as part of local government costs. New models of funding need to be devised that recognize the responsibility of the community to support the library, at least to a substantial degree. This is one of the key issues for the future.

TECHNOLOGY

Information technology in the library can be divided into two parts: the technology necessary to manage the library and the technology used to provide service. Great strides have been made in both areas. In the development and adoption of ways to manage the collection, we have gone from the date due stamp on the pencil to bar coding and now to Radio Frequency Identification (RFID), which allows the borrower, with a wave of the book, to self-check out materials. Like many business-related advances, RFID had been around for a long time before its value to libraries was seen. This technology has made circulation services much easier and more efficient.

Librarians need to learn by walking around, and not just in the library. Go to the grocery store to see how they handle inventory, go to the coffee shop to see how they handle marketing, and observe how businesses handle online purchases. Attend not only library-related conferences but also other events that showcase business applications of new and/or existing programs. Attend workshops on new uses for information technology held by other agencies in the community. Ask other agencies in local government what they are doing differently that you might try in the library. Not only does this have the potential of finding new ideas, it is also a good way to build connections for the library.

Stay current with communications technology. Considering the view that broadband Internet service is central to keeping the United States competitive and that it will gradually displace the telephone and broadcast television, how does/will the public library take advantage of this technology? As with any federal initiative that affects libraries, it is important to stay in touch with the ALA Washington Office to take advantage of its analysis of plans and initiatives that impact libraries.

The ALA Office for Information Technology Policy issues reports eight times a year that are also a very helpful means of keeping up with tech developments of importance to libraries. For example, *Fiber to the Library; How Public Libraries Can Benefit from Using Fiber Optics for Their Boadband Internet Connections*,[9] provides an overview of this technology and identifies numerous Web sites for additional information.

The New Media Consortium's Horizon Project produces an annual survey, the *Horizon Report*, is "a long-running qualitative research project that seeks to identify and describe emerging technologies likely to have a large impact on teaching, learning, research, or creative expression writing learning-focused organizations.[10] Although its primary focus is on academia, there is much that the public librarian can find useful. It is published annually and is available on the Web.

Numerous tech savvy librarians have set up blogs in which they review new technology, critique existing systems, and make suggestions that will simplify, augment, and/or replace existing technology. For example, The Librarian in Black Blog (librarianinblack.net/librarianinblack/2010/01.tech.html) suggests free software that can replace costly software. Librarians who investigate and evaluate technology with other librarians as their intended audience are among the very best sources for staying current with technology. And unlike vendors, they do not have a product to sell.

Test devices for reading books and other materials in electronic form. Amazon's Kindle is one of numerous devices that provide a different kind of access to print materials. What are the benefits of downloadable books (portability, being lightweight) and are there individuals who do not benefit (vision-impaired readers)? How useful is the text-to-speech capability that actually reads an e-book aloud in a computerized voice? Not only is it important to become familiar with the devices, it is equally important to be sure that the procurement policies of vendors guarantee accessibility for their products and services.[11] What kinds of contractual arrangements can be made with vendors?

Social Networking

Social networking, with its peer-to-peer connections, is another interactive place and has become an increasingly important communication medium. By 2009 it was used by 22 percent of the population, and the number continues to grow.[12] Social networking sites such as MySpace, Facebook, Twitter, and LinkedIn have become a useful means of communication among and within groups. Research has shown that different social networking sites are used by different age groups and that a site can lose popularity among a particular group. It is therefore necessary not only to know which sites are available but who uses them and for what purposes. Public libraries have found that announcing programs via social networking is a very positive means of connecting with those who twitter and text.

Technology in Support of Programs

Though each of the tech solutions to library management problems impacts the user, their purpose is to provide more cost effective, more accurate, and more efficient solutions related to business activities and collection management. Members of the community come to the library to find information, learn, or improve on a skill, and for many other reasons, and expect to have access to the latest and best information resources in a variety of formats.

A study conducted by the University of Washington's iSchool in 2009 reported that 77 million Americans (one-third of the population) use public library computers to look for jobs, connect with friends, do their homework, and improve their lives. Those living below the federal poverty line (families of four with a household income of $22,000 dollars or less, about 44 percent) reported using library computers and Internet access during the previous year. Nearly half of the nation's 14- to 18-year-olds (about 11.8 million) reported using a library card last year, and a quarter of teens used the library at once a week. The most common use of computers included gaining access to government agencies, searching for jobs and filling out applications, doing homework, communicating with friends and family, banking, seeking health advice , running a business, completing online courses, and seeking financial aid for college.[13]

In difficult economic times, the public library provides online access to job information sites. Many of those seeking work do not have the language and computing skills necessary to access these sites without help. They don't know where to start and often don't know what questions to ask. Library staff members work with individuals during a stressful period in their lives to teach them basic computing skills, how to access job information sites appropriate to their needs and interests, and how to apply for a position. More and more employers are requiring online applications, and where does a person who has no computer access at home go to apply for jobs? How does someone who has never written a resume prepare one? Federal and state governments also require that many of the forms to request assistance be submitted online. These tend to be complicated and an almost insurmountable barrier for those who are most in need of support. Public librarians work with people who need help in a difficult time in their lives and do so in a respectful way. Unlike many employers and government agencies, librarians do not expect everyone to have a computer and sufficient skills to respond to complex tasks, and they are willing to answer what might be the most mundane questions.

Today's reference librarians are ahead of the curve in helping individuals who don't know which questions to ask when Googling, or when they ask the right question, what to do with the results. Library users can connect to the reference librarian in the virtual library via e-mail or by texting and will receive a response. Librarians keep up with the latest advances in online reference services and share them with those who are not satisfied with their own search results. The line between public service and technical services staff is blurring because questions about content and how to access content often need information from both sets of experts. The best way to stay ahead of the curve is to continue to question and to learn about the latest online reference sources while at the same time incorporating hard copy resources when they are more appropriate.

Public libraries now have strong connections with the schools in their community. At one time there tended to be competition between the two, as there was concern that children belonged in the school library and should not clutter up the public library. Students are now welcome in the library, and the range of programs to attract them is limited only by the imagination of the librarian and the students. After-school study programs for at-risk students provide an environment where students can "focus on their schoolwork, receive tutoring, and access the library's collection of free learning tools."[14] Tutoring in the library, access to computers to complete homework assignments, and just having a place to go to study have become increasingly important in the community.

For fun, teenagers at one public library wanted to write a play. Then they wanted to produce it. The library provided resources and space for them to do this. They charged an admission fee of a can of food, which they donated to a local food bank. The learning experience and their desire to give back to the community added to their sense of responsibility as citizens, and they enjoyed the activity so much that they did it again.

Children's librarians are among the busiest individuals in the library. They conduct storytimes for different age groups and teach age-appropriate skills that will help them once they start their formal schooling. Librarians have introduced pajama storytime at 7:00 pm so that working parents can bring their children to the library. Babies now belong in the library.

Pediatricians are part of the informal communication network that introduces babies and mothers to the library. Initially, baby social times are introduced (20 minutes twice a week) and the mothers get to know one another, which is another element of building community. New parents having the opportunity to meet one another and share experiences is one of the oldest forms of community building and an important opportunity to learn from one another. Librarians have organized blogs focused on young children that report research studies relevant to the age group, suggest sources of information, and announce programs at the library of interest to parents and care givers of the very young.

Preschool children learn to enjoy arts and crafts. They may be visited by animals accompanied by their owners who live in the community. The snake guy gives them an opportunity to pet a snake. The hawk guy can tell them about the bird, its history, and how the hawk has helped men who were hunting. Guide dogs are a particular favorite, as they can do many things and are kind and gentle. These activities build and enrich the feeling of community.

The public library's local archives are a rich resource for students, who can learn how their community came to be where it is. Invited guests ranging from performing artists, to sculptors, to noted environmentalists, to community figures who have made a contribution or have a story to tell, inform not just students but everyone in the community. In celebrating the community and its residents, the library is building community in an era when the concept of community is fragile.

The virtual library, which provides many services in an online mode, is not just for convenience. It is also the way in which those who cannot use the physical library are able to ask a reference question, order a book title to be sent to them, see programs that have been presented in the library, and take advantage of other services available on the Web. They can also access blogs and be part of an ongoing discussion. Those who don't come to the library may have many reasons other than lack of transportation, lack of time, or difficulty in maneuvering. They may dislike crowds or may feel uncomfortable in public places, and there may be many other reasons why the virtual library is their library of choice. The library's Web site and related elements will continue to expand. Some public libraries have already hired virtual librarians to manage this very important activity. Learning who uses the virtual library, for what purpose, and how this relates to use of the physical library is an important component of the library's planning activities.

How will outreach services change as the virtual library grows? Will book collections still be placed in off-site locations? Will a library staff member visit those unable to come to the physical library? For many of the elderly, the information revolution and social networking are not part of their comfort zone, so will we still need the personal touch of a personal visit?

All of these programs can be tailored to meet the needs and interests of various groups in the community. Once one knows the demographics of the community, storytime in Spanish or Korean or any other language may be conducted, and if a member of the library staff does not speak a particular language, cooperation with a member of the community is always possible.

Demographics

Because communities can change so quickly, it is necessary to stay current with the demographics of the area. Some communities remain stable over time, with the numbers in each age group remaining fairly steady. In others, the building of a new development may increase the number of children, or the building of a retirement community may increase the number of seniors. A new industry being built or an existing industry closing down or leaving the area will change the population mix. Some communities have relatively few members of other ethnic groups; others may have many. In one Virginia county, more than 100 languages are spoken.

Planning for services, identifying new community needs and interests, and phasing out programs for which interest has waned are all dependent on current demographic resources. It is also important to work with municipal planning groups and other local agencies to ensure that each is working with essentially the same demographic data and that there is no unnecessary overlap among programs and that an area of need has not been overlooked.

SUMMARY

When asked how to stay ahead of the curve, one very savvy public librarian said that it is very important to have a personal vision that is ambitious and difficult to achieve. Then "think more visionary thoughts, learn more, and take more personal initiative." Be aware of your community; don't accept no as a final answer, but find another way to serve the community even better. Listen to members of the community and their wants and needs. Be creative. Learn about community assets—local history, local arts and crafts, local industry—and use them as a platform to build programs that inform the community about itself.

The public library is a place, both virtual and physical, where people can come together to discuss issues and enjoy the company of others, where they can learn, where they can bring their children to learn and enjoy, and where they can be part of a community. The best of all possible worlds is when one social community enriches and strengthens the other, when on the Internet one can search globally, and when in the library one can act locally.

Librarians have an important role in fostering community and in connecting that community to the world. Combining knowledge of the community with understanding of the library's role as the place where people and information meet with research-based problem solving and technical, informational, and social expertise, the public librarian will continue to stay ahead of the curve and contribute to the community served.

NOTES

1. Marilyn Johnson, *This Book Is Overdue: How Librarians and Cybrarians Can Save Us All* (New York: HarperCollins, 2010), x.

2. Ann E. Prentice, *Managing in the Information Age* (Lanham, MD: Scarecrow Press, 2005), 2.

3. Denise Davis, *The Condition of U.S. Libraries: Trends, 1999–2009* (Chicago: American Library Association, 2009), 12.

4. *Libraries Connect Communities 3,* ala.org/plinternetfunding (accessed August 11, 2010).

5. Ibid.

6. Davis, *Condition of U.S. Libraries,* 18.

7. Prentice, *Managing in the Information Age,* 3.

8. Vernon E. Palmour, Marcia Bellassai, and Nancy V. De Wath, *A Planning Process for Public Libraries* (Chicago: American Library Association, 1980).

9. John Windhausen Jr. and Marijke Visser, *Fiber to the Library: How Public Libraries Can Benefit from Using Fiber Optics for Their Broadband Internet Connections* (Chicago: American Library Association Office for Information Technology Policy, 2009).

10. *2009 Horizon Report,* www.nmc.org/pdf/2010-Horizon-Report.pdf (accessed August 11, 2010).

11.Peter Blanck, "E-Books Must Be Accessible and That Means Audio," *The Chronicle of Higher Education* 56, no. 26 (March 12, 2010): A81.

12. Donna Blankinship, "Study: Third of Americans Use Computers at Libraries," *Wilmington (NC) Star News*143, no. 162 (March 25, 2010): 2A.

13. Ibid.

14. Robert Rua, "After School Success Stories," *American Libraries* 39, no. 10 (November 2008): 45–47.

ADDITIONAL READINGS

Aleman, Ana M. Martinez, and Katherine Lynk Wartman. *Online Social Networking on Campus; Understanding What Matters in Student Culture.* New York: Routledge, 2009.

Blossom, John. *Content Nation; Surviving and Thriving as Social Media Change Our World, Our Lives, and Our Future.* Indianapolis, IN: Wiley Publishing, 2009.

Bridges, Karl, ed. *Expectations of Librarians in the 21st Century.* Westport, CT: Greenwood Press, 2003.

Cortada, James W. *How Societies Embrace Information Technology; Lessons for Management and the Rest of Us.* Hoboken, NJ: Wiley, 2009.

Dyson, Esther. *Release 2.1: A Design for Living in the Digital Age.* New York, Broadway Books, 1998

Turkle, Sherry. *Falling for Science: Objects in Mind.* Boston: MIT Press, 2008.

Turkle, Sherry. *Simulation and Its Disconnects.* Boston: MIT Press, 2009.

Watkins, S. Craig. *The Young and the Digital: What the Migration to Social-Network Sites, Games, and Anytime, Anywhere Media Means for Our Future.* Boston: Beacon Press, 2009.

Index

About the Author

ANN E. PRENTICE is Professor Emerita at the University of Maryland and former Dean. Dr. Prentice is the author of numerous books dealing with library administration and related topics.